A MEASURE OF ENDURANCE

A MEASURE OF
ENDURANCE

The Unlikely Triumph of Steven Sharp

WILLIAM MISHLER

ALFRED A. KNOPF   NEW YORK   2003

THIS IS A BORZOI BOOK
PUBLISHED BY ALFRED A. KNOPF

Knopf, Borzoi Books, and the colophon are
registered trademarks of Random House, Inc.

Library of Congress Cataloging-in-Publication Data
Mishler, William.
A measure of endurance : the unlikely triumph of Steven Sharp /
William Mishler.—1st ed.
p.   cm.
ISBN 0-375-41133-X (alk. paper)
1. Sharp, Steven, 1974–   2. Manning, William (William H.)
3. Handicapped—Oregon—Case studies.
4. Accident victims—Oregon—Case studies.
5. Case Corporation—Trials, litigation, etc.
I. Title: Unlikely triumph of Steven Sharp.   II. Title.

HV1555.O7M57 2003
346.79503'23'0269—dc21   2002043326

Manufactured in the United States of America
First Edition

To Marie

What is the body?
Endurance.

—Rumi, thirteenth-century Persian mystic

No living thing was moving throughout the vast landscape, except
the lizards that darted over the sand and through the rank grass and
prickly pear, just at our feet. . . . And yet stern and wild associations
gave a singular interest to the view; for here each man lives by the
strength of his arm and the valor of his heart. Here society is
reduced to its original elements, the whole fabric of art and conven-
tionality is struck rudely to pieces. And men find themselves suddenly brought back to the wants and resources of their original
natures.

—Francis Parkman, *The Oregon Trail*

A MEASURE OF ENDURANCE

CHAPTER ONE

S TEVEN SHARP woke in the night to the percussion of hooves on the thin mountain soil. With only a folded blanket between his ear and the ground he could sense their approach before he could hear or see them. Elk. Then he felt the commotion of their heavy bodies pushing through the brush and the low branches a stone's throw from the clearing where he'd built his fire. The early June night was chilly and moonless. Unmoving, he lay in the dark, his lanky body folded in on itself inside the thin sleeping bag, inured through long habit to the pebbly bumpiness of the cold ground, reading the sounds of the herd's movement for the number and size of them. They were heading for the new grass in the lower meadow that bordered Hidden Lake, now passing close enough through the undergrowth for him to distinguish the guttural grunting and snorting of bull, cow, or calf. To be on the ground among large animals, potential prey, though with no thought of hunting them, brought him to an alertness indistinguishable from joy. All game commanded his attention, perhaps elk most of all, for to the hunters in the Pacific Northwest elk were a prestigious prize. What drew Steven, however, was not the allure of the animals as trophies so much as the force of the connection he had established with them half his young life ago. His father, R. E., had first brought him up into these mountains in the fall of 1981, when Steven had turned seven and was first capable of sitting a mule. Since then Steven had never missed a hunting season, which began early in October. Usually the weather could be counted on to be decent—cold, but still free of snow.

On that first trip, however, which had begun in bright sun while he and his father spent half a day packing in on muleback, snow surprised them. It fell in the night, starting sometime after midnight and silently blanketing the world. At dawn father and son had emerged from their tent to find the pine branches loaded and the meadow below covered in nearly a foot of snow. The air had a sharp, ozone edge to it, frosting the insides of their nostrils. Scanning the apron of the meadow, R. E. found fresh elk tracks. Hurriedly he pulled on his high boots and heavy jacket, then bundled Steven in an extra flannel jacket and a hunting cap with earflaps. The two of them set out after the tracks, wading in the snow toward the lake. The trail led around the rim up into Box Canyon, and was so fresh R. E. couldn't resist heading over to see whether he could catch a glimpse of the elk on the canyon trail.

Assuring Steven he'd be gone no more than ten minutes, R. E. posted the four-and-a-half-foot boy as lookout in a level expanse of snow that flowed seamlessly over the meadow and across the lake, telling him to stand there and to shout if he saw something. With that, R. E. was on his way, stepping storklike through the drifted snow, rifle slung on his back. For some moments Steven watched as his father disappeared while silence settled around him like a transparent bell. In the stillness he became aware of the sound of his breathing. Whenever he moved the cold clustered around him like invisible bees. The light off the snow flooded his eyes. His boots creaked on the new snow with a squeaky sound. Minutes passed. And then, without warning, turning again, he found himself staring at a five-point buck at no more than twenty paces, poised atop a slight knoll, as if it had bloomed there or as if the air had opened and it had stepped through, coming into view so quietly and matter-of-factly that its presence seemed totally expected and yet as strange as if a mountain had taken a step closer to him. The buck was huge, particularly seen from the boy's lower vantage. Vapor puffed from its nostrils. The animal dropped its wonderfully encumbered head and snorted. Sober curiosity and wild excitement warred within Steven while he and the buck stood measuring each other. Finally Steven shouted for his father. Again the bull lowered its heavy head with a clearing sound in its throat. Again Steven called, his cry echoing clearly off the canyon walls. This time, faintly, his father answered.

At a leisurely pace the buck advanced in Steven's direction. The boy watched it come with eyes that ranged as eagerly as hands over the long shaggy body, from the massive antlers to the heavy knobs of its forelegs to the ragged and uneven coat that hung in ropy tatters off its belly. The long hair on its back inner thighs was matted with urine and excrement. As it drew nearer, the boy caught a whiff of the animal's rank musk. Steven stood utterly still, heart racing, scarcely breathing. Moving past, the buck gave him a glance with a swing of its heavy head, then kept on toward the woods, grunting softly, its forelegs articulating stiffly, a forlorn dignity in its stiff, measured gait.

Then it was gone.

And now Steven's father was crossing the snow toward him, running.

R. E. gave a whistle when he saw from the tracks how close the buck had come to his son. He clapped Steven repeatedly, as if to congratulate him for somehow having conjured the animal into appearance.

Then he took the boy's hand and they followed the tracks back into the trees, but the elk was not to be found. "That's OK," R. E. said, meaning it sincerely, "that's OK," from which Steven understood—not in so many words but nevertheless clearly—that what counted most for his dad in the matter of hunting was not necessarily getting the animal lined up in his scope but the encounter.

Since that first trip Steven had been coming back regularly with his father or grandfather or brother, and then later, during his teen years, as often as not, alone. Hunting with a buddy was fun, but it could be distracting from what he was gradually discovering to be his real purpose for coming into the wilderness—namely, to push himself, to test his capabilities, to use every part of himself. Hanging out with buddies could be done anywhere, and never offered the kind of satisfactions available only in these pristine surroundings. There was risk, of course, in camping alone in the mountains. One slip could, and occasionally did, send him sliding down a sheer rock face or tumbling among boulders, but that was a price he was more than willing to pay.

More than once, while bandaging Steven or applying a splint, his mother, a trained nurse, would try to get him to agree always to take a buddy with him. "Stevie, you could *die* up there, and we wouldn't know for days."

"Right," he would say ambiguously, hoping she wouldn't try to pin him down.

But if she did and he was forced to declare himself, he'd tell her that, sure, of course he'd try to be more careful. He wasn't interested in hurting himself. "On the other hand, Mom, once a guy's taken reasonable precautions he might as well do what he feels like. Otherwise, he'd spend his life being scared and that's hardly living at all."

NOW, IN the June night, Steven felt the herd moving down into the same pasture where he had been left standing that snowy October morning ten years before, the sound of their passage dying away, skittering and scurrying noises returning in the dark. In moments he was asleep.

At dawn, which came prior to the sun as a spill of light from the higher snow peaks, he rolled out of his sleeping bag, stowed it near a fallen tree, and pulled on his bill cap. Around him the trees swayed like silvery ghosts in the drifting ground fog. His breath smoked. He drew the charred remnants of last night's fire together, banked them with twigs, then held a match to them. Once the flame caught, he headed with a steel pot to the meltwater creek that fed Hidden Lake. The icy dew drenching the silver grass stung his bare feet like fire. Balancing on a rock in the middle of the stream, he snagged some water with his coffeepot. He squatted close to the flame until the coffee came to a boil.

From his pack he took his rod and reel and assembled them, his hands going easily through the routine motions; then he set out through the meadow between him and the oval of Hidden Lake. He moved in slow zigzags, scarring the dew, scraping with his toe at any likely brown or green speck, for it was too early in the day for the grasshoppers to be stirring on their own. At every telltale twitch or flicker he sprang and stomped. By the time he reached the lake, some hundred yards, he had a pocketful of the trampled insects. Rounding the east shore, he came in a matter of minutes to a point that had been his grandfather's favorite fishing spot, and then his father's as well. In Eagle Valley below, and even in neighboring Pine Valley, beyond the mountain twelve miles distant, you could for brevity's sake refer to the Sharps' point at Hidden Lake and most people would nod.

Steven dropped his fly not far from a ripple and began to reel it in. A blue heron stood on the other side of the water, smudged by mist. The first fish to strike was a bluegill. Then a sunny. For upwards of an hour he continued to cast and pull fish from the lake, releasing most of them, the wet line singing by his ear with a thin whistle. Casting a line was as exhilarating to him as pitching a baseball, feeling the flow of energy in his arms and in the roll of his shoulder as he canted back from his waist in order to pinpoint his target; he also loved the subtle draw of the line through the water when his fingers and wrist and forearm were functioning like an antenna tuned to the slightest strike.

The sun moved above the rim of the mountains and filled the upland valley with light. Steven felt its soft heat on his shoulders as he continued to flex and whip his fly rod. Now he was hungry. He secured his hook and locked his reel. He chose a trout from his stringer, and with his folding knife gutted and filleted it. Grasshoppers were starting to sing in the grass and sail waist high through the air as he headed back through the meadow to his clearing. He noted the droppings and trampled grass where the elk had trekked the night before. There was birdsong and a distant woodpecker. The day was heating up. As the sun climbed the canyon it swept shadows from the granite walls and kindled the surrounding peaks, the light immense and yet insistently tuned to particulars, stopping him in his tracks and inviting him to look around. He never tired of resting his eyes on these mountains; at moments like these it was as if the light came from them.

Years later, when he was required to spend several months in the Midwest, he discovered he sorely missed the mountains. He told R. E. that driving between Milwaukee and Racine, Wisconsin, he would look around but find nothing to see, really, by which he meant nothing to raise his eyes up to. So he hung on fiercely to the memory of these Eagle Caps, and they served him as a kind of shelter for the sweetness of things as they used to be, before they became radically otherwise. He had no way of knowing, that June morning in the upland meadow, at the beginning of his seventeenth summer and with a feeling of leisure as rich as the unplanned day stretching before him, that he was about to become engaged in a chain of events that in a few short months would lead him up to a very narrow gate in his life. How could he know it, since he'd glimpsed it only in nightmares that were full of warnings but empty of particulars? On the other side of that narrow gate everything would change for him and for his family, and for some in his community. And eventually, the ripples from his ordeal would move outward and come to touch other lives in other places, years later and thousands of miles away.

CHAPTER TWO

E AGLE VALLEY forms a pocket—geologically, a volcanic trough—
in the Eagle Cap Mountains, themselves part of the Blue Mountains of eastern Oregon. Ten miles as the crow flies west of the
Idaho border, the sparsely populated valley is nearly landlocked. Eighty
miles separate it from Baker City (population 9,880), the county seat
and nearest city of any size, and twelve miles, over a mountain, separate
it from the city of Halfway in neighboring Pine Valley, where the nearest supermarket, Laundromat, drugstore, video rental, Catholic church,
lawyer's office, high school, and library are to be found. Highway 86, a
two-lane strip of asphalt, connects these three points. After leaving
Baker City it runs northeast for a dozen miles through fields and farm-
land, then begins a winding ascent through mountains and desert,
eventually to arrive at Richland (population 175) in Eagle Valley, where
its name changes from 86 to Main Street. Roughly a mile farther on, it
exits at the eastern end of town and becomes 86 again. You can stand at
either end of the town and stare straight through to immensity, for it is
surrounded by miles of plain—first of cropland and pasture, and then,
where the irrigation ceases, of rolling hills that flow into a desert landscape of stark beauty—of rock and sand, juniper, sage, cactus, and tumbleweed. Circumscribed by the surrounding peaks, the desert sky
nevertheless seems wider than the land it overarches, perhaps because
it appears to be without upward limit. In any direction, dawn to dusk,
you see predatory birds—hawks and buzzards and, of course, the eagles

that gave the valley its name—slowly circling, drifting so high above the plain they look like specks of floating ash.

The valley, twelve square miles in area and a pear-shaped oval in form, is enclosed on three sides by the Eagle Cap Mountains and bounded on the south by the Powder River. Thanks to its south-facing orientation and a lower elevation, Eagle Valley has a milder climate and a longer growing season than the neighboring valleys. Its bottomland, carried inland millions of years ago from the floor of the Pacific Ocean by the shifting of the earth's plates, is rich and fertile. Irrigation, a necessity in this arid climate, is provided by the mountain runoff into a network of creeks, chief among them Eagle Creek, which distributes the water through a tightly regulated grid of ditches and sprinklers. Most of the roads in the valley are narrow and unpaved. They run, rutted and dusty or muddy, depending on the season, among hayfields and pastures grazed mainly by cattle and horses but also by sheep and a scattering of mules, and even, here and there, some llamas. Campers began using llamas, lighter and quicker than mules, around 1990, to the intense irritation of many of the old-timers, who claimed that their urine burned the grass. Beef cattle, a mix of Angus, Shorthorns, and Herefords, graze the rich low pastures in their final months of fattening. In early summer they are herded by cowboys into the many thousands of acres of ranch and government land in the foothills of the mountains, a collective effort in which the men from the area's ranches and farms participate. Outwardly, cattle raising is a way of life that has changed little since the first immigrants arrived.

Originally, they came not to farm but to mine and pan for the gold that had been discovered in 1863, in an area they named Sparta, in the mountains about nine miles northwest of the valley. Colossal amounts of gold were extracted during the following twenty years, and Sparta boomed. But by the nineties, the gold was played out and Sparta quickly lapsed into a ghost town, one of several in the area. Prosperity that had seemed limitless vanished overnight, producing the first cycle of boom-and-bust that was to be replayed in other sectors of the region's economy several times during the ensuing hundred years.

After gold came the timber industry. For roughly fifty years the old-growth forests in the area underwent clear-cutting, and then that resource, too, dwindled to a trickle. The sawmill in Richland closed in the sixties and the one in Baker City in the nineties, eliminating an important source of jobs. During that time dam construction flourished. From the 1950s to the 1980s a series of dams was constructed on the Snake River, which forms the border with Idaho, erasing towns and villages in the process. Trout and bigmouthed bass now swim above the roofs of the former mining town of Robinette, for example. Dam construction brought an influx of workers and their families, drawn by the high-paying jobs, and for a while money flowed into the area and the new families took root, as evidenced by the new grade school in Richland and the new high school in Pine Valley. But when the construction was over, the money dried up and an exodus of families ensued.

Even in farming, which along with ranching had been a stable livelihood in the valley, a slow version of boom-and-bust was also at work. When the settlers arrived toward the end of the nineteenth century, the valley's relatively temperate climate favored fruit growing, and they quickly planted orchards—apple, cherry, plum, apricot, and peach. For the next eighty years the orchards grew and flourished and became an important industry. But then, around 1950, a cool shift in the climate set in, so by the time Steven Sharp was born, in 1974, all the large commercial orchards were closing. J. W. Sharp, Steven's great-grandfather, an emigrant from Missouri who bought his ninety-five-acre farm in 1914, earned much of his life's income from his orchards, but in the years when Steven and his older brother, Ed, and sister, Lori, were growing up, the orchards' output had shrunk to just enough to maintain a roadside summer stand.

Even cattle ranching became precarious as cattle prices nose-dived during the final decade of the century. Ranchers who were wealthy in terms of their landholdings were finding themselves living from bank loan to bank loan as they tried to use this year's profit from the sale of yearlings to pay off the previous year's loan and meet their current expenses. A number of the valley's version of aristocracy, many of them third- or fourth-generation landowners, went riding around in ancient pickups and put off equipment purchases from year to year. In short, during the final quarter of the century in which Steven was growing up

in Eagle Valley, the familiar notion of the closing of the American frontier was not so much a theory in a book as the lived aftershock from the
slamming of several giant doors. They echoed through a region where
equipment from the gold rush days could still be found in occasional
use, or where a cabin still stood with rifle slots in the walls for firing at
Indians, or where wagon ruts from the Oregon Trail were still discernible in the desert sand—but also where the forward thrust from
that era had spent itself in successive waves of frantic enterprise that
had given way to the grimmer mode of simply hanging on and making
do. People in the thinly populated valleys might still be as dependent
upon one another as in the days of the frontier, but whereas they once
had bartered and exchanged food and services in the spirit of an unfold-
ing adventure they now struggled simply to make ends meet.

Most of the young people left after high school. Some returned in
later years, drawn by family ties or the harsh beauty of the place, mostly
to retire. Those who stayed often worked several jobs, struggling to
hang on, but finding it harder as the years went on. Inevitably a certain
darkening of mood, a feeling of possibility curtailed, settled over the
valley as the century entered its final decades.

But little of this decline was particularly noticeable to Steven in the
years when he was growing up. For him, conditions in Eagle Valley were
simply the air he breathed and the way things were. Besides, during his
childhood and early adolescence, it was neither Eagle Valley nor Richland that was most immediate to him, but the Sharp farm, to which his
family returned in 1982, when he was seven, after R. E. had served a
couple of tours of duty in the Army and then worked for several years as
a lumberjack in Washington. "Why lumberjacking?" Steven once asked
his dad. "Just something I needed to get out of my system," R. E.
explained. "But I should of done it in my twenties, not my forties, when
I was just kind of too fat and wore out to really enjoy it."

When Grandpa Randolph and his wife, Leora, bought their farm,
they moved into the original rambling farmhouse with a wide front
porch nestled in a willow grove; later he added a modest bungalow on
the other side of the property, and it was into this that R. E. and his
wife, Betty, and their three children moved. It was in urgent need of
repair and expansion when they arrived, having only two bedrooms, an

unfinished attic, and no basement. Nevertheless, soon after settling in, Steven woke up one morning on his portable cot in the living room, his eyes alerted by the first stripes of light through the window blinds, and sensed from the tingle reaching him from the coming day that they'd come to a kind of paradise.

CHAPTER THREE

EVERYTHING ON the Sharp farm seemed like virgin territory to Steven, inviting and no greater in scope than could be thoroughly known on foot. Step out the front door and on one side was his mother's flower garden, and on the other the vegetable garden. Straight ahead, a short flagstone walk led to a plank bridge over the irrigation creek that bordered the property, then the dirt road, on the other side of which was the tall slope with Great-grandpa's apricot orchard, where their mules, Popcorn and Turbo, grazed. To the west the road led past farms out into the hills, and to the east, a quarter mile to his cousin's house, and then another quarter mile to the center of Newbridge, the village to which, technically, the Sharp farm belonged, although all that remained of Newbridge was the ancient bridge itself and a crossroads where the white Grange hall stood beside the smaller white clapboard Church of the Nazarene, where Steven's grandmother Leora was pastor. When he exited the church on Sunday morning, he could take the upper fork back home for lunch and afternoon football with R. E. and Ed in front of the TV; or he could take the lower fork to his grandparents' house for a large family dinner that included aunts and uncles and cousins; or, in season, he could climb on his bike and head the other way into town for a game of baseball with his buddies. These were the first easy interlocking orbits of his life, none of them imbued with the shimmer of the first mornings, perhaps, but known so well that in recall he could faintly taste the shifting weathers through which, during the endless days, they were learned.

Step out the back door and to the left was an aspen grove and a run for the hunting dogs; to the right, a path that led down the long slope through fields and orchards to the barn and outbuildings around his grandparents' house. Steven, who liked to care for the dogs, had the calm persistence required to train them, as he also did for the pigs he raised for 4-H. They were skittish as mice when he bought them in April, but by the end of May, Betty would glance out of the kitchen window and see them trotting behind him as he led them on a string. Steven and Ed were required to help Grandpa Randolph with his chores, and milk and feed his four Jersey cows and clean out their stalls. During the summer those chores included digging ditches and changing pipes to irrigate the orchards and pastures. Grandpa was a large, quick-tempered man, not particularly sociable to outsiders, still robust in his eighties despite a slow-growing prostate cancer he saw no point in doing anything about. These chores weren't particularly demanding for the boys, but needed to be done with unfailing regularity. Occasionally R. E. would assign additional work, although whether they did it depended to a certain extent on their own sense of its urgency. One project, however, that engaged their forces was excavating the basement for their bedroom because they were eager to stop sleeping on cots in the living room. This they did in the fall of their first year, working with a pick and shovel and wheelbarrow under a swinging lightbulb. From time to time the boys, who were largely unsupervised, got into trouble. R. E. occasionally had to discipline them severely.

If such incidents, however few, had no place in paradise, they were far outweighed by the freedom. Other than a few simple, strictly enforced rules, Steven and Ed were at liberty to range, explore, and experiment to their hearts' content. They would get off the school bus in mid-afternoon, and from then until chore time were free to ride bikes, play baseball, fish, or even pan the Eagle Creek for gold. When Steven turned ten he asked R. E. for a BB gun. R. E. refused, saying they were too dangerous. "First thing you know, you and Ed'll be shooting each other's eyes out." Instead, he took Steven hunting, as he'd done earlier with Ed. After shooting a quail, R. E. probed its feathers with his leathery mechanic's fingers in order to show Steven what buckshot did to flesh. On another occasion he gave him a similar lesson with a deer he'd shot. And now that he felt Steven had grasped the difference between the magical guns of television and the lethal guns of reality, he told him he could save his money and buy himself a rifle if he chose to do so. This was an important decision for Steven. It opened a door in the midst of childhood that led directly into the adult world, where his safety became his own concern. He understood that his father's permission was given not without apprehension, but despite it. R. E. would not let fear constrain him. So that fall, with money he earned from his 4-H pigs, Steven bought himself his first rifle, a Stevens 20-gauge shotgun, and soon was matching his father and brother in accuracy.

R. E. instructed Steven in the various skills that were directly relevant to their life and could serve him later, like pruning trees, caring for the cattle and mules, making leather boots and saddles, repairing engines, building, and doing carpentry and basic electrical work. He became all the more intent on giving Steven this practical grounding when, as he and Betty had feared, they received confirmation that Steven had inherited the dyslexia from which both he and his father suffered. Like the two of them, Steven would probably never read beyond a third- or fourth-grade level. The discovery devastated Steven, and from one day to the next, a shadow fell over his world.

"When Steven's reading trouble became definitely established, I guess in the second grade, it was like he took a bullet," said Millie Shold, Steven's special ed teacher in grade school. "He threw himself into overcoming it with the same kind of determination he put into everything. He wanted to be like everybody else. But with reading, he just couldn't. It had nothing to do with his intelligence. Steven was plenty bright, but he just had this glitch."

"When I'd look down at the page, the letters would start to move," Steven remembered. "The harder I tried to hold them steady, the more they'd move, like they were heating up in a frying pan. Or like my eyes were pushing them off the edge of the page."

This gave his mother even more cause to worry about him. He had been born less than robust physically; he suffered from asthma, allergies, and migraines. When he was young she would sleep with one eye open, and when his barking coughs began she would hurry him outside and sit with him until the damp night air relieved his lungs. For days thereafter he would scarcely stir from her side, skipping school, sitting at the kitchen table, and drawing. Ed had R. E.'s build and general toughness, and was well suited for the kind of ranch work he'd wanted to do since he was a boy. But Betty thought Steven would need some kind of indoor work, perhaps as an architect, given his obvious skill at drawing, but then again his dyslexia would be a hindrance.

She cried when she talked over his prospects with her mother-in-law, Leora, who was one of the most literate and well-educated people in the valley, with master's degrees in both theology and education. In addition to her pastoral duties, Leora had taught all eight grades in Richland's two-room schoolhouse, and later, English, math, and Spanish in the high school in neighboring Halfway. By the end of her career she had risen to become school superintendent of Baker County. She was a woman of great energy, with a quick wit and an occasional prickliness that was balanced by a boundless capacity to listen to people without judging them. "This is not the end of the world," she told Betty. "Dyslexia hasn't prevented Randolph or R. E. from having a good life. You tell Stevie to come see me."

When he showed up, Leora sat him down in the kitchen and had one of her little talks with him. She told him she knew how hard this disability was for him, but that it had nothing to do with his intelligence. "You're plenty smart, Steve, I know you are, so I know you're going to find ways of dealing with this."

"I know, Grandma," he replied, downcast and wounded.

"You are just as special as you ever were, and in some ways even more so."

"Why?"

She decided to tell him a difficult truth. "Well, because now you'll have a special eye for the underdog."

"What's an underdog?" he asked.

"The kid nobody plays with. The kid who gets picked on. Not that *you'll* get picked on, exactly, because somehow I don't think you will, but now with this setback of yours you'll always know how those other ones feel. And maybe some you'll be able to help."

"I don't know," he said, still forlorn. "I just wish I could read."

"I know you do, Stevie," she said, and hugged him. "I do too."

In fact, Steven was occasionally picked on during his first years of grade school not because of his dyslexia but because he was a short, shy kid who tended to stick close to his sister for protection. Lori, five years older, defended him with the quick fury of a mother bantam. Socially, the Sharp children occupied an ambiguous position on the Richland playground, for they did not belong among the town kids, the ranchers' kids, or the kids whose families were on the social margins. Their situation mirrored that of R. E., who, as a skilled independent mechanic living on his own land and supporting his family comfortably if modestly, was a figure who also escaped easy pigeonholing. Perhaps for this reason the Sharp kids looked like inviting targets on the playground, not least of all because of their casual air of self-sufficiency.

When Steven was in the second grade, a seventh grader chose him and Lori as preferred targets. The bully started picking on them in the spring, and resumed again in the fall of Steven's third grade. "But one day," Lori recalled, "when this guy was teasing me and trying to pull my hair, something happened to Steven. He walked up to where the two of us were fighting, watched quietly for a minute—we paid no attention to him—and then all at once, he jumped up and punched this big kid so hard in the nose that the blood just gushed. The guy was stunned, he turned and ran away, and he never bothered either one of us again. And from then on Steven lost all fear of fighting. After that, I never had to protect him; he would take on anyone, no matter how big. And Steven didn't really start to get tall until the seventh grade, so he took a licking now and again. But he didn't care. Not that he liked to fight. He just never would back down."

Ed noticed the change in his brother. Steven no longer ran from him. Ed was much bigger and heavier than Steven and was used to beating him up, in the way of older brothers, forcing him to cry uncle. But from the time Steven hit fourth grade, he refused to give in, and soon was holding his own. Ed could throw him but no longer pin him. Steven, lean and wiry, could twist out of his grasp. Several years later they gave up fighting altogether.

Leora turned out to be right about Steven's intelligence. Neither his problematical health nor his dyslexia managed to hold him back. His friends took turns taking notes for him at school and reading to him in the evening, and in this way Steven kept abreast of his schoolwork. He had a quick mind and a retentive memory. Betty was understandably much relieved, as she watched him grow and become more independent with each year. He was getting taller, with the thick dark hair and handsome good looks of Leora's father, who was half Ojibwa. Steven was popular at school, had a wide circle of friends, and was turning into a good athlete, and even something of an entrepreneur with a fledgling pig business that had developed out of his 4-H activities. His mother was pleased with his progress but couldn't help feeling a little nostalgia for their former relationship, which had been so close.

Betty had grown up in Eugene, and although she had lived more than twenty years in Eagle Valley, she shunned the world of hunting and fishing that so fascinated the men in the family. When first married, she had tried one fishing trip, but that had sufficed. She was appalled by the dirt and discomfort of wilderness camping. When the men headed up into the mountains, she liked to take Lori, who also had an urban temperament, and head for a Holiday Inn back in Eugene with a hot tub and room service. Consequently, in her view of the outdoors world in which Steven spent much of his time, a certain sentimentality remained that occasionally sounded a jarring note between them. One spring day, for example, when Steven was thirteen, she happened to glance out the window and spy him sitting on the grass in the backyard, nursing a piglet with a bottle. It looked to her like a tender scene, and she was pleasantly moved. A few minutes later when he stepped through the door and went to the refrigerator, she asked him in a sunny tone, "What are you going to name that new baby pig of yours?"

Steven poured himself a glass of milk. "Nothing," he replied shortly. "No name."

"But, Stevie, you always name your animals. Last year you had Blackie."

He set down the glass. "That was for you, Mom."

"For me?"

"I know you like to give animals names. But me, I'm not going to give a name to something I'm going to take to slaughter in a couple of months. I'm not going to be its *friend*."

"I see," she said. It made her a little sad, this realism of his, the distance it implied between them.

But then, occasionally he would talk to her again in the old way, particularly if she happened to catch him off guard, as she did very early one June morning when he was fifteen. Hearing a noise in the kitchen, she came out to investigate. A bright moon was flooding the kitchen with milky light. She found Steven sitting at the table, motionless. She asked him what was wrong, suspecting a recurrence of his asthma.

"I had this dream," he replied quietly.

She pulled up a chair. "What kind of dream?"

"A nightmare," he said. "I've had it a couple of times."

"Tell me about it."

He said that in the dream it was Sunday, and they were all in church. Grandma Leora was preaching, as she usually did, standing behind the lectern up in front and walking back and forth. He tried to hear what she was saying, but could not make out her words. Her mouth was moving, but her words were submerged by a low machine rumble that seemed to be coming from the rear of the small church. He looked around, trying to locate the source, but no one else seemed to hear it. He tried to ignore it too, but the rumble grew louder, as if coming nearer. Again he turned and peered at the back, because now the rumble was a roar and was shaking the walls. Just as he was about to yell to his father, the back wall burst open and a huge baler came crashing through. It was not pulled by a tractor but, unlike any baler he had ever seen, seemed to be self-propelled; it was working as it came, its belts turning, chains clanking, and metal arm moving up and down. And still everyone's eyes were fixed forward on Leora, as if frozen. Then suddenly he found himself outside the church, alone. He could hear the machine roaring inside, and he knew it was destroying anything in its path. Desperately, he felt that he had to go back inside the church, but he stood frozen, unable to move.

"The worst thing about it," he told his mother, "was that because I'd had this nightmare before, I knew at each step of the way what was going to happen, but I couldn't do anything to stop it."

His shoulders were hunched in his T-shirt, and his voice was thin with fatigue and apprehension. Betty wondered why he had never told her about the dream. She leaned over and hugged him. "There's no such baler," she said with warm conviction. "You know that. Dad works with them all the time. And now you're running Grandpa's. Maybe that's what gave you this dream."

"What about the times when I've had it before?"

"Maybe it's from watching Dad work."

He said nothing.

"It's just a dream, Stevie. It doesn't mean anything." She drew him to her and held him close. Then he detached himself and padded back downstairs to his bedroom. Betty returned to her bedroom, lay down beside R. E., and said a silent prayer.

But such glimpses into Steven's private inner world grew rarer. Most often he was flying out the door, busy with a dozen projects. During eighth grade and freshman year, he was particularly occupied with 4-H and Little League baseball. Thanks in no small part to Ed's coaching, Steven had moved into the long coveted position of pitcher for the Richland team. With his friend Matt Halley in the outfield, and another good friend, Barry Neal, at second base, the team had two undefeated seasons. Ed had taught Steven his whole bag of tricks—fastballs, change-ups, curve balls, sliders, and sinkers—and through long practice Steven had made them his own. It helped that the catcher on their team, who had moved to Richland from Baker City, was familiar with the batting habits of many of the kids in the area. His signals, coupled with Steven's hard-earned control, enabled the team to pull off the nearly miraculous feat of going all the way to the state finals two years in a row, something the minuscule town of Richland had never done before. Steven was in his glory during those long summer afternoons of 1990 and 1991.

By the following summer those heady days were gone for good. The families of several players had moved during the winter, leaving the team undermanned. Heading into his junior year, Steven had only eighteen months until the onset of a lifetime of work. Ed, who had completed high school two years previously, was by then working as a cowboy on a local ranch.

"Got any work on that ranch of yours?" Steven asked him one late spring evening at supper.

"Not summer work," Ed replied. "But if you were thinking more long term, then maybe."

"Stevie's too young to start working full-time," Betty protested. "He's got two years left of high school."

"Young or not," said R. E., "he's not going to find any work on the ranches around here this summer. From what I hear, nobody's hiring."

"You talked to the Saunderses?" asked Steven.

"Just have. I been out there looking at their equipment, and they don't need anybody."

Well, at least he could work with his pigs and maybe make some money in the fall. Last year he'd won a blue ribbon with a pig at the county fair, which had boosted its price to three times the market rate. Perhaps he could repeat his success. He was saving his money to buy a secondhand pickup like Barry's. Then he would expand his business.

"If nothing else," he said, "I could spend some time in the mountains catching rattlesnakes." There was decent money to be made from the taxidermist for good-sized rattlers. Betty wasn't sure about the rattlesnake business but was pleased that he was going to spend one final summer without a regular job. He was seventeen. Real life would close in soon enough, she felt.

CHAPTER FOUR

THE LAST HYMN SUNG, the congregants filed out of the small church into the May sunshine, twenty-five or thirty people counting the children. At the door they shook Leora Sharp's hand and thanked her for the sermon. Some headed for their cars but many dawdled in the warm sunlight for a little conversation, among them R. E. and Steven. For the most part, the men, their faces and arms newly sunburned, wore laundered blue jeans, shined riding boots, and ironed sport shirts. They stood in a loose group making small talk about the planting season now in full swing while their wives moved about busily, checking schedules and making arrangements for meetings and outings of the 4-H club, the Boy Scouts and the Rainbow Girls, Little League and the preparations for the upcoming Grange supper. Leora and Betty were finishing up inside, stowing the Bibles, prayer books, and sheet music. After the first set of departing cars and pickups had left the parking lot, a few people remained clustered at the crossroads.

"Steve, what you got in mind for the summer?" asked Dick McNulty, a retired welding contractor who had moved to Richland several years earlier and joined the Nazarene congregation. He and R. E. had become hunting partners and good friends.

"Nothing much, looks like. Can't find a job anywhere."

"You been looking around?"

"Yeah, me and my friend Barry been riding around to ranches for weeks, but nobody's hiring."

"Well, if you want a job real bad," McNulty said, "you could come work at my shop for a while." McNulty had set up a small shop in town that manufactured doormats out of old tires.

"Well, thanks," Steven said, considering the offer.

"I don't know if you'd really be interested, Steve. You'd be inside all day, and it's hot, smelly work."

"Well, it wouldn't be forever, just two or three months."

"It's up to you."

There was a pause. "Sure, I could do that," he said, not wild about the idea but not about to turn down a paying job.

"Appreciate it, Dick," said R. E.

"Hey, I need the help," McNulty replied.

The following morning Steven showed up for work at McNulty's shop. Almost two weeks later, on a Saturday morning, Barry Neal ran into Steven in town, having a cup of coffee before work, and told him he was going to drive out to the Saunders ranch one last time to see if they were hiring. Steven said there was no point in doing that because R. E. had just told him that Debbie, Dwight Saunders's fiancée, had just moved out to the ranch and would be helping out with the summer work—driving one of the tractors when they planted and later cut the hay, then raked and baled it. Barry said what the hell, he felt like driving out there anyway, he hadn't talked to Dwight in a while, and besides he had nothing else to do.

He headed west out of town, content to be at the wheel of his first pickup. The weather had been dry that spring, but today sporadic winds were tumbling heavy clouds over the wide valley sky. On either side of the dirt road ranks of sprinklers hissed and clicked, sending jets of water in high arcs over the fields while behind the pickup the plume of dust kicked up by the tires was whipping around like a turkey tail. Six feet seven, Barry sat hunched at the wheel, beating out the rhythm of the radio's country-western tunes and driving slowly, so as not to bury the oncoming tractor drivers in dust. As each driver approached, Barry would raise two fingers of his steering hand in greeting, and each in turn, equally measured, would return the polite salute. It was not necessarily a friendly greeting, more like a gesture of reassurance among acquainted men that everything was pretty much under control.

The Saunders ranch, roughly a thousand acres, had been in the family for three generations. Both Stan and his son, Dwight, had been born in the house where Stan, age sixty-seven, was presently living. It was a small frame structure, once painted red, but so long ago licked clean of paint by wind, dust, and snow that the wood had silvered. Dwight and now Debbie lived a quarter mile down the road in a bungalow built in the fifties. The Saunderses owned a herd of about five hundred beef cattle, and struggled to stay afloat during the bad cattle market years. It was plain to the eye that their resources were stretched thin. Here and there were signs of neglect—fences unmended, broken windows in the sheds, gates attached to their posts with barbed wire. Stan's health had been declining in recent years. The previous fall he'd suffered a heart attack, so at present his work was restricted to driving a tractor three or four hours a day. Dwight, thirty-four, had taken on the lion's share of the work. He was a husky man, about five feet eleven, weighing about three hundred pounds, and strong as the proverbial ox. He'd known Steven and Barry and their circle of friends from the time they were kids, and was friendly with them. He was nowhere to be seen when Barry pulled up at his gate and got out of his truck.

Behind the yard fence, Dwight's border collies raced and yapped. Barry knocked on the back door of the house and Debbie told him Dwight was moving sprinkler pipe in the hayfield below Stan's house. Barry drove over there and parked. Below him in the field he caught sight of Dwight's squat figure as he bent and carried sections of aluminum sprinkler pipe, four inches in diameter and twenty feet long. To Barry, Dwight looked like an incongruous tightrope walker as he staggered over the uneven ground, attempting to keep the springy pipe from bouncing on his shoulders. Even on a day with no wind, one good wobble could knock a man down, even one as stout and strong as Dwight. Thus Dwight's risk was compounded when a sudden wind gust caught one end of the pipe he had just placed on his shoulders and began to rotate it. Dwight tried to keep his balance by moving about beneath his burden, but inadvertently he placed one foot in a narrow irrigation ditch, which clamped it like a vise. Meanwhile the wind, like a hand on a giant corkscrew, continued to twist the long pipe. Instantly, before Dwight could drop or heave the pipe away from himself, his body was twisted beyond its limits. Disks snapped in his lower back. With a howl, he crumpled to the ground in agony. Barry ran to him and dropped to his knees. Dwight was gasping for breath against the pain.

Several hours later in Baker City, when Barry was permitted in the hospital room, Dwight was lying in traction, his massive arms incongruous in his short-sleeved hospital gown. Debbie sat at his bedside. The pain medication was making him drowsy. In a voice much reduced from its usual vigor, he murmured to Barry that he was going to be laid up for at least three months, and asked him whether he would be willing to hire on for the summer. Minimum wage. Barry replied that oddly enough, that's why he'd driven out that morning, to ask for a job. He could start on Monday. Debbie thanked him. She said she thought he was looking for a job. Good thing she hadn't turned him down at the back door, then Dwight might have lain there in the field until lunchtime.

IN THE COURSE of the summer, the Saunderses planted and harvested three crops of hay. Barry's working day began at five with irrigating, which meant either moving pipe and sprinklers or opening the head boxes and directing water into ditches with a shovel, partially redigging them. Once the sun had burned the dew off the grass, he would climb into the cab of one of the ranch's three tractors and work until nightfall cutting, raking, or baling hay. It was hot, dusty work with old equipment in mediocre repair. On rainy days or in the gap between haying cycles, Barry repaired fences, dug ditches, or worked in the shop sharpening cutter blades and, in general, maintaining the equipment. It was his first full-time job, and he earned his pay.

The equipment he was using, a Case 970 tractor and Heston baler, was machinery that R. E. knew well. In the years since 1972, when Stan had bought the tractor, three times R. E. had repaired the Power Take Off (PTO), the unit that supplied power to attached machinery, because its clutch plates inside the unit had burned out. It was a mystery why these plates, which ought to have lasted the life of the tractor, were frequently so short-lived. When R. E. called the local Case representative, a so-called block man, he was told that the problem, which was a familiar one on that model tractor, sprang from the fact that operators were not pushing the PTO lever fully forward, thereby producing only partial engagement of the clutch plates, which then spun against each other, instead of locking, and overheated. He asked R. E. whether the tractor had been retrofitted with a sloped ramp that Case had designed to cause the operator to push the PTO lever fully forward. R. E. told him that the Case did have such a ramp. The representative said then that it was just one of those quirks that tended to show up on the 970s. The only thing to do was to install a new PTO unit.

"Couldn't it be repaired?" R. E. asked.

No, he was told, it was a sealed unit. The only thing to do was to remove the old unit and replace it with a new one.

R. E. had last replaced the PTO unit three years before, the same summer that he had welded a bar above the rollers on the Heston baler to make them grip tighter. Dwight had noticed that the hay was starting to slip between the rollers as the twenty-five-year-old machine got older and he thought such a bar would make the rollers grip more aggressively. R. E. made the repair and it did the trick.

A couple of weeks after Dwight injured his back, R. E. swung by the Saunders ranch to service another tractor. Steven was free that Saturday morning, and had ridden along with him to see how Barry was doing. While R. E. set to work at Stan's place, Steven walked back to where Barry was sharpening and reinstalling the sickle bar on the swather (the machine that cuts the hay). It was around eight in the morning and the sun had not yet burned off the ground fog, which happened to be particularly dense. Steven located Barry in the machine shed and the two of them chatted while Barry finished sharpening the cutter bar. All at once, they heard frantic dog barking mingled with even more frantic bleating of sheep. They rushed to the yard behind the shed and peered into the sheep pasture, where the fog stood like a wall. The bleating, high pitched and shrill, sounded like screaming women, and the barking had become raw and feral. Heading toward the uproar, Barry and Steven made their way through the fog and found one sheep already dead, its throat torn, with one of Dwight's border collies working on it, and the other collie tearing at another sheep, this one still alive. A third sheep had plunged into a nearby swamp, where it stood bleating with a torn shank. The scene of ferocity was intensified by the dark fog. Barry and Steven grabbed the collies by their collars and yanked them from their prey, then dragged them back to the barnyard where they tethered them, crazy and straining, to separate fence posts.

Dwight had come to his back steps, alerted by the uproar. When Barry and Steven told him what had happened, he had difficulty absorbing it. His beloved collies had never shown any feral tendencies before. Dwight told the two of them to wait. A couple of moments later he hobbled back with his .38 service revolver, which he handed to Steven.

"You put the sheep out of their misery first," he said.

Steven shot the sheep and then the collies, tethering them close and firing at point-blank range so that they would not suffer. While Barry dug the holes for the carcasses, Steven walked back to Dwight. Dwight pocketed the revolver. When he took the collars from Steven, he began to cry.

"Thanks, Steve," he said. "I couldn't have done it."

"I know how you feel, Dwight. We've had dogs around home that I've had to put down, for one reason or another, and it ain't ever easy."

"It's 'cause I been laid up. I ain't had the time to spend with them. That's why they went crazy on me."

"I don't know, Dwight. Sheepdogs'll turn every now and then, all on their own. Chasing and snapping at sheep is what they're bred to do, after all, and it don't take much for them to slide over that line, sometimes."

"I know, Steve, I know. You don't have to try to make me feel good."

"It's a fact, Dwight."

"Yeah, well, come on inside and have a cup of coffee, why don't you, while you're waiting on your dad."

Debbie fixed coffee and Steven asked Dwight how his back was mending, and how they were doing in general that summer. Dwight said his back was still very painful and that it would be months before he could think of doing any kind of work. He also said that Stan's diabetes was getting worse, so he had to be careful how much he worked. Debbie set out some doughnuts and Steven drank his coffee. The three of them talked until R. E. showed up. R. E. turned down an offer of a cup of coffee. The start of haying season was his busiest time of year.

"Come on, son," he said. "We gotta get moving."

"Barry will run him home later, if it's OK," said Dwight. "I've asked Steve if he'd be willing to help out this summer, along with Barry, and he's agreed to do that."

"What about McNulty?" asked R. E.

"I'll talk to him," Steven said.

"Well, suit yourself."

Barry was happy to hear that Steven would be working on the ranch, because there was way too much work for him, Debbie, and Stan.

As for McNulty, he said, "Sure, Steve. If you got a chance to work on a ranch running some big equipment, take it. Be good experience. I can always get somebody to fill in here. Might as well be working outside and learning something useful."

CHAPTER FIVE

T HE FIRST DAY Steven reported for work, Dwight, propped on a cane, instructed him in the use of the baler.

"This ain't a new machine. As a matter of fact, it was the first round baler in the valley. We got it when I was seventeen, same age as you. But your dad has taken good care of it over the years, and she'll run fine if you just pay attention and know what you're doing."

He showed Steven how to grease it, how to install the baler twine, how to thread the twine through the knotter, and what to do in case the machine got clogged, as it tended to do because of some missing tines on the uptake rollers. Dwight told him to keep an eye out for hay bunching up in front of the intake, because if he let the machine get truly clogged he would have to power down the engine, turn it off, take a wrench and crank the rollers backward to discharge the stuck hay—a long, sweaty, dusty process.

Steven nodded.

"Just one last thing, Steve. Don't ever get off the tractor with the PTO running. And don't ever try to do anything around it while it's running."

"I ain't stupid, Dwight."

"I know you ain't stupid, but you're still a kid, and most kids think they can't get hurt. Just like me when I was your age, and was working with this baler that first summer. She jammed up on me, and I went back to clear it, and I didn't turn off the PTO. I don't know why not.

Maybe I thought I'd already shut her off, since she wasn't turning over. Anyhow, soon as I pulled out a clump of hay, she started up. Quicker than I could pull my hand back, she'd bit off the end of these two fingers."

He held up his right hand, and Steven saw that the tips and nails of his middle two fingers were missing, and that shiny, dead-looking skin now covered the bones.

"Close call."

"Damned right," said Dwight. "Now today I want you to ride with Barry while he bales, so that you can get the hang of it."

"Dwight, I've already done plenty of baling for my grandpa."

"Not with this tractor and this baler, you haven't, so do what I tell you."

All day Steven shared the cab of the Case with Barry and they baled hay. Barry sat in the driver's seat and Steven leaned standing against the wheel guard. The hours rolled by in clamor and heat. The boys kept their eyes on the windrow as it lifted endlessly off the uneven ground into the intake of the baler, and occasionally stopped to fork the hay into more manageable shape or to tinker with the complicated machinery. Barry found the work monotonous, but Steven had his dad's interest in and unending patience with machines, both when they were running smoothly and when they went out of whack. Still there was ample time for the two of them to discuss the girls they were currently dating, and the girls who as yet only loomed as possibilities. In the summer of their junior year, they were at the point where the females in their circle were emerging on their own, losing their identities as someone's sister, cousin, or daughter. That evening, when Barry and Steven rolled back into the yard, Dwight was sitting with Debbie in their car.

"You got the hang of it?" Dwight asked Steven.

"Yeah, it ain't that different than Grandpa's. That's a round baler too, you know."

"Well, good. From here on, it's going to be mostly you doing the baling. Barry can stick to cutting and raking."

He made this assignment based on his assessment of Steven as the more careful and cautious of the two. Recently, to his horror, Dwight had caught Barry getting down from the tractor and approaching the baler while it was functioning, despite the warning lecture he had received. Dwight had hollered at Barry until he was hoarse.

"I wasn't going to touch the baler, Dwight," Barry eventually protested. "I was going to move a stone that was in the way."

Dwight told him to do what he was told and not make excuses.

The arrangement suited both Steven and Barry equally well. Barry was happier working with the Saunderses' newer equipment, cutting and raking with the Ford, and not having to deal with the Case tractor or the Heston baler, which were temperamental. Steven, on the other hand, his father's son particularly in this respect, derived satisfaction from his ability to elicit smooth performances from the machines. Built in 1969, the Case tractor was six years older than he was, and he approached it with something of the same wariness he used around Stan Saunders or his own grandfather or even his dad's ancient mule, Turbo, all creatures who had toiled long enough to claim the privilege of crankiness. The Case had lost most of its comforts and amenities. The seat had lost its padding, the floor of the cab was slippery with oil from some undetermined leak, the emergency brake was shot, and the cab radio unaccountably picked up only a conservative talk show station.

The heat in the enclosed metal cab was often intense, over a hundred degrees if the outside temperature was in the nineties. On one of his first days of solo baling, Steven returned from lunch to a tractor cab so hot the heat shimmered in waves off and around the nearly incandescent exhaust pipe. Stan's order was never to turn off the engine until the end of the day, unless there was an emergency, to save wear and tear on the starter. Sweat drenched Steven's shirt the instant he sat down in the cab. He flipped on the air-conditioner switch. Gratefully he heard the fan start up, but instead of cool air a stream of angry yellow jackets flowed from the vents, buzzing and stinging. He snapped off the switch and jumped down from the cab, swatting the air around his head with his bill cap and slapping his arms and shoulders as he raced to a safe distance. Then he sat in the shade of the single tree in the field while he waited for the cab to clear. Later, he would recall the serenity of that moment in late June as he sat with the sweat drying on his skin and his breathing coming back to normal.

Baling was repetitive work, but Steven was not bored by it. There were sixteen forward gears on the tractor, which he was constantly shifting in accord with the terrain while he watched ahead and behind, twisting in his seat, listening to the tenor and rhythm of the equipment, slowly swerving the intake of the baler from side to side to distribute the flow of hay over the entire intake. There were fittings to be greased, gauges to be checked, twine to be added. He watched the bale as it formed, keeping track as it approached its target weight of one ton. When that occurred, he would halt the tractor and activate the mechanism that tied and knotted the bale; then he would pull a lever that dropped the bale to the ground. All of this required constant attention.

And so the months of summer went by, three cycles of cutting, raking, and baling, each cycle producing a little less tonnage as the hay grew thinner, but the work was equally arduous. Barry and Steven continued to arrive before dawn and work until dark. Lunch was a welcome highlight. They would climb down from their cabs, nearly deaf in the sudden silence, startling short-eared jackrabbits or quail from the windrows as they walked back to the barnyard. Most days they would climb into Barry's truck and drive into town to get a sandwich and soda at Flip's Coffee Shop, maybe pick up some Copenhagen at The Hitching Post. They took their time over lunch, an hour or so. On rainy days they worked inside. Occasionally, between cuttings, they would take the afternoon off and drive out to the marina on the edge of town with whatever girls and additional buddies they could collect, where they would swim and horse around and leap off the high bluffs into the river. On a hot July afternoon, few pleasures could match taking a running leap into that tall space and plunging into deep cold water, feeling the squeeze as you went down into the abruptly soundless dark, and then even deeper, and then sensing the release as you kicked back up to the surface.

Then, on the evening of Friday, August 21, Stan handed them both their final checks and thanked them for their summer of hard work. But he wondered if they could help him with one last job—the field below his house, which he'd cut on Thursday and planned to rake and bale over the weekend. His asthma was bothering him and Debbie was busy. It would take him two full days to do it himself, but if one of them could drop back and help him out, bale while he raked, they could do the whole field in four or five hours. Barry begged off, saying he was going to visit his girlfriend. Steven said he was going to meet a guy with a pickup to sell, but not until around four in the afternoon, so he could come by.

"Your money burning a hole in your pocket?" Stan laughed, aware that for teenagers like Steven and Barry buying a pickup was an essential step into manhood. Steven laughed and said he guessed so.

On Saturday morning, he drove R. E.'s car to work, parked it at Stan's in the light of a blanched moon, and set about moving sprinkler pipe, just like any other day. Then he mended fence for an hour while the sun dried the grass. Stan emerged around nine-thirty and started raking, rolling every two windrows of the thin late hay into a more substantial single one. Half an hour later, Steven turned on the Case and began baling, and for several hours thereafter they raked and baled past each other in slow ovals, working their way from the center to the perimeter of the field. At noon, Stan had finished raking, and drove his rig back to the yard. Steven considered stopping for lunch, but with only three rows left to bale he kept on working.

He noticed as he approached the single tree in the field that the hay around it was still slightly damp, where it had lain in shadow. There was a swale there, and each time he guided the baler into it, the hay tended to bunch up and snowball in front of his baler. Twice he corrected the problem by stopping, backing up, and then hitting the windrow at an angle, but the third time the maneuver did not work. The hay stayed piled in a bunch. The last thing Steven wanted, this close to finishing the job, was a clogged baler, so he stopped to remove the pile by hand. He took the tractor out of gear, reduced his rpms, turned off the PTO, got out of the cab, and walked back to the baler. He gathered the piled hay in his arms and redistributed it in the windrow. Then he reached into the intake for the armful of hay that was in front of the rollers, and this too he spread out in the windrow. Checking for good measure, he saw that there remained another couple of handfuls of hay in the intake. Placing his left hand on the lower roller for balance, he leaned into the baler to scoop the remaining hay with his right. Most of his weight was now thrust forward on his left hand. At that instant the baler sprang into full activity, its belts and chains moving at normal speed, its rollers turning.

His left hand vanished instantly between the rollers. He pitched backward and grabbed his left wrist with his right hand in an attempt to pull it out. Then his right hand was seized as well, vanishing between the rollers. Now he was in a struggle for his life, his hands and wrists already destroyed. The baler was working with the force of 90 horsepower behind it, drawing him in like any sheaf to be crushed. An instant ago the day had lain around him in baking placidity, the sun pouring down, the diesel imperturbably putt-putting, his body swaying to its slow progress, the end of the job just two rounds away—and now without warning he was pinned at the narrow gate in his life, the focus of panic that he had often glimpsed in nightmares. He was utterly alone. Barry was two hundred miles away, Stan was snoozing after lunch in his La-Z-Boy. But Steven cried for help until his voice gave out.

By bracing his forehead, stomach, and knees against the unmoving parts of the baler and pulling with all his power, he was able to slow the rate at which he was being drawn into the machine. At first his body had been too startled to register pain, but as the minutes dragged on the pain returned with howling intensity. He was losing blood rapidly. Waves of faintness and exhaustion began to roll through him, obliterating him, inviting him to give in and let go and allow death to happen quickly. The prospect of dying did not so much frighten him as fill him with sadness. For a moment he thought of his family and friends and sensed their grief, and it summoned an animal-like drive. He would stop at nothing.

Thirty to forty minutes later he broke free of the baler.

He was alive.

He stumbled back from the baler and drew breath. Something like a wave of exhilaration went through him when he realized he could still function. He knew he had to get back to Dwight's and get help as quickly as possible, but how? He could barely see; his glasses were gone, and his eyes were full of chaff and sweat and blood that he could not wipe away. He thought to himself, logically but unclearly, that the best thing he could do would be to get on the tractor and drive back, because to walk the roughly four hundred yards to the farmhouse seemed utterly beyond his forces. He made his way to the tractor and put his right foot on the mount. Then he reached up with arms and hands that were no longer there and closed his missing fingers on the handrail, whose weight and metallic coolness and hardness he could feel in his palms as vividly as ever, and gave a pull. Midway in his rise he pitched backward and fell, striking his head on the baler hitch. He passed out.

When he woke it was not to steady consciousness, but rather to a condition like that of an exhausted swimmer or drowning victim who bobs to the surface and sinks again. The midday sun glowed through a fiery membrane. A huge thirst had seized him. He struggled to his feet and started moving up toward Stan's house. But because he could discern only vague shapes and colors, and because he kept fading in and out of consciousness, he wandered for a while like a drunken man. When he found himself back at the baler for the third time, he understood that he had to strategize. Peering about, he made out the fence line at the edge of the field. What he had to do, he realized, was to make his way over to the fence, even though that would increase the distance to Stan's house, and follow it up to the barnyard. Once he had the wire against his leg he would not wander off course.

Balance posed great problems as he tried to mount the rise without arms. If he leaned back too far, of course, he tumbled backward. He fell down repeatedly, momentarily passing out. At one point he returned from one of those empty spaces and found a large black bird, an eagle or a hawk, close enough for him to feel and hear the clattery commotion of its wings—the same bird, he thought, as the one he had seen hovering overhead at one point during his ordeal with the machine. As much as anything, the bird terrified him, clearly taking him for carrion. He struggled to his feet and continued moving along the fence line up toward Stan's house.

At last the house loomed up, a reddish gray blur with a green blur of grass around it. His thirst had gotten worse. He stumbled against an obstacle at shin height, which had to be the porch. Stepping up on it, he let his shoulder find the wall of the house, and bumped along it until he came to Stan's kitchen door. The door was open but the screen door was shut. He gave the open door a kick.

No response.

He gave another, harder kick.

"Who's there?" Stan called drowsily from the den, which was off the kitchen.

Steven stepped back.

"It's me, Stan."

"Steve? Come on in."

Steven kicked open the screen door and found Stan in a chair in front of the television. He looked at Steven, but at first could not make out his condition, other than that he was filthy from head to foot, his eyes peering out from a black mask of grime, because Steven was standing at an odd angle, backed up a little distance from the door, as if shy. Then even before his mind could register what his eyes were seeing, apprehension put a massive squeeze on Stan's ailing heart. He grabbed his chest and collapsed.

CHAPTER SIX

MILLIE SHOLD, who lived about fifteen miles from the Saunders ranch, was standing at her kitchen counter pinching shut the crusts on half a dozen apple pies when the familiar warning tones sounded. For hours she had been working in a silence mellowed by the hum of a distant tractor and confirmed by an occasional whinny from the corral, and now this—an emergency on a day when she was the sole EMT on call in the valley. All her colleagues were attending a conference in Baker City that dealt, ironically enough, with new emergency first-aid techniques. Despite her years of experience, Millie dreaded responding to an emergency alone, for fear that her level of training might not be adequate. Compounding her reluctance was the fact that she generally knew the victims, and so could not hide behind the mask of an impersonal professional. Almost always she had crossed paths with them—in school, in church, in 4-H, or in any number of other community organizations—just as afterward she would continue to encounter them. It was hard for her to smile casually in the aisles of The Hitching Post to a person whose bleeding she had stanched or whose wound she had sewed up.

As she called in, she hoped it was not a suicide attempt, of which she had seen her share.

"Some kid got hurt at the Saunders place," the dispatcher told her.

"How?"

"Not real clear, Millie. Stan said something about him getting his hand bit."

She rinsed the flour from her hands, removed her apron, and scribbled a note for her husband. Then, easing open the screen door where the barn cat lay nursing her swarming litter, she hurried to the barn for the station wagon. Overhead, gathering storm clouds were turning the hot August sun to brass. A bite may not be too bad, she thought as she sped along, her medical kit beside her, as long as they have the dog. Clean the wound, apply antiseptic, maybe some stitches, bandage it, make sure the dog doesn't have rabies. She was feeling fairly reassured by the thought of these orderly procedures when she turned into the overgrown and rutted lane that led to Stan's house.

When she saw the look on Stan's face, her anxiety flared again. His lips were bloodless and trembling, his eyes darting; he seemed disoriented. He was rubbing his chest as if it ached. She knew about his bad heart.

"You doing OK, Stan?"

"Me? Yeah. He's in there." He pointed at the den. "He's hurt bad. His arms . . ." He was trying to explain, but suddenly she snapped a command. "Boil me some water and bring me some clean towels. Can you do that?"

"Yeah."

"Well, hurry up."

In the pine-paneled den the curtains were drawn, the only light in the general murk coming from the large TV screen. In its flickering bluish glow she made out a long figure slumped on the couch with a blanket covering the torso. For a change, it was no one she recognized. She knelt down and gingerly lifted the blanket.

"Let's see here," she said as she glanced, clamping down on her voice to hold it steady against her impulse to cry out. She gave a little cough and looked again. She felt a heat in her face as if from an opened stove, coupled with a chill at the roots of her hair. She rocked back on her heels.

"Hi, Millie," said the figure in a thin, tired voice.

It was a voice she knew, and her eyes darted to his face.

"Why, you're *Steven*," she breathed in a long exhalation, and her mind raced to bring the boy she'd known for years as a special ed pupil and Cub Scout into accord with the mangled figure before her. "My Lord, what's *happened* to you?"

Taking the question at face value, he repeated what he had said to Stan: "The baler ate my hands." A plain fact delivered with immense fatigue.

"Ate your hands?" she repeated, stunned.

He could go into shock, she thought. Why wasn't he screaming? Perhaps he was dying. How much blood has he lost? His shirt and jeans were caked with it, but it appeared to have stopped. Why? She placed two fingers on the artery in his neck and stared at her watch.

"Stan, I need light in here."

The pulse was weak and elevated.

Grabbing her scissors, she carefully started snipping his shirt away from his stumps, which were filthy, mangled, and reeking of char. Ah, she thought, there was no blood because somehow he had found a way to cauterize them. Not much remained. His right arm was severed three or four inches below the shoulder; the left, a little longer, a couple of inches above the elbow. She was about to ask him for more information when his weary voice intruded into her racing thoughts, "How's Stan?"

"Stan?" She had to made an effort to recall. "He's OK."

"He kind of collapsed when he saw me. I was afraid the shock might give him a heart attack."

God, wasn't that Steven all over, she thought, a foot away from death's door and worrying about Stan.

Stan brought a basin of steaming water and some washcloths and towels.

"Sheriff's here," he said.

"You heard anything from the ambulance?" she asked.

"Just that they're on their way."

Gently she began cleaning the areas around the wounds. "Hang on, Steve. I know you must be in terrible pain, but I got to clean off as much dirt as I can before it hardens."

"I'm awful thirsty," he said. "Can you get me some water, Stan?"

"No, he can't do that, Steve. I'm real sorry. We can't let you have any food or liquid because they're going to want to operate at the hospital. Maybe some ice, though. Get him some ice, Stan."

As he turned to leave, Steven said, "Do me a favor, Stan."

"What's that?"

"Turn off the TV."

Stan hit the button, blanking an infomercial for Japanese steak knives.

"Thanks. It was making me kinda sick."

Carefully Steven let his long frame fold back into the couch cushions.

In the kitchen, Stan put in a call to Dwight, who, at the moment, was resting on the couch. Debbie took the call and handed the receiver to Dwight. A moment later he was on his feet and moving out the door, Debbie at his heels. "Honey, be careful," she warned. Not soon enough. Charging ahead, Dwight stumbled as he stepped off the porch, and fell heavily on the flagstone walk, twisting as he went down. "God *damn*," he screamed. And there he was forced to lie until the sheriff, Dennis Parr, could help him back into the house.

When Parr got back to Stan's, Millie handed him an ice chest. "Go down there and find his arms."

Parr hurried into the field just as the ambulance pulled in.

"Where you guys been?" Stan demanded.

"Lost," was the reply. "You know, none of these little roads are even marked around here."

"Kids use the signs for target practice," said Stan.

DWIGHT LAY on the floor of his living room gritting his teeth while he waited for the handful of pain pills to take effect. He was having trouble grasping the disaster that had just occurred. He'd thought Steven had already finished baling the field and had left, securing the hay before the rain. Now this. The desolation he felt for Steven, of whom he had grown particularly fond over the summer, flowed together with the pain transfixing him like a skewer, and in the process turned into something like rage. Had he been on his feet, this disaster would never have happened. All his months of foreboding at having to rely on kids had turned out to be justified beyond his wildest fear. How had this thing happened? He knew that Steven was planning on meeting someone later that day to look at a used pickup. Maybe he'd gotten careless in his hurry to finish.

He told Debbie to go over and see what was going on. She met her father-in-law stepping off his porch.

"Come on," he ordered. "You got to help me."

"Do what?"

"Help Parr look for Steve's arms."

As they moved into the field they saw Parr straighten up from where he had been hunting in the baler's intake. He was holding an arm.

"Keep looking," he said as he hurried past them. "I couldn't see the other one and the ambulance is going to have to leave."

Debbie felt ill when she glimpsed the limb.

"Go ahead, Stan," she said. "I gotta stop a second."

She faced away from the men and took a couple of deep breaths. The wind gusts before the rain tasted good to her. A handful of fat rain-drops spattered down. Stan walked to the rear of the baler and began poking in the hay.

"Is it in there? You see it?" she asked moments later.

"No."

"Maybe it's already baled."

"COME ON, SON," one of the medics said, "lay down on this stretcher and we'll get going. We gotta get you to the hospital."

"You got my arms?" Steven asked, standing up from the couch. He'd seen the sheriff hand one to the medic, who'd then radioed that they were about to depart with one arm in an ice chest. "I ain't leaving without both my arms."

"We got one," the man said. "The quicker we get there, the more chance you got they can reattach it."

Steven turned to Millie. "I ain't leaving here, Millie, till they got both my arms."

"Hey, guy, we got no time, let's go," the medic commanded, his voice taut with urgency.

Steven gave him a flat look. "I ain't leaving here till we get both my arms, and I ain't laying down on that stupid stretcher."

"Leave him alone," Millie ordered. She drew up a kitchen stool.

"Just set here a sec." To the medic, "We can take another minute."

"You know as well as me that he could go into convulsions any second, Millie."

"We can take another minute."

"LOOK. There it is, Debbie. See it?"

Stan was pointing with the end of the pitchfork he had been using to probe the hay. Debbie saw the badly mangled arm lying tumbled among the hay in the rear of the baler.

"I got to turn on the tractor to open that rear gate," Stan said.

He climbed into the cab and turned the ignition. To his astonishment, the baler, which from the position of the PTO lever he judged to be off, sprang into activity the instant the tractor's engine ignited. Stan jumped in his seat. *What the hell?* What was going on today?

"Turn it off, Stan!" Debbie screamed. He swatted the lever. He was shaking. Then carefully he pulled the hydraulic lever and the rear gate lifted. Turning off the motor, he dismounted. They peered into the narrow opening.

"Go on in and get it, Debbie."

"I ain't crawling in there, Stan, for that. You can't ask me to do that."

"Hells bells, Debbie. That's Steven's arm, what's left of it. Maybe they can use it. No way with my knees and legs I can crawl in there. But you can."

Fighting a wild mixture of revulsion and pity, Debbie crawled under the gate. Gingerly she retrieved the damaged limb from the hay. She clambered out and handed it to Stan. They hurried back to the house.

"Finally," yelled the medic. "OK, we're going to put you on the stretcher."

But again Steven refused. Somehow it had become an irrational sticking point for him not to lie down on it and be carried from the house.

"Steven, please," Millie asked. "This is how it works."

Steven lay down on the stretcher. Quickly the medics carried him outside and eased him into the ambulance.

"OK. Let's go," said one of the medics.

Millie climbed in. They shut the doors, and, red lights flashing, they took off to Baker City.

As they did, Sheriff Parr raced back to Richland to pick up Betty at home and then R. E. at a nearby ranch. Debbie had called Betty. At The Shorthorn on Main Street, where a police scanner sat next to the toaster, the cook and waitresses had already spread the news to the Saturday lunch hour crowd that the younger Sharp kid had lost both of his arms in an accident at the Saunders place, but only one had been found.

THE RAIN SPATTERS turned to a downpour, forcing the ambulance to move with caution around the winding turns in the mountains. Millie had wrapped Steven in several blankets. As they careened along she swabbed his mouth, eyes, and nostrils with cotton, and moistened his lips with ice. She monitored his pulse and his breathing. Her training instructed her to remove all of Steven's clothes in preparation for emergency treatment at the hospital, but she refrained. Something in his manner forbade it. She felt that to invade his privacy when he could no longer defend it would be too gross an infringement of his basic dignity. She wondered what he possibly could be thinking. Clearly he had some hope that the damage would not be irreparable, because at one point he asked her if she thought they could reattach his arms.

"I don't know. I just don't know," she said.

Thirst tormented him. As the ambulance approached the rickety pop stand at the halfway point to Baker, he asked that they stop and leave word for the owner of the pickup he'd intended to meet there. Millie told him they had no time. She asked him if he wanted to tell her what had happened in the field, for she thought if she could keep him talking he would have a better chance of not lapsing into a coma.

"I don't know," he said. "Some hay got clogged. I was taking it out, and the baler turned on."

"How?" she asked.

"I don't know, Millie. It just did."

She didn't press him with additional questions, not wanting to add to his suffering, which obviously he was working hard to master, for he gave no sign of pain, not even a moan, except when she touched him, however lightly, and then he winced and chewed his lips. She kept track of his vital signs. She watched his face. He seemed to withdraw to a remote place. His lips were blue. The thought of the coming meeting with Betty and R. E. oppressed her.

"Millie," one of the medics said, "we got Baker on the line here. They want to know if you want Life Flight to take Steven directly to Portland. Or do they treat him first right there?"

"Who's on call in Emergency?"

The name he reported was one she recognized as belonging to an elderly internist. Panic seized her. She, the lowest person in the medical hierarchy, was about to make a decision that might determine whether Steven would ever regain the use of either of his arms. Fly him at once by jet to The University Hospital in Portland, where the specialists and good facilities were, or rush him into Emergency in Baker and put him in the care of a doctor perhaps not fully competent to deal with his condition?

"I can't answer that," she replied after an agonizing pause. "That's not my decision to make. I'm no doctor."

"All right," the man spoke back into the receiver. "They'll treat him first in Emergency in Baker, then fly him out after that."

WHEN SHERIFF PARR arrived at the hospital with R. E. and Betty, Steven was already in surgery, and they took up their vigil in the waiting room with a gathering group of family and friends. Among the first to arrive were Grandma and Grandpa Sharp, along with the minister who had replaced Leora as pastor when she retired. The mood in the room was anguished and uncertain, because little information had been reported other than the simple fact of Steven's devastating injury. In the meantime, the doctor told Steven he needed to make a decision.

"Your right arm is too damaged to be repaired," he reported. "That's certain. Your left is in slightly better shape."

"Can it be reattached?"

"Possibly. But it's doubtful it can become functional again."

"It won't work?"

"Probably not. There's been too much damage to the nerves."

"So, basically, it'll just hang there."

"Well, you might be able to regain some minimal use."

"I got no use for an arm that's no better than a hood ornament. Throw it away."

"OK," the doctor said. "We're going to sedate you now, Steven. You're not going to remember much of the plane ride to Portland."

But the sedative had little effect. Steven spoke more or less normally with his parents when he was wheeled into Recovery. There they were soon joined by Lori, and finally Ed, who after a search had been located on the large ranch where he was working.

"Hey, pardner," Steven said, greeting his brother with a ghost of humor. "Got myself messed up real good this time."

Ed took one look at Steven, and it was as if he'd been punched. He exchanged glances with R. E. and Lori, but could barely look at Betty.

"You sure as hell did," he said softly, then turned and left.

"We're taking him now," said the orderly.

R. E. and Betty stood up, ready to follow by helicopter.

"R. E., you going like that?" the pastor asked him. R. E. was wearing his grease-stained coveralls; he'd had no time to change.

"I guess. I ain't going home to change."

"Here, take mine," the pastor said. "We'll switch. We're about the same size." And they did.

Steven remained lucid on the way to the airport, and lucid when they loaded him into the diminutive Life Flight Learjet, where there was just enough room for his stretcher, emergency equipment, and a medic. It felt like sliding into the belly of a large animal, except that everything was metal. An inch from his cheek was a porthole through which he watched the pattern of raindrops change to lateral streaks as the plane took off, then stall into trembling beads as the plane rose. It was his first time in an airplane. It ascended steeply into thunderheads that began tossing it about like a shuttlecock. The medic kneeling at his side clutched the stretcher frame, his face taut as the plane dipped and bucked.

"Is this normal?" Steven asked, after a violent toss.

"It's a little rougher than normal, I gotta say that," the medic replied, his face drawn. He attempted a smile. "But we'll make it."

"Hope so. After what I been through today, it'd be a heck of a thing to crash."

WHEN DEBBIE AND STAN arrived home, they found cars parked along the road. Below in the hayfield they could see beams from flashlights and torches moving about, an unsettling sight, the veering probes of light like some kind of alien invasion. "What's going on?" Stan shouted at the gate into the mist that had followed the rain. A figure reported that they were looking for Steven's other arm. They'd heard on the scanner that one was still missing.

"Go on home," he said. "We got them both."

He turned back to the house. Debbie put her hand on his arm. "Come on, Stan. Have some supper with us. You better spend the night at our house."

"Sure," he replied. "Let's go see how Dwight's doing."

When they entered the house, they found Dwight on the phone. He gestured for silence. When he hung up, he said he'd been talking to their insurance agent. Then he'd made another call to his lawyer.

"It's a terrible thing that happened to Steven," he said later, when they sat down to dinner. Debbie was crying. "No question about that." He put his hands flat down on the table and added, "But, you know, we could lose the ranch on this kind of deal. Easy."

CHAPTER SEVEN

*D*ON'T AIM *at the water surface but about three feet higher so the fly lights above the bulge where they're feeding. At the last minute drop the rod tip and the fly'll settle right above that rainbow's nose and chances are he'll go for it, but if he don't well then just let it drift back and hope that he'll chase it while slowly, slowly you bring the rod back up slanty by your right ear. And take up the slack with the line hanging in a loop down past your shoulder. But now is the time to whip it so you push forward hard while at the same time snapping your wrist and the line whistles up off the water and past your ear and rolls over in the air in a loop like a wave with a wet bead of light running out to meet the fly. This time that rainbow's going to hit, and if he don't well then it's because . . . Look, actually the fly's not even put together yet, it's just a number two hook that for some reason keeps sticking holes in your fingers as you're winding a back-fanned mallard feather with black thread around the hook shank. It's freezing cold in the tiny attic room where the heater's working kind of in spasms under the bench where Dad sits patiently loading powder into shells under a hanging lightbulb when he turns and says careful, careful now that the two of you are down in the kitchen and Mom's gone. So now is our chance to heat lead in a saucepan on the stove and pour it, careful now, all trembly like bright blobs of mercury into the bullet molds, for if even a smidgen of it should happen to splash on your hands. . . . So stand back and here's Mom, not coming through the door with groceries and a puzzled look but leaning down over your hospital bed with a worried look, asking, "Stevie, you awake?"*

SLOWLY THE DREAM gives way to the hospital room.

"They'll be taking you soon," Betty said.

"Taking me where?"

"To surgery."

"Wasn't I just . . . ?"

"That was last night."

He moaned as he stirred, the fragmentary memory of last night's ordeal returning.

"I know, Stevie . . ."

"It ain't my arms, Mom. There's something wrong with my legs. It's like they're all itchy and on fire."

"That's where they took skin . . ."

"Why'd they take skin?"

"For grafts, honey. They have to take skin from your legs to make patches."

And then he was under way again, his IV dangling from a hook, jolting on a gurney down corridors smelling of disinfectant and discombobulated by flashes of people striding past and lying exposed in open doorways and voices and bells coming over the PA system, and then bumping into a green-quilted elevator to emerge with a bump into more corridors that led finally to a prep room where they hooked a different bag to his IV and, in a moment or two, darkness again.

There was day after day of this, with no way of distinguishing the days or keeping count of them, so sleeping and waking grew porous and flowed randomly into each other. Whenever Steven opened his eyes in his room, he found his mom and dad there, sometimes sleeping in beds on either side of him or sometimes sitting in chairs. At times there was food and they fed him; at times TV; often it was dark. About midway in the week the doctors switched to pigskin grafts rather than take more skin from his thighs and hips. After these had had time to take, they said, fresh grafts would again be made from his own skin.

Reeling under the impact of the multiple surgeries and groggy from anesthesia, even with the pain medication, he was constantly in pain. At times it was bright and jagged, searing, and at others dampened, but even then as active in his nerves as the dull pounding vibration of snow tires on a clear road, pooling at reclusive spots in the roots of his teeth, in the backs of his eyes, in the base of his skull. He would lie back on his pillows and stare down his skinny length, fixing his eyes on the thick wad of bandages that capped his stumps in an effort to distinguish between the pain in his actual nerves and flesh and the pain of his phantom limbs, which was just as intense. He struggled to muster his mental forces in the same ways he'd hit upon as a kid in the grip of asthma and migraine. One of his maneuvers was to go into the pain as if it were a knot and try to disentangle its strands. Each one by itself was more tolerable, easier to work on—easier to empty of its heat, somehow. But with pain flooding him from so many sources he had to resort to cruder methods, as if he were digging a kind of trench against a forest fire, on the near side of which he would position himself in full view of the pain, but out of its immediate embrace.

Ed had inadvertently revealed to him a similar technique, potentially more powerful, one day during their first summer on the family farm. Ed had taken him fishing with two other boys, and on the way back through the woods Ed had accidentally led Steven through a patch of nettles, which the other boys hadn't paid attention to because they were wearing jeans. Steven was in shorts, however, and by the time they emerged from the woods his legs were covered with painful welts. Dreading his mother's reaction if he showed up with his brother in this sorry state, Ed ran to the house for some medicine. Moments later he returned with half a glass of a green liquid that Steven, dancing with pain, downed in a couple of gulps despite its fiery, nasty taste. Then, sure enough, to both his and Ed's considerable relief, the pain in his legs began cooling; in less than an hour it was more or less gone. Not until that evening when they were getting ready for bed did Ed confess that he'd given him straight Listerine—a revelation that shocked Steven. He stared at his brother in amazement, not so much at the trick but at its effectiveness. How could the mind do that? If welts in flesh could be dispelled by mere thought, then thought was a lot more than what he'd known it to be. Clearly it was a force, one that perhaps he could direct consciously.

A short time afterward, Steven tried using the mental trick during an asthma attack, and at first it didn't work, but that was because he wasn't sufficiently focused. But then when he managed to get a clear picture of himself breathing clearly, it actually brought him some relief. As a kid he used to make use of a similar kind of focused concentration when he would sit in the dining room and draw and paint, oblivious of the conversations and comings and goings of the people around him. Before diving off a forty-foot bluff, he would picture himself entering the water as clean as a knife, or when winding up to deliver a crucial pitch, he'd see the pitch already completed; he would see these things so clearly and with such single-mindedness that at times the world had no choice but to give way before it.

But his present pain was too constant and multifarious to dominate. He would give way under the onslaught and be swept and swirled like a wood chip in white water, and then he would have to ring the bell for more pain medication. The drugs produced a restless sleep full of hectic dreams in which he often found himself back at the Saunders ranch try-ing to perform tasks that went on forever. In one he found himself try-ing to string barbed wire all the way to the mountains.

For seven days the surgeons at The University Hospital operated on him, first cleaning the wounds and attempting to deaden the raw nerves, then cutting away and shaping the exposed bones, and finally performing multiple skin grafts. When he was out of immediate danger and his condition sufficiently stable, they sent him home to recuperate.

He left with a prescription for pain medication. Betty had already begun changing his bandages and caring for his wounds. The doctors at the hospital told Betty and R. E. to bring Steven back in a month, when he would be sufficiently recovered to undergo more surgeries and begin therapy.

At home Steven faced the task of beginning his life over again. He was unable to feed, clean, or otherwise care for himself, or manage many of the myriad small tasks of daily life, like opening doors or turn-ing on lights or tying his shoes. R. E. helped out when he could, but was away at work during the day. Thus Betty bore the direct emotional and practical brunt of it all. Both were equally saddened. It helped that they were able to commiserate with each other, at least out of Steven's hear-ing, for in his presence he would tolerate no talk of regret or of what might have been. Once during his first week home when Betty was changing his bandages, she inadvertently pulled away some of the newly grafted skin with the last layer of gauze. Faced with the raw wound, she exclaimed, "Oh, Stevie, it's so awful what's happened to you."

He snapped: "Don't say that, Mom. I never want to hear you say anything like that again."

"But Stevie . . ."

"Look, it's done. It's happened." He was absolute. "It can't be fixed."

She drew a troubled breath.

More gently he asked her, "Do you think it helps me to have you say something like that?"

"No," she replied.

"Does it help you?"

"No, I guess not," she said.

"It really don't. Both of us, Mom, we have to just look ahead and be strong. Otherwise we'll just go under. But we'll be all right."

Thereafter Betty rarely gave Steven a glimpse of her grief. She kept her pain and worry about the prospects facing her sorely handicapped and dyslexic son to herself, or shared them with R. E. It helped that they could pray together, which they did on a daily basis, and thereby consciously acknowledge that their dilemma exceeded their resources on every level. They had always been religious, but until now had tended to see themselves as competent, self-sufficient people, more comfortable in the role of helpers in their community than receivers of help. Now they had no choice but to modify that sense of themselves and accept the outpouring of comfort and aid provided by their neighbors, their church, and the general community in the two valleys. People stepped forward to help in a variety of ways. An acquaintance of Betty's, for example, a professional nurse, volunteered to come by every day and change Steven's bandages, a service for which Betty was hugely grateful. Gifts of food and helpful items showed up for months. Various groups took up collections. And in all the churches of the area, people prayed for them. It was all a great comfort to Betty and R. E. Whether Steven himself prayed, or put much stock in prayer, however, is unlikely. He had nothing against it, or against religion in general, but felt that for the time being it was all he could do to keep his focus on managing his pain and staying psychologically intact. On the other hand, he never for a moment doubted that he was at the mercy of forces far beyond his control.

Barry dropped by not long after Steven's return. Full of misery, he sat on the edge of an easy chair and contemplated his friend, who was stretched out on the living room sofa, wrapped in a blanket, drowsy from his pain medication, but grateful for the visit. "Steve, I am so sorry," Barry said. "I would have come to the hospital, but I didn't know."

"How could you? You were out of town."

"Well, to tell you the truth, I actually had a feeling that something was wrong," he replied. "One night during the week, it got so strong I called my mom, but she didn't tell me anything. She just acted weird."

"Weird?"

"She kept asking me if I was OK, and I said, 'Mom, of course I'm OK, what's gotten into you?' And then she started to cry, and she said, 'Oh, I just worry about you so much. I don't want anything bad to happen to you.' I kept asking her why anything bad should happen to me, but all she kept saying was that she was worried.

"Then when I got into town, first person I ran into was Jason [a mutual high school friend] and he said, 'Did you hear what happened to Steve?' 'What?' I asked, and he said, 'Steve got his arms cut off in a baler,' and I refused to believe him, because you know Jason."

"Always goofing around."

"Right. So it wasn't until I visited my mom and I asked her point-blank: 'Is anything wrong with Steven?' and she started to cry again that it hit me that maybe Jason was telling the truth. So I made her tell me."

Barry fell silent, the pain of his discovery rolling from that moment to this, threatening to overwhelm him.

"Hey, there was nothing you could have done," Steven said.

"Damn, Steve, I am so sorry."

"I know you are. But this ain't the end of the world. I'm going back in the hospital. I'll get me some new arms. Maybe electric ones, I don't know, but something."

"But I keep thinking, if only I had been there that day."

"That's crazy, I knew you weren't going to be there."

"I know." Barry gave him a wan smile. "Strange to think that the last time I saw you away from work was when we went to the rodeo."

Steven smiled at the memory, a lifetime ago, a day when they'd finished baling early, each gone home and cleaned up, slicked back their hair, pulled on their cowboy boots and blue jeans, their wide-buckled belts and fancy shirts, and headed over to Baker City in Barry's truck. They'd pulled up in the dusty parking lot to the raucous midway music and the bellowing of cattle, the odors of cotton candy and deep-frying, the distinctive mix of county fair excitement they'd been breathing every year since childhood. They'd watched a couple of the roping and riding events and a tractor pull; checked out the livestock barns where Richland's famous blue ox stood in all its immensity; cast an eye on a few of the contests, like pie-eating and watermelon-seed–spitting; bought some beer and a couple of burgers; then did some swanking around until eventually they'd hooked up with a couple more friends, and with them had gone looking for girls they either knew or didn't know to take to the dance. And they'd danced till the band shut down, swing and old-time rock and roll, with some slow numbers thrown in. Then they drove home in the early hours, sipping beer and smoking cigarettes with the windows down and the cool night air blowing in, riding along in the desert night immensely fatigued, because they'd been up since five, but knowing that evenings like these stretched before them in an endless array.

"And now here we are. And here you are."

"Hey, Barry, next year, this time, we'll be back at that rodeo."

At that Barry had to smile, because he could hear that Steven meant it. If anybody could make it happen, he could. Then Barry left so that Steven could sleep. Barry's misery had been partially relieved by Steven's refusal to be pitied, his resolve to go on as much as possible as before. During Steven's recovery, Barry would give him tireless help.

ON AUGUST 30, Betty received a phone call from Gerald Beverage, the senior compliance officer of Oregon's Occupational Safety and Health Administration (OSHA). He asked whether he might drop by the following day to get a statement from Steven concerning the accident. Betty advised him that Steven was still heavily medicated and so not in the best condition for talking, but Beverage said that it would just be a matter of answering a few simple questions. Prior to visiting the Sharps, the inspector spent the morning of the thirty-first at the Saunderses' talking to Dwight about the accident and generally checking out his equipment and conditions on the ranch. Dwight had been concerned about the visit because he knew that a thorough inspection could not help revealing violations of Oregon's safety code. Beverage took four pages of notes and told Dwight that he had indeed found several significant violations, which he would present to him in an official report. Beverage held none of these directly accountable for Steven's accident, but then again it was not Beverage's function to determine the cause of Steven's accident. Beverage's only job was to check the site for infractions of the OSHA code.

But, of course, he and Dwight discussed the accident, and it seemed to them both that the primary fault lay with Steven. He must have failed to turn off the PTO, they decided. Dwight mentioned that he had nearly lost his fingers himself, some years ago, by pulling clogged hay from between the baler's rollers. What other explanation was there? Sure, Steven was a careful worker, far more meticulous than Barry, but maybe on this last day of work he'd been in a hurry. Dwight recalled that Steven had had an appointment to see a guy about a truck.

Regardless of the views he had begun to formulate about Steven's responsibility for his accident, Beverage showed up at the Sharps' later that afternoon wearing the face of a sympathetic and neutral public official. For the first forty-five minutes of his visit he sat with Betty at the dining room table, leading her through the thickets of workmen's compensation procedures, while Steven rested on the couch in the adjoining living room. Steven's medical expenses, both now and in the future, were going to be considerable, particularly if later on, after his therapy was completed, his doctors decided to fit him for myoelectric prostheses, each of which cost several thousand dollars. But even for these expensive devices, Beverage told Betty, Steven could apply for the appropriate compensation.

When they were done with procedural matters, Beverage moved

into the living room and questioned Steven. Betty observed the interview but did not participate in it.

Beverage asked about the equipment, whether the chain guards were missing from the baler, for example, or tines from the intake rollers. Steven answered yes. As for the Case tractor, Beverage had noticed some oil in the cab, and Steven said there was some kind of leak. The parking brake was shot.

"Was that a problem for you?" Beverage asked.

"Not really. You just had to park it on a level, or across the hill, rather than up and down."

Then Beverage asked about how Steven had been trained, and about his daily routine, whether he was supervised or not. He also asked whether, on the day of his accident, Steven had been in a hurry to finish. "Not particularly," Steven replied.

"Not hurrying to see a guy about a truck?"

"That wasn't until four."

Beverage requested that Steven describe how his accident had occurred, asking in particular whether Steven had fully turned off the PTO. Steven replied that he had. Beverage wanted to know how he accounted for it turning back on, and Steven said he had no idea. "A freak accident, then?" Beverage asked.

"I guess," Steven replied.

Beverage had been writing down Steven's answers, and now that the interview was over, he read back through them aloud. Steven listened wearily. "Do you have anything else to add?" Beverage asked. "Can you think of anything about this accident that I might have overlooked?" Steven said that he couldn't, and Beverage thanked him for his cooperation. He wrote at the bottom of the form: "Victim read this statement and stated it was accurate to the best of his recollection. Because of his injuries, he was unable to sign his name, my initials, GB, August 31, 1992. 5:10 p.m."

Beverage had been working at OSHA for eleven years. In the course of that time he had investigated three previous accidents. Most of his time was spent investigating industrial sites. Several years later, when Steven thought back on the inspector's visit, the image that came to mind was that of a snowball. He realized that it was on that afternoon that Dwight and Beverage had tossed their impressions back and forth and given them a preliminary shape that subsequently took on weight, mass, and solidity. And then the two of them had rolled the snowball to him, and he, in his distracted condition, had given it a little answering nudge with his foot, whereupon, although not immediately, the ball of presumed cause and effect had started to pick up its pace, increase in size, and somehow start heading back in his direction.

CHAPTER EIGHT

I N ONE of the double bedrooms on the plastic surgery ward of the Oregon Health Sciences University one afternoon in mid-September 1992, a staff psychologist was checking on Steven's emotional condition. He leaned back in the bedside armchair, made a little steeple with his fingertips, and asked Steven how he was doing. Steven was recovering from his third surgery in as many days.

"Can't complain, for the moment," he responded drowsily, savoring a stretch of euphoric disembodiment in the wake of the anesthesia administered to him that morning. On the other side of the drawn curtain, in the neighboring bed, his roommate, a sixteen-year-old boy from Portland nicknamed Buzz, lay unmoving, staring at the ceiling.

"That's good, Steven. That's good. I understand the skin grafts are taking satisfactorily."

"It's where they're taking that hide from, on my legs and butt, that hurts."

"I understand. But they're nearly done. At least for this round. In a few more days we'll be ready to let you go home again, so you can rest and recuperate."

"Sounds good."

"What you need now, physically speaking, is time. Time to let those grafts heal and the swelling in your stumps to go down."

"Feel kind of like footballs right now. And *man*, they're sore."

"Right. And that's to be expected, of course."

"What bothers me most is the pain in the parts that aren't there."

"That's called phantom pain."

"I know."

"You see, the centers in your brain don't know your arms are gone. They just register that there's been a lot of trauma to your nerves. And then neuromas develop, which add to the pain."

"What's that?"

"A neuroma is like a little tumor, a bundle of fiber that can develop at the end of a traumatized nerve. They will have to be removed."

"More cutting."

"Unfortunately. How extensive it will be they'll be better able to tell once your swelling has gone down. And then," he said, his voice rising warmly, "you'll be ready to move next door to Shriners and start being fitted for some prostheses. New arms."

"How long you figure that'll take?"

"For the swelling to go down? Maybe a month. Maybe a little longer. I think we're looking at around mid-October."

"Hmm," Steven replied, letting his eyes shut.

"That might seem like a long time to stay cooped up at home, a month or more, missing school, but before you know it it'll be behind you."

Steven opened his eyes and gave the psychologist a level look. "You mean I can't go to school?"

"Would you want to?" he asked in surprise.

"Well . . . yeah. I don't see why not."

"Before you get your prostheses?"

"Yeah. I still got the use of my legs."

"Well, Steven, you'll probably want to think that over. Before getting your artificial arms, what would you be able to do? You won't be able to open a door, hold a book, pick up a pencil, or eat a sandwich, none of those things. I understand that you're eager to get on with your life, but think about it realistically."

As if taking him literally, Steven chose not to respond and turned his face to the wall. The silence between them stretched out beyond the bounds of politeness. Was he falling asleep? The psychologist made a note on his clipboard. "Steven?" he asked gently, leaning forward. In a surprisingly vigorous tone, Steven said, "You know, Doc, I'm kind of tired right now. And by the way," he said, turning back to face him, "you ain't a *real* doctor, are you?"

"I don't know about being a *real* doctor, I'm a psychologist."

"Like a shrink?"

"Well, like a therapist."

"That's what I figured, and like I said, I'm kind of tired right now. Maybe we can talk later, if you want."

"Fine, Steven. It's important that we keep talking," he said, rising from his chair. "Go ahead and catch some sleep." He exited the room, leaving the door open behind him. Steven let a minute or two go by, then asked, "Buzz, you awake?"

"Yeah, Steve."

"Do me a favor and shut the door."

Buzz got up to comply. "You don't much care for the therapist, do you?"

"I got to admit he's starting to get on my nerves. Every day when I'm waking up, there he is, sitting there, wanting to yack. It's a little aggravating."

"How come?" Buzz sat down in the chair beside the bed.

"'Cause he wants to get inside my head, and that annoys me. Last thing I want is some shrink messing with my head."

"Give him a break, he's just trying to help."

"Did I ask him?"

"He's helped me."

"Yeah, how?" Steven countered, then instantly regretted it, fearing he'd offended his roommate, who spent hours talking to the therapist.

One warm day last June, Buzz had been sitting at the end of a dock with his skis resting on the surface of the water, uncoiling a tow rope that was looped around his arm, when the powerboat to which the rope was attached had unexpectedly leapt forward. Before the engine roar had reached his ears, the rope had run out and severed his left forearm as if with a cleaver. Now he was dealing with an extreme depression that had pushed him into a recent suicide attempt. Buzz was a large-framed, athletic kid with classic blond lifeguard good looks whose life no longer made sense to him. The psychologist's strategy for relieving his despondency, in addition to administering antidepressants, was to lead him through Dr. Elisabeth Kübler-Ross's five stages of grieving laid out in her popular book *On Death and Dying*: denial, anger, bargaining, depression, and acceptance.

"I don't know. Just talking to him helps me," said Buzz.

"Well, for you, that's good, then."

"I mean, I'm still really depressed, but at least I don't feel like killing myself all the time."

"That's a step in the right direction. No point in being dead at your tender age."

"On the other hand," Buzz said wearily, "I don't feel much of anything."

"Man, don't you think that's from all those pills he's always having you take?" Steven asked almost pleadingly.

"Yeah, I guess so. They flatten everything out. And pretty soon you get like you just don't give a shit. But, you know, that's better than any minute feeling like you're going to want to jump out the window."

"Buzz, I got to admit, that's something I just don't understand, wanting to kill yourself. I mean, wanting to kill yourself because of your accident."

"Don't you ever feel that way?"

"No, I really don't."

"Steve, I don't mean this in the awful way it's going to sound . . ."

"Yeah."

"But from my standpoint, I don't understand why you *don't* feel like killing yourself. I'm not saying you *should*, you understand, I'm just asking why you don't."

"You think losing my arms would make me want to kill myself? How come?"

"Well, obviously because of how it's changed you. Because of all the things you can't do anymore."

"I don't know about what I'll be able to do or not do, you know, we'll have to see about that. And sure, my life has changed, but that doesn't mean that *I* have."

"How can you say that you haven't changed?"

Steven paused to formulate his thought. "Well, because I'm not just my arms. My arms aren't *me*. You follow me?"

A couple of days later, after the last of the current set of surgical procedures, Steven returned home. Before leaving he had an exit interview with the psychologist, who again wanted to know how and what he was feeling.

"I'm anxious to get home."

"What do you have planned?"

"Get a good night's sleep, for starters. It's hard for me to sleep in a hospital."

The therapist wanted to know about Steven's feelings, any regret or disappointment that he'd be willing to share.

"For the moment, the main thing I'm unhappy about . . ."

"Yes?"

"Is that I missed the Baker County Fair last weekend. I wasn't there to show my pig."

"Your pig?"

"My 4-H pig."

"Is that something that's important for you?"

"Well, sure it's important. Last year I won first prize."

The other made a note. He could tell from Steven's voice that his regret was real. It was a start. Perhaps it was the end of a thread on which he might gently tug in the months ahead. That year Lori had shown another pig Steven had raised, and had won second prize. During the judging, the animals were considered without reference to their owners, but when the bidding started, the auctioneer took a moment to introduce the petite, dark-haired young woman in a jean skirt and plaid shirt leading the 275-pound Yorkshire as the sister of Steven Sharp, the teenager from Richland who'd recently been tragically injured. He reminded the crowd that the family was now facing a mountain of medical bills, and he encouraged them to put some heart into the bidding. Lori stood solemnly beside her brother's pig, lightly scratching its back with her leading stick while the bids began to fly. They closed around $400, a generous sum, the final bid coming from a rancher from Eagle Valley. The auctioneer banged down his hammer and thanked the man by name, at which point the rancher promptly rose to his feet and announced that he was donating his pig for sale all over again.

Happily surprised, the auctioneer thanked the man for his generosity and launched into an even more animated second round of bidding.

Once again the pig was sold for an amount well in excess of its market value, and again to a purchaser who offered it for resale. Now the crowd was whistling and cheering, warming to its own spontaneous show of generosity. In all, Steven's pig was sold five times that afternoon, and netted more than $2,000 for the family.

"So you see," Steven said to the psychologist, "I'm not really that sad that I wasn't there. We still won second prize."

AFTER A COUPLE of weeks of convalescence at home Steven told his parents he wanted to start attending class. They questioned whether he was ready. His limbs were extremely sensitive and could be easily damaged, and there was little he could do for himself; he could not open a door or pick up a pencil or turn the page in a book. But Steven was adamant, and soon they conceded. Perhaps it would be good for him to get back to his network of close friends. During the early days of Steven's recovery at home, most of these friends dropped by to see him, but these meetings, which took place in the Sharps' living room, tended to be awkward. Steven was eager to get out of the house and start connecting with them as much as possible in the old way.

One morning in mid-October, R. E. held open the door of his pickup while Steven climbed in. R. E. pulled out of the driveway and rolled down Newbridge Road. The surroundings felt strange to Steven, as if a pane of glass had inserted itself between him and the well-known landscape. He found he was actually *seeing* the Grange hall and the Nazarene church as they slid past the windows, seeing them as a visitor might rather than as a familiar blur. There was something puzzling and dreamlike about the clipped autumn fields and pastures with their patches of chilly morning fog, their grazing cattle, and scattered hay bales. In former years this view would have meant that hunting season was about to begin, which would have meant that he and R. E. would have spent their short ride into town talking about their camping plans. This morning, however, they said little as they drove along, the near silence suggesting to Steven that try as he might, nothing was going to be available to him in the old way.

It was all indeed behind glass, inaccessible. He would never again set foot on the baseball field next to the Adventist Church, where he'd spent countless hours in recent years. It was right *there* but totally remote. That was true of each familiar site and building on Main Street in Richland, not all of them equally interdicted, to be sure, but all of them standing as much in memory as in actual space: the pumpkin field at the end of the block, site of the annual Halloween party; Flip's Coffee Shop, where he and Barry had eaten lunch a couple of times a week during the summer; the gas station, where if time was too short for lunch they'd buy some chips and a can of soda, and where earlier he and Jason Blade used to tinker with Jason's motorcycle. To the right, across the street, were the Longbranch and The Shorthorn, Richland's two restaurants, The Shorthorn particularly familiar because it was there that members of the Nazarene church regularly ate Sunday brunch. Then the bait shop and the post office, and finally, The Hitching Post, and The Hitching Post Motel. Nothing on the four blocks composing Main Street had changed in the six or seven weeks since he had last visited, but he had aged so much, a twist on Rip Van Winkle.

They pulled up in front of the grade school, where the Richland kids waited for the high school bus. R. E. leaned over and pushed the door open, and Steven got out, slamming the door behind him with a shove of his boot. R. E., careful not to embarrass his son by hanging around, drove on. And now the feeling of invisible glass grew stronger as Steven approached the waiting kids. He could see himself with their eyes, an outsider scary in his radical disfigurement. His face drained of color and his throat dried as he approached, but his smile remained in place. He gave a little cough and steadied himself with a toss of his head, greeting the wall of familiar faces, "Hey, how y'all doin'?" The ordinary words delivered in his slow familiar drawl prompted a chorus of relieved replies and counterquestions, and then he was into it, running through the ceremony of reacquaintance whose success, he instinctively understood, depended on speaking the same old familiar words with the same old familiar humor. He had to convince them that he was still the same old slow-talking, understated Steven. "Yeah, messed myself up *pretty good* this time," he said with a grin and a cock of his head. Then, once he'd put them more or less at ease, he frankly avowed his temporary helplessness: "You guys are going to have to open some doors for me and other stuff like that for a while, until I get me a new set of arms."

When would that be? they wanted to know. In a month or two, he told them. And with that he'd won them back, for he'd met them in a way that neutralized their dismay and set limits to their pity. Not that they had been at all difficult to win, for Steven was one of the most popular kids in town, and they were eager to help him. Patiently he answered their questions, using a kind of nuts-and-bolts realism that did much to defuse the horror of his ordeal. He might have been speaking about a damaged machine or an injured mule. The only thing he would not say much about was pain. When they asked him about that, he would report briefly on his sensations, many of which were indeed painful, but he spoke of them as localized, specific, strictly finite; he never gave a true indication of his actual state. To those few of his friends in the days ahead who, presuming on their friendship, came right out and asked him: What was it like that day? or even What did it feel like? he would give an impersonal response. "Well, when a person loses a lot of blood, it's easy for them to go into shock," or "When pain passes a certain line, it almost stops hurting." Downplaying, deflecting, he gave no one admittance to his subjectivity.

He was equally dismissive of attempts to give a romantic tinge to his ordeal. A local newspaper had made much of the bird that had hovered overhead, presenting it without question as an eagle, as if to inject some element of the uncanny, but when people asked Steven about the eagle he would laugh and say it was probably just a buzzard looking for a meal. His goal was always to present himself as normal, ordinary, at most a guy who had solved a very tough problem in a very tough way. For this reason he was careful never to mention his recurrent nightmare about the murderous baler, nor would he allow Betty to mention it either.

His friends were happy to follow his lead and continued to tease him or, in their terms, harass him in the old way, grateful to find the same friendly, sassy Steve Sharp they'd always known. They accommodated his handicap with a minimum of fuss, opening doors for him, helping him with his locker and books, even partially deflating the basketball during gym, so that he could clamp it under his left stump and run with it up and down the court. One or two of his male friends

— 65 —

assisted him in the bathroom, and various girls took turns feeding him at lunchtime, showing him an attentiveness he pretended to enjoy.

The school counselor had been alerted by the staff psychologist in Portland to expect Steven to fall into a state of depression once the newness of his situation had worn off, and invited him to her office. Steven was willing to talk to her, but not about his condition. She was savvy enough not to push him. They had talks about his activities, his relationships—occasionally stressful with authority figures—and, as time went on, about his progress at the Shriners Hospital, where he returned periodically, first for additional surgeries and physical therapy and then for his prosthetic arms. In time she put more trust in Steven's emotional equilibrium, to the extent that she even began using him as a peer counselor for certain of her troubled students.

CHAPTER NINE

AFTER THREE or four weeks of recuperation at home and school, it was time for Steven to return to the hospital in Portland for additional operations, after which he would begin his treatment at the adjacent Shriners Hospital. Ed volunteered to drive Betty and Steven because R. E. was busy with his work. When Ed arrived mid-afternoon on the last Saturday in September, no one was about. Kicking off his boots, he moved on saddle-weary legs to the narrow galley between the refrigerator and the sink, and glanced out the window. He is a big man and his shoulders practically filled the confined space. Snow lay in patches on the stubble fields. He heated a cup of leftover breakfast coffee and lifted the lid on the pie cozy. He was sitting down to a slice when Steven's disheveled head appeared in the stairwell from his basement bedroom. "Hey, man, I didn't think anyone was here," Ed said, "the house was so quiet. Where's Mom?"

"You got me," Steven replied, a little bewildered. He'd been sleeping. "She was here when I went downstairs."

"She often leave you alone?"

"I don't think so."

"Probably down at Grandpa's. How you doing?"

"OK, I guess. Better."

Steven was doing better in the sense that his wounds were healing, but the pain in his muscles, nerves, and bones remained intense. Nevertheless, he'd cut down on his pain medication because of its side effects; he found he preferred specific distress to gray, melancholy stupor. As a consequence, his sleep suffered, the firing of his ravaged nerves filling it with confused dreams, which he nonetheless tended to leave with regret, for in them he often had his arms. He found it strange to wake and find Ed sitting in the kitchen, because the two of them hadn't spoken in person since that first day in the hospital, and a certain awkwardness now hung in the air between them. Ed had moved away from home several years ago, so the brothers had fallen out of the routine of banter and insult that used to facilitate their interaction. To add to the awkwardness, at least on Ed's part, was the fact that he was sitting there fork in hand with his slice of pie. Should he offer Steven one? He would have to feed him, of course. Would that be awkward? Perhaps it wouldn't be for Steven, who, from what Ed had heard, was adapting to his situation with little fuss—but for Ed? Fortunately, Betty came through the door.

"Why, hello, stranger," she said. "I didn't expect you till later."

"Where you been, Mom?" Steven asked.

"Down at Grandma's for a little bit. They're coming for dinner. They want to see you." She smiled at Ed. "You were sound asleep when I left, Stevie."

"Yeah, I was, till I heard Ed banging around up here. Thought maybe a moose had wandered into the house."

That was better. That was more the tone. It helped to have Betty there.

"How you been, Ed?"

"Real busy, Mom."

In recent weeks he'd been taking part in the fall cattle drive, working with crews from his own and other ranches to move the herds down from their summer grazing grounds in the mountains to ranches where they would spend the winter. Ed liked the work, spending his days on horseback and camping at night. From the time he'd been a kid he'd wanted to be a cowboy, and indeed it was work that suited his reserved and solitary temperament.

After chewing the fat with Betty, the brothers stood up to leave for a walk. Betty helped Steven into his jacket and boots, then stood watching from the front window as they crossed the bridge and entered the apricot orchard on the far side of the road, Ed burly as a bear, with a forward roll to his walk, while Steven maintained his armless balance with a compensatory tilt to his lean frame, like a man striding into a wind or a wading crane. They were walking among the trees that in Grandpa's time had supported the family, and that after his retirement, when Betty and the kids had taken over—irrigating, pruning, spraying, and harvesting—still produced enough fruit for their small circle of regular customers. It used to be Ed's job to carry the heavy bushel baskets and ladders from tree to tree; she and Lori would pick, while Steven would scramble barefoot and agile as a monkey into the upper branches. It seemed only a season or two ago that they'd been working together, the four of them, yet the overgrowth of the trees declared that it had been more like a decade. The trees were no longer the neatly trimmed ovals that the eyes of memory expected to see; they had bolted into tangled clumps of spiky branches. It was painful for Betty to see her boys reuniting among the unkempt trees, although on the other hand she was relieved to see them talking together again. Lori was married now, living in Baker City, but had kept in touch with her brothers.

Steven showed Ed the new mule R. E. had recently bought, a temperamental three-year-old named Henry that was proving something of a challenge to break for camping use. It tended to balk at fallen trees across the path, or pace too close to the mule in front of it, which would then kick and buck, behaviors that could be dangerous for R. E. on high, narrow mountain paths. "Next year," Steven said, "once I get my arms, I'll help Dad train this guy."

"Well, you got the patience," Ed replied after a pause. "You always been good with animals. Like with your 4-H pigs."

"You, too," said Steven.

"Not like you, man," said Ed. "Me, if the little pig didn't want to walk nice, I'd just hitch it to the tractor and trot it up and down the road a few times. Then he'd mind. But you, you'd coax yours along."

Memories. Steven's condition had turned the most mundane of them into a source of sadness. The brothers left the orchard and continued walking down the road, away from the house. "You know, Steve, I'm real sorry I haven't been by to see you sooner," Ed said. "I been meaning to, but I just been so damn busy."

"Yeah, I figured."

Ed looked away. "No, look, that ain't the real reason. The fact is, I been kind of putting it off. That day when I first saw you in the hospital, man, I just about lost it. I had to get out of there."

"Hey, I would have felt the same way if it'd been you."

"Yeah, I guess you would. But you more than likely would of stayed. Yeah, c'mon, you know you would of. But your deal coming on top of everything else, I just needed some time to think."

Ed was referring to the death of a close friend of his, Tom Smith, we'll call him, in late July, someone Steven had once known fairly well, too. The death of young people was unfortunately not that uncommon for Eagle Valley, where the suicide rate in the nineties was eight times greater than the national average. But Tom had a high school education and reasonable intelligence, and he could have escaped the hard times in the valley and made a life for himself elsewhere, had the town not had its teeth in him, or vice versa, in ways that would find echoes in Steven's life in coming years.

Most of Tom's unfortunate story was familiar to Steven. When Smith was about five, his parents divorced in such a hostile fashion that Mrs. Smith took out a restraining order against her husband. He defied it, however, by climbing through a first-floor window of his former house, late one night, in order to retrieve some of his personal belongings. On the point of climbing back out again, his suitcase on the lawn outside the window, he changed his mind and stepped back inside, in order to visit his son. He opened the door of his son's bedroom, but his wife, who had heard an intruder, had holed up in there with a shotgun. For an instant Mr. Smith stood silhouetted against the hall light, unidentified, and in that instant she killed him.

In itself, the killing would obviously have been enough to cause severe damage to the young boy, but what turned the sorry affair into an endless source of damage was that town people tended to view the shooting not as a mistake but as a murder, perhaps not a premeditated one, but a murder nonetheless. Mr. Smith had been a popular figure in town, and sympathy gravitated toward him. Nothing could be proved against his ex-wife, but rumors and suspicions circulated. Rather than try to mollify the town, Mrs. Smith eventually started a lawsuit against one of her outspoken accusers, which then dragged out into a long and bitter feud. It was in this poisoned atmosphere that Tom Smith had grown up, a collateral target of gossip and ill will, which he tried to counter during his childhood and adolescence through defiant and flashy behavior. In his teens he drove fast cars and loud motorcycles, drank too much, partied too hard, and made a fair number of enemies in the process. To a few friends, however, like Ed and Steven, he showed a more serious and occasionally more wounded aspect of himself.

As the brothers continued to walk, they mounted a rise in the road that gave a sweeping view of the valley and surrounding desert, the stubble fields and the wide snow-streaked sand. Hunching his shoulders against the chilly wind, Ed nodded at the road ahead and told Steven that was where Tom had died, a fact he had not revealed to the deputy sheriff or anyone else in order to ward off gawkers. He said they'd had breakfast together in town, then gone out hunting. Around three, with the light failing, they'd called it a day. They hadn't spoken much in the course of the day, but that was normal. On the way back into town, Tom had begun to complain about the mess his life was. He'd been laid off from work, his girlfriend had broken up with him, and his mother, as usual, was suffering from her long ostracism. Ed listened sympathetically to his friend's troubles, but since none of them were, in essence, new, he gave his standard response. He advised Tom to get away from Richland, look for a job elsewhere, make a change.

"And then all at once he asked me to pull over," Ed said. " 'Why?' I asked, and he said, "Cause I want to get out.' So I pulled over, I thought maybe he was sick or needed to take a leak or something, I mean, he seemed OK. Then he got out and went about twenty paces up the road, then turned around and looked at me with a funny grin on his face, and the next thing I knew he put the barrel of his shotgun under his chin, reached down, and pulled the trigger."

"Damn."

"I sat there and watched that," Ed said. "Then I had to pick up what was left of him and put him in the back of the truck and take him home."

It was not an unfamiliar tale in Steven's and Ed's circles, but never had the victim been this close. Steven and Ed continued to walk, turning over the details of that final day and final conversation, but came no closer to figuring out what specifically had moved Smith to inflict the outrageous spectacle of his exit on perhaps his closest friend. "You'd think," said Steven, "he wouldn't want you to see that."

"I don't know, Steve. Maybe that was his way to show me how desperate he was, that this time he wasn't crying wolf. 'Cause he'd been talking about his depression off and on for years."

How many of their mutual friends or near acquaintances had committed suicide in recent years? Four? Five? What was the undertow that seemed to be operating so powerfully in these valleys, exercising such an insidious allure, particularly among young people—male and female—barely out of their teens? For Ed and Steven, the effect of these multiple voluntary deaths produced a sense of enormous bleakness, of flat and sterile unanswerability. Close as they had been to Tom, they sensed they could speculate all day about his motivations and still be left with the same blank wall.

But to some dreadful questions there were answers, or at least living people to pose them to. Having addressed his friend's death, Ed took advantage of the moment to turn to the other topic that was heavy on his mind. He said, "Look, Steve, before we get back inside, there's something I got to ask you."

"Shoot."

"Just between you and me, and I hope you don't think I'm trying to make you feel worse than you already do, but," he took a breath, "how come you didn't turn that damn baler off?"

"But I did, Ed."

"What do you mean, you did?"

"You ain't the first one to ask me that, you know. Everybody wonders the same thing. There was an OSHA guy came out and talked to me about how come the baler turned on, and I told him I didn't know. He called it a 'freak accident,' but it was pretty clear he thought I'd left it on. But I know I turned that sucker off."

"Well, then, how come it turned on?"

"All I can say is, I did what I always did. I pulled the lever back, cut down my rpms, same as always."

"You're sure?"

"How sure are you that you put your truck in park when you pulled up today? You got a specific memory of that?"

"No."

"But you're sure?"

"Course."

"Well, that's how sure I am. Even surer, 'cause I had to go through three or four different steps."

"Well, that's a relief to hear that, Steve, even though it don't make sense."

"It's bad enough losing my arms," Steven said, "without having to go around for the rest of my life thinking it was because of some dumb-ass mistake I made."

"That's what I was thinking," Ed agreed. "I was thinking you're way too smart to screw up like that."

Ed brought the matter up with R. E. while they were sitting around waiting for Grandma and Grandpa Sharp to arrive for supper. In their brief conversations on the topic, Steven had told R. E. that he had no idea why the baler had turned on, and from his taciturn response Steven had taken it that R. E. felt he must have done *something* wrong. R. E. had been servicing that tractor since 1972, and saw no other explanation. Yet when Ed reported on his just completed conversation with Steven, R. E. was willing to listen. Then Steven and R. E. talked.

"Dad, I can see myself reaching down and yanking that PTO back, just like I always did," said Steven.

"You can, huh?"

"Yeah. So is there some way it could have turned back on?"

"Not that *I'm* aware of," R. E. replied, but then added, "which don't mean it ain't possible."

"Well, in one way it makes no difference," Steven said, "at this point. The harm's done. And no matter what I say, most people are going to go on thinking that I screwed up. But you know, at least I want *you* to know I did what I always did."

And then, to his great credit, R. E. told Steven that he believed him, overcoming what all his years of experience as a mechanic had led him to believe initially. "If you say so, son, I don't doubt it."

"Well, that makes me feel better."

Ed's mind was forging ahead. "You know, if it turned out that there was something wrong with that tractor or baler," Ed added, "we could sue the Saunderses."

"Don't think that thought hasn't occurred to Dwight," R. E. said with a humorless chuckle. "I understand he's hired a lawyer."

"That'd help with Steve's medical expenses," Ed said.

"Yeah, I know," R. E. said, "but we got workmen's comp. We ain't going to start suing the Saunderses. It wasn't their fault."

"Well, whose fault was it?"

"Ed, everything bad that happens don't mean someone's gotta be at fault, necessarily. Sometimes things just happen."

If Ed was frustrated by his father's response, he may have been equally so by Grandma Leora's lengthy table grace, which concluded by thanking God for the healing Steven was receiving. Rather than healing, wouldn't it have made more sense for God to have prevented the accident in the first place? But Ed kept quiet. Grandma was the authority on spiritual matters in the family, and although Steven and Ed might have grown out from under her direct tutelage, it would not have occurred to either of them to challenge her. Neither of them was religious in a conventional sense, yet neither was interested in repudiating the family's bedrock faith, perhaps because Leora never attempted to impose it as a framework of explanation or a set of blind beliefs. For her, faith was rather a tool for dealing with the world, particularly its painful aspects, as, for example, when she had recently learned that her husband's heart condition gave him only a short time to live.

"No, *accept* is not the word, Stevie," she told him when they had talked about it. "I don't accept it. I don't think I could. Just like I don't accept what's happened to you. But I hand it over. It's that simple."

SUNDAY MORNING Ed drove Steven and Betty to Portland, about a seven-hour trip. On and off they listened to cowboy music interspersed with the evangelical Christian music Betty favored. Steven sat in the backseat and held himself upright so as not to put his stumps into contact with any of the car's hard surfaces. After a couple of weeks of progress, his right arm had taken a turn for the worse. The tissue covering the stump had become ulcerated, the bone beginning to break through the skin graft. On both sides Steven had developed fresh neuromas, new tangles of barely shielded nerve fiber that at the slightest touch sent electric shocks through his system. Managing pain from all these sources was hard work. Exceptionally, he took several doses of pain medication during the drive. After lunch he drowsed, periodically awakened by the swaying of the car and the jolts it inflicted. By the time they pulled up to the hospital, he was groggy and tired. He was relieved that the uncomfortable trip was over, but now he tensed at the chemical odors, the long, dully gleaming surfaces, and the robot-like voices coming over the loudspeakers. He felt the sort of unlocatable sadness that haunts a locale where a forgotten punishment has been administered. Here the doctors had cleaned his wounds, snipped his nerves, disarticulated the elbow of the right arm, and with both a power saw and a guillotine had shortened his bones, so his skin, like a long sleeve, could be made to cover them.

Betty and Ed took Steven to his room. Betty could see from small telltale signs on her son's face, like the stiffness of his smile and the tiny patch of bloodless white at the tip of his nose, that he was struggling to maintain his composure, and that in itself was sufficient to threaten her own. She helped him out of his clothes and into his hospital gown. Then she and Ed drew up chairs by his bedside and made small talk until he fell asleep, which he soon did. They wouldn't see him for a month.

CHAPTER TEN

I N THE VIDEO he is lying facedown on the massage table. The masseuse begins at his head and proceeds methodically to his feet, her hands moving over his body, gently palpating, tracing the deep impact of his trauma for the benefit of his medical team—which includes a surgeon, an occupational therapist, and a prosthetist. "The plates in his scalp are separated," says the masseuse. "He resisted the pull of the rollers by bracing his forehead against a bar, and the pressure opened a gap. Until we can get that to close, he will continue to have severe headaches. His jaw is rigid and he has what we call a 'military neck,' like a marine standing at attention, with his chin pulled in and the back of his neck tilted at a rigid angle. Here you can see how his shoulders have drawn up. The muscles of his back are still in spasm, so his rib cage can't expand adequately, which makes his breathing shallow and labored. It's important we loosen up the entire area or it will lead to future pulmonary problems.

"See how rigid the muscles in his legs are. Like armor. That is constricting the flow of blood to his feet, as you can see by their slightly bluish color. He doesn't have a lot of sensation in them. Swimming would help."

She moves back up to his shoulders. She takes his short right stump in her hand where it was severed midway in the bicep and that now tapers to a rounded point. The skin at the extremity is puckered with the skin graft. "This scar tissue is going to need a lot of work. It has formed these adhesions as it healed." She runs her fingers over the ridges. "Folds that have gotten fused. This is contributing to his neuromas. They're pretty painful, aren't they, Steve?"

"Yes," he replies in a voice muffled by his facedown position.

"When the surgeons made these grafts, they simply took the exposed nerves and bundled them together and sewed a patch over them. As a result, there's a lot of nerve confusion. The same applies to the left stump, which, however, is in a little better shape than this one. The scarring there is not as severe. Thanks to the fact that it still has an elbow, it would make sense to fit it first for a prosthesis. I'm assuming it will become the dominant limb, which will mean that he'll have to switch from being right-handed to left-handed."

In the days ahead, the surgeons attempted to solve the problem of the neuromas by clipping the nerve endings, but the neuromas grew back. Then the doctors tried burying them in the marrow of Steven's bones, but for some reason the painful twinges and phantom pain continued. Surgery followed surgery. The doctors wrapped his stumps tightly after each surgery to prevent swelling. At the end of his second week, Steven was ready to be fitted for artificial limbs. With his physical therapist, Kristin Gulick, he visited the prosthetics lab for a plaster impression of his left stump, preliminary to fashioning a socket on which to build a prosthesis.

Initially, Steven and his family had placed great hope in myoelectric arms, artificial limbs controlled by nerve impulses in the body that look like human limbs thanks to a lifelike plastic skin. But that turned out not to be an option for Steven because the nerves of his right stump were too damaged and sensitive to tolerate a prosthesis of any sort; only the left was available. Moreover, a myoelectric arm is ill suited to a double amputee because it is relatively slow and clumsy, best used as an auxiliary to a normal limb. The device the prosthetist chose for Steven's left limb was a relatively primitive affair. Assembled from about $50 worth of materials and looking something like an industrial tool, it consists of a plastic tube for a forearm, on which were mounted several small pulleys and caliper-like brackets for guide wires. The tube attaches to a flexible wrist joint, which in turn attaches to two large stainless-steel hooks. These are controlled by wires across Steven's chest that run through brackets to a harness of canvas straps worn outside an undershirt, and anchored at his right shoulder. All the movements of the hooks—up, down, lateral, opening, closing—are controlled by subtle flexes of the right shoulder. Weeks of experimentation were required to determine the proper proportion of wire and canvas strap.

When the device first came from the lab, the canvas straps were hooked together by safety pins so that ad hoc adjustments could be made as Steven worked with it. Whatever functionality he would eventually obtain with the prosthesis would depend on retraining the relatively obscure muscles of his upper back and shoulder, bringing them under conscious control in order to achieve a differentiation comparable to that of the hand. In the beginning, he was nearly helpless, barely managing to open and close the hooks, picking up objects like a slow and clumsy lobster. It wasn't only a question of grasping, there was also the question of maintaining the proper tension so as not to drop the object. Steven shattered water glasses and pulped bananas. But little by little, as his physical therapist made the requisite safety pin adjustments, he achieved better control and precision. It was a slow, tedious process. Hours lifting a fork and setting it down again, hours to get food on the fork and lift it, and then more hours for fork and food to complete a successful transit to his mouth.

But that mouthful was a victory. A start.

He spent his days at the Shriners Hospital reconquering the elementary tasks of daily life one by one. He would squeeze toothpaste onto a brush with his elbow and then struggle to get his clumsy hooks to grasp a toothbrush. He would brush the right side of his mouth and then stop to strategize about how to coordinate muscles, straps, and wires to reposition the brush for the left side. Each previously automatic sequence of movements—slipping on an undershirt, pulling on his pants, tying his shoes—had to be broken down into separate gestures, then recombined. The muscles in his back and shoulders ached from the unfamiliar work. Forty-five minutes of practice could exhaust him. Kristin would shift his tasks from complex to simple, interspersing them with ones requiring simple precision, like picking up a quarter and moving it from the desk to the dresser.

A couple of weeks into his training a video was taken to document his progress. In one of the scenes he faces the complicated task of putting on his glasses. How to hook the flexible frames over his ears? If he succeeds in hooking one bow, he jerks it off when he tries to secure the other. He bends the fragile bows, he pokes himself in the eye and forehead. He sits for a moment in apparent defeat, thinking. Then he places his glasses facedown on the bed and opens the bows; he kneels down on the floor, bends forward, and inserts his face between the bows; he holds the bridge in place by pressing down on the bed, then he reaches up and secures each bow over an ear. Slowly he raises his head. A couple of additional tugs and pats and he has solved that particular problem for good.

In another scene he tries to put on his socks. But he can grip only the top at one side. He inserts his toes and pulls the sock along his sole, helping it move along by shuffling his feet, but is unable to get the sock past his anklebone. He tugs on one side, then the other. He shreds the top of the sock. His hook pulls away with a tangle of thread. His expression turns grim with disgust.

Kristin visited him twice a day, once in the morning and once in the evening, to monitor his progress and assign him new and more complicated tasks. Once he learned to move things on a level plane, she had him move from plane to plane. Drop a shirt and pick it up. Drop a book and pick it up. Pick up a comb, try to use it, and put it on a shelf. Pick up a deck of cards and put it on a countertop. A pencil. A grape. For each object there was a different strategy. He had to be careful with each thing he touched, for his hooks are as heavy as a hammer. Occasionally he was struck down with headache or fatigue.

Morning and evening she checked the tension in his wires and straps and made the requisite adjustments with the safety pins. As the days went by he learned to get some help from his toes. Several of his friends at the hospital were burn victims with arms encased in bandages. He watched how a particularly agile one fed himself with his toes. His own legs and hips, however, are too stiff for such maneuvers. He ate in the kitchen with a towel tied around his neck to catch the splatters and spills. As often as not he flipped the fork in the opposite direction from his mouth and fired the food into space. The nurses helped him when the process went on too long.

As patient-oriented as the Shriners is, it still makes for a depressing environment. Serious injury is a prerequisite for admission, and many of the children were understandably frightened and depressed. When Steven was not practicing with his prosthesis, rather than attend classes he preferred to sit at the bedside of some new friend, finding it easier to keep up his own spirits if he could use some of his common sense to cheer somebody up. This was his own self-devised form of therapy, to which the only serious threat came from one or two staff psychologists, who refused to take his emotional equilibrium at face value. To them it seemed medically impossible to undergo Steven's sort of loss without a process of mourning. They were convinced that he was covering up deep feelings of loss and probably rage. Periodically the psychologists visited with him and invited him to open up and deal with his putative depression. At the end of one such session, Steven, normally accommodating, reached the limit of his patience. Angrily, he told the psychologist that the only serious threat to his emotional equilibrium was coming from the psychologist himself. "Every time I talk to you, I do get depressed, but you're the one who's driving me to it. Tell a person often enough that he's supposed to be depressed, and eventually he'll go along with you." The psychologist protested that he was simply trying to get Steven to be honest about his feelings. At that Steven blew up. He asked the man whether he'd been assigned to his case. "Yes," said the psychologist.

"So that means, in a way, you're working for me, right? You're trying to help me?"

"Yes," said the other.

"Well, then, I'm firing you. Good-bye."

The following day Steven got a phone call from his mother, asking him to be kinder to the psychologist, he was just trying to do his job.

"Well, he ain't doing it on me, Mom," he told her.

AFTER THREE WEEKS, Steven was approaching the end of this first extended stay. It was time to go home, to allow his swellings to continue to abate, and continue to train himself in the use of his prosthesis. After a month at home, he would return for more medical attention, followed by another home stay, and then one final return to the hospital. Kristin told him that in a week he would be ready to leave.

Why a week? he wanted to know.

By then she thought he would have sufficient dexterity.

Why not now? he asked.

"I tell you what, Steve," she said. "I'm going to give you a beanbag. You practice with it by yourself and with your friends. Take three or four days. As soon as you can toss and catch it half a dozen times, you can go home. That'll be your exit exam, OK?"

He took the beanbag and practiced with his friends, off and on, for the remainder of the day. After lights out, he continued to practice. The following morning he told Kristin he was ready.

Bemused, Kristin positioned herself at about fifteen paces from him.

"Ready," she said.

They tossed it back and forth, slowly and easily at first, and then more rapidly. He caught the bag a dozen times, and then over and over.

Kristin was startled.

"What did you do, sit up half the night practicing?"

"More like all night, actually."

"All night? Didn't you sleep?"

"Yeah. I woke up this morning lying on my bed in my clothes."

"How did you practice? Obviously, you didn't have a partner."

"Until bedtime, I practiced with my friends."

"And after that?"

"I just kept tossing that bag up in the air and trying to catch it."

"Are you *that* eager to get home?"

"Like I told you, Kristin, I been having trouble sleeping. So I was just lying there, and pretty soon I started wondering what my buddies at home been up to. And if my dad was doing any hunting. And since I was lying there awake, I thought I might just as well be doing something productive."

"You are something else, man."

"You know me, Kristin, I'm not the sort of guy who gets depressed. That's not me. That's not how I was raised. On the other hand, if a guy ever was the least bit prone to getting depressed, a couple of weeks in a hospital, even a hospital as nice as this one, would do the trick."

"Well, a hospital is not a happy place, I grant you . . ." she began, but he cut her short.

"Happiness really got nothing to do with it," he said. "I mean my personal happiness. It's got more to do with how everybody's thinking. If you got everybody all together here thinking, I'm in the hospital and I'm depressed, well, pretty soon, little by little, it's going to wear on you, and you're going to get dragged down too."

"I hope you don't mean to tell me, Steven Sharp, that people in your hometown don't get depressed."

"I ain't saying that. We got our share—yeah, maybe even more 'n our share—of depressed folks in Eagle Valley. I guess I'm talking more about my family."

He was desperate to get out, she could see that now. He wouldn't say that directly, he would speak in generalities, but the fact was implicit in how he had spent the last twenty-four hours. It occurred to her as she stood there mulling over his request that while she had been stacking her dishes in the dishwasher last night, he had been tossing that bean-bag. Dropping it, bending over, grasping it, tossing it. And that while she had been watching the ten o'clock news, he had been tossing it. And that during the hours when the corridors in the hospital were quiet and across town she had been getting ready for bed, he had been tossing it. He was swinging his stump, flexing his shoulder, periodically cranking his neck to shed the stiffness settling into his back and shoulder muscles. And that later while she had lain reading her novel in bed, he had been tossing the bag. And then through the night until the first birds stirred in the shiver of dawn, most of that time he had been flexing his stump in a rhythm finally as routinized as a metronome's.

"OK, Steve," she said, shaking off her reverie. "You're ready. Go on home."

CHAPTER ELEVEN

IT WAS PAST SIX and Grandpa Randolph still hadn't come in from mending fence, so Leora sent Steven, who happened to be sitting in her kitchen, to fetch him. He found the elderly man sitting by a fence post, his tools beside him. He couldn't get up because his chest ached and he felt weak. "Better get R. E. to drive down here with the wagon," he said. "You'll be OK till I get back?" Steven asked. "I'll be fine," Randolph replied. "I'm enjoying the scenery." That episode, the first of several, was for Leora the tolling of a bell. Worry weighed on her for the rest of that Saturday evening, most of which she spent sitting in her study trying to prepare the Sunday sermon; she was filling in for the new pastor, who was otherwise occupied.

She sat in her rocking chair, a lamp at her elbow, her feet propped on a low stool, favoring the leg she'd broken nearly a decade ago. A writing tablet and her Bible lay in her lap. Quarter hours and full hours gonged on the hall clock and still she sat idly clicking her ballpoint, the normal flow of her inspiration dried. Normally she would have welcomed the opportunity to preach, for next to her family the local Nazarene church had the greatest claim on her. The church had been established when she'd come to the valley fresh from the seminary so many years ago, and the small band of welcoming congregants had jacked the small log building onto rollers and dragged it by mule and brute force to its present site beside the Grange on Newbridge Road.

Leora had married Randolph five months after meeting him. He'd been part of the committee that welcomed her, and they had quickly fallen in love. Outwardly it was a surprising match, given her urban background, education—a B.A. in classics, two master's degrees, and training in classical piano—and literate tastes, for Randolph was a farmer whose dyslexia had prevented him from going beyond the eighth grade. Physically and temperamentally they were a disparate pair: she, petite, vivacious, pretty; he, tall and taciturn. Yet they had thrived together, each with the clarity to perceive beyond their dissimilarities a genuine ally in the other. Affable and witty, Leora got along well with people, while Randolph was a strong-minded, relatively solitary individual whose good judgment was nevertheless sufficiently respected in the community to get him elected to the school board. And it was in that capacity that he had invited Leora to become the head teacher at Richland's two-room grade school. At the time, her three children were in grade school, so she had accepted. Later he prompted her to teach high school in Halfway—Spanish, English, math, and home ec—where, incidentally, she'd been the first high school teacher in the district to offer a course in sex education, an eyebrow-raising venture in the fifties. In the meantime, she continued to serve as minister to the Nazarene church, over the years baptizing, confirming, marrying, and burying a large number of three generations of the valley's residents. She played her music both in her own church and at other venues, like town dances, weddings, homecomings, and funerals.

Randolph had already been moving into semiretirement when Leora was offered the most eminent job of her teaching career, the position of superintendent of education for Baker County. She consulted with Randolph about whether to take it. A major drawback in both of their eyes would be the daily drive to Baker City, a distance of sixty miles on winding mountain roads that could be dangerous in bad weather. Randolph advised her to wait a day or two before making her decision, and then, unbeknownst to her, he drove to Baker City and managed to get himself hired in the same building where she would be working—as a janitor.

"As a janitor?" She could scarcely believe it. "You're not serious."

He was entirely serious. Prestige and social esteem mattered little to him. He had no problem with the prospect of pushing a broom and emptying wastebaskets in the office building where she would be serving as an important public official.

"It'll be a change for me," he said, "and besides, it's a paycheck."

"Which you hardly need."

"Leora, look, there's some repair work involved with this job, and I'm good at that. But the main thing is, it'll finally give us a chance to spend some time together."

At that, her resistance melted and she accepted the position. For three years thereafter, five days a week, they drove together to Baker City, the school superintendent and the janitor, except for the weeks of the spring planting and fall harvest, when Randolph remained at home. Three years of daily conversations. Thank God, she thought now, thinking back, that she'd said yes to the arrangement.

Now the house was silent, the TV mute in the den. She glanced at her watch. It was past ten. The writing pad in her lap was still blank. Overhead Randolph's footsteps creaked on the bedroom floor. With a final click she set her ballpoint on the table beside her and opened her Bible to the familiar verse in Ecclesiastes:

> *Two are better than one; because they have a good reward for their labor.*
>
> *For if they fall, the one will lift up his fellow: but woe to him that is alone when he falleth; for he hath not another to help him up.*
>
> *Again, if two lie together, they have heat: but how can one be warm alone?*

Sunday morning at ten-forty-five, Leora sat in the tiny vestry trying to gather her thoughts while Betty accompanied Bob Taylor on the piano as he rehearsed the hymn he would sing solo during the service. Betty was the church's music director, if such a title could be applied to a job that consisted of selecting the day's hymns, handing out and collecting the hymnals, and leading twenty to thirty indifferent and self-conscious singers in song. Bob was the exception. He had a big, resonant voice that he was not shy about using. Indeed, he was currently taking singing lessons in the hope of supplementing his disability payments by singing at local events. He was a large man in his late forties, muscular and big-boned, who until about a year ago had made his living as a lumberjack. Then he had suffered a near-fatal accident in the woods. He had cut a large fir and seen it start to fall. Then he had turned and moved on to the next one. But the falling tree had snagged on its downward plunge in the branches of its neighbors, which had yielded at first, and then at the point of maximum tension had snapped back, catapulting the fir in Taylor's direction. Unsuspecting and absorbed in his work, he soon lay buried and unconscious. When they had found him the following day, he had had no feeling in his lower body. He had left the hospital as a paraplegic.

Today he was practicing "Precious Memories," a favorite hymn of Leora's father, Martin. She had decided to preach about her father, the man who had led her into the ministry. She would tell his story to give a long view of the working of grace, for at the present, grace in the short run was hard for her to discern.

Outside the church, Steven and R. E. were standing around with the other men, chatting. It was Steven's first appearance at church since his accident, and under the guise of small talk he and R. E. were more or less consciously negotiating his reentry into the community. On the one hand, the men were pleased to see Steven, relieved that he was on his feet and functioning, many of them taking a detailed interest in the workings of his prosthesis, its straps and wires; on the other hand, Steven detected a certain awkwardness in the group, a reserve beneath the banter, which, if translated into plain speech, might have come out something like this: He's R. E.'s boy, and how ironic is that? Maybe the best mechanic in the area, and one of the safest, not a nick on his fingers after a lifetime of work, and now he's saddled with a son who was careless enough to stick his hands into a moving baler. Can you beat that?

At a signal from Betty, the men moved inside, and R. E. and Steven took their accustomed places at the back of the small church, which had five pews on each side. Betty sat at the upright piano on the right, Leora on the left, and between them was a small table beneath a large bare wooden cross. There was no other ornamentation on the plain white walls or on the plain window glass; overhead was a rough-hewn roof beam. During the opening hymn, R. E. held up the hymnal for words and music that he and Steven both knew by heart. Then two congregants came forward and read Scripture passages, following which, after a moment of silence, Leora rose from her chair and placed herself at the lectern. She gazed out over the sparsely filled pews with their well-known faces. She knew the stories of these people and many of their secrets. Today, she was speaking as much to her own condition as theirs.

"In times of sadness," she began, "it can help to be reminded of grace. Just a couple of minutes ago, listening to Bob singing 'Precious Memories,' I got to thinking about my father, Martin, who loved that hymn. Some of you met him when he used to visit, and I was thinking about how his life was changed by an act of grace one day about seventy years ago."

In his pew, Steven relaxed. He'd heard parts of the story before, and he much preferred Grandma Leora in her storytelling rather than Bible-interpreting mode, especially when the stories concerned Great-grandpa Martin. Steven never knew him but felt a certain link with him nonetheless, because Grandma often told Steven how much he resembled and, as he got older, even acted like Martin.

"My dad was born on the Chippewa Falls reservation of an Ojibwa father and an Irish Roman Catholic mother. In those days, of course, non-Catholic spouses of Catholics had to promise to raise their children in the Church, and so for the first six years of his life, Martin went to Sunday Mass with his mother. Then he rebelled. He refused to go. Grandma talked to Grandpa, but Grandpa said he didn't have to go if he didn't want to. 'If he goes unwillingly, church won't do him any good anyway,' he said. 'Instead, he can come fishing with me.' Grandpa loved to fish. And so, from then on, my dad spent his Sundays fishing, and later, hunting as well, and Grandpa taught him everything he knew about the outdoors, which was a great deal.

"And so my father grew up, technically, as a heathen and, I guess, a fairly happy one. He had a great appetite for life and the kind of personality and good looks that made it easy to satisfy. Unlike his two sisters, who favored their fair Irish mother, he resembled his father. He had jet black hair and chiseled Indian features. He had talents that brought him lots of friends. He could play the guitar; he had a good singing voice; he liked to have fun; and he liked to fight. As a kid he was a fighter. Fortunately, at sixteen he joined the Army and so directed that fighting spirit into boxing. He boxed on the Army team and won some awards. He stood six two and was strong as a bull. I'm telling you all this so that you'll understand that serving the Lord was the last thing on his mind.

"After he left the Army—that was in 1919, after four years of service—he looked around for a gym where he could continue to work out and box, and he found one in a YMCA not far from where he lived, which happened to be run by a secretary who was both a good boxer and a devout Christian. Now he and my dad began to work out together, and soon, despite their religious differences, they became friends. After their boxing sessions, they'd often have a meal or a cup of coffee together, and each time the director would invite my dad to a small-group Bible study or a prayer group. Each time, my dad would turn him down.

"This Y was located in a seedy part of town. Outside, there were usually some hard-luck types, down-and-outers, hanging around, waiting for the soup kitchen to open. This particular Saturday morning, my dad and the secretary worked out as usual, and afterwards, as usual, the secretary invited him to come pray with a few of the other men. For some reason, that day the invitation particularly annoyed my dad. Maybe it was the man's persistence. So my dad decided to take a minute and clarify his position. He told the secretary that he was not interested in praying with him or with anybody else, not today or any day. He wanted to make that clear. It had nothing to do with their friendship, it was just something he didn't need in his life.

" 'Why not?' the secretary wanted to know.

" 'Why not?' my dad replied. He said things were perfect as they were. He was young, he was healthy, he had some money in his pocket, he had friends, he was enrolled in trade school. God and religion and all that were the last things he needed. He wanted to make that clear.

" 'Fine,' said the secretary. But then as my dad turned away, the secretary got in a parting shot. 'Martin,' he called after him, 'watch out for perfect. Perfect will snap back on you every time.'

"But my dad paid no attention. He walked outside and then stopped to button up his coat. And as he was doing that, something happened. He saw something, or heard something, or felt something, I'm not sure what, but something touched him. Maybe it had to do with one of those unfortunates who hung around the place, because my dad, when he'd tell me this story, always mentioned them. Did someone come up and talk to him? Ask him for something? Maybe a handout? Or simply smile at him? I don't know, but whatever it was, it struck my dad to his core. One minute he was buttoning his coat against a cold October day, indifferent to the world, and in the next he stood there with a broken heart. He was not unhappy, mind you, in the worldly sense, but he was penetrated by something deeper than the world. Saved. By which I mean, run through and filled with a sense of divine grace and mercy.

"So he turned and went back into the Y in search of the secretary. It had only been a minute or two. My dad tried to tell him what had happened, but the man said, 'I know, Martin.'

" 'What do you mean, *you know?*'

" 'You've been walking on risky ground for a while now.'

" 'Risky? What do you mean, risky?'

" 'Because,' the secretary said, 'don't you know when you turn down invitations to pray with people who put their whole heart into it, the risk is that they'll turn around and pray for you? And the force of that prayer can be hard to withstand.' "

Leora paused.

"The reason I wanted to share that story with you today, friends, is not only because it's one of the clearest examples I know not only of how grace can strike at any moment, it also shows how it goes on working. For my father, his life was changed, as Saint Paul writes, in the twinkling of an eye, but then it took him further. It took him into the ministry, into a different life altogether, a life in the Lord. And from that day to this, just look at the connection. I wouldn't be standing here today, nor would you be sitting here listening to me, had my father not been touched by grace that day. Think of the years we've spent together, what we've lived through, how we've helped each other, prayed together, done what we could, which otherwise we would not have done, except for grace."

There was one final pause.

"We need to keep this grace in mind, in the midst of our sadness, which otherwise would surely overwhelm us."

Then Leora led them in prayer, after which Bob Taylor sang a reprise of "Precious Memories." He sang it forcefully, bracing himself on the armrests of his wheelchair and lifting his head, giving himself space for air.

In the car, on the way to The Shorthorn for brunch, Steven said to Leora, "When you started talking about Great-grandpa and his love for the outdoors, I was wondering if you were going to tell them that he could talk to the animals."

"Why would I tell them that?"

"Wasn't there an eagle that followed him from Chippewa Falls to Boise, when he came out to join the seminary, followed him every stage of the way?"

"There was indeed, Steve," she said, "but that's not a story for church. That's a family story."

"How many people around here know that you can talk to the animals too?"

Leora said there was no particular reason for people to know about that, either.

THE SHORTHORN, Richland's unofficial gathering spot, was a dim, pine-paneled, mildly reeking locale where little had changed in decades. A lunch counter ran along one side, booths along the other; in between was a scattering of Formica-topped tables. At the far end, the kitchen was set off by a half-wall with a serving window, and where the lunch counter ended, the room opened laterally into a murky bar. Odors of coffee, tobacco smoke, beef, and bacon fat pervaded the place. The wooden floor was scuffed and scored by boots and spurs. Hunting calendars and framed photos of Western movie stars, Clint Eastwood being the most prominent, decorated the walls. Over the hum of conversation could be heard the occasional crackle of the police scanner in the kitchen.

A group of nine or ten regulars from the Nazarene church seated themselves at the pushed-together tables the owner had reserved for them. Steven and R. E. found themselves sitting next to Dick McNulty, an arrangement the latter had deliberately engineered. After everybody's first couple of sips of coffee, while the others in the party were busy talking or ordering, McNulty broached the topic that was on his mind to Steven and R. E.

"You know, Steve," he said, "your dad and I were talking the other day about your accident. And he says you're sure you turned off that PTO before you got out of the cab, is that right?"

"Yeah, it is."

"Yeah, well, then the two of us got to talking about what might have made the PTO turn on."

"You got any ideas, Dick?" R. E. asked.

"No, not really. But the funny thing is, R. E., our conversation jogged something in my memory."

"Oh, yeah? What's that?"

"Now, it might be nothing, but after we talked I vaguely remembered seeing a little notice in the back pages of this farm journal I subscribe to. Something about the Power Take Off on a Case tractor. This goes back about three years, you understand."

"Right," R. E. replied, pricking up his ears.

"So I went home and started looking for the magazine. After I moved here, I put all my old ag journals in the barn, and I went out there and started hunting. And wouldn't you know, I found it."

"Found what?"

"This little notice." He took a small folded piece of paper from his breast pocket and opened it.

"What does it say?" R. E. asked.

McNulty read: " 'If you have experienced difficulty with the PTO on a Case 970 or 1070 tractor, call this number.' Now, that was a 970 you were operating, wasn't it, Steve?"

"Yeah, it was."

"What do you think this is, Dick?" R. E. asked, excitement sneaking into his voice.

"Got me, R. E. Maybe just a survey of some kind. But who knows?"

"How did you even happen to remember this, Dick?" Steven asked. "You don't own a Case, do you?"

"No, I don't. I really can't explain it. It was just one of those things that got stuck in my head."

"Yeah, but from *three years ago?*"

"Right. Strange, ain't it? Anyhow, it might be worth giving that number a ring."

"You think so? If it's three years old?"

"What's it hurt?"

"Right. Worst that can happen be that they say the number's no longer in service," said R. E. "Yeah, read me that number, Dick, and I'll write it down." He fished in his shirt pocket for his pencil and the small spiral notebook in which he kept note of parts numbers and prices.

Slowly McNulty read the ten-digit number.

R. E. wrote. "Wait a minute," he said, staring down at the number. "There's too many numbers here."

"What do you mean?"

"Well, you got three, and then another three, and then four. What are those first three?"

"That's the area code," McNulty replied, wondering why he was stating the obvious.

R. E. gave him a puzzled look: "What's an area code?"

CHAPTER TWELVE

ABOUT THREE WEEKS LATER, mid-afternoon, halfway across the country in a conference room on the twenty-sixth floor of an office building in downtown Minneapolis, two lawyers and a legal investigator were winding up a meeting when a call came in over the intercom. It was for Chris Olson, the investigator. While he took it, one of the lawyers, Leo Feeney, happened to mention to the other, Bill Manning, that he had just received a settlement check for $350,000 from the J. I. Case Corporation, a Wisconsin-based manufacturer of agricultural equipment.

"Today? In today's mail?"

"Yeah. It came this morning."

"Great. What was that family's name again?"

"Tautges."

"Right, and his name was Raymond, right?"

"Correct."

"Have you called them?"

"Not yet."

"Well, they'll be happy to hear from you."

The settlement was the end result of a suit prompted by an accident that had taken place on September 9, 1987, on a family farm in Brainerd, Minnesota, the day Michael Tautges, twenty-five, the owner of the farm, and his father, Raymond, fifty-seven, were finishing up the corn harvest. Not a farmer by profession, Raymond worked as an accountant for the Potlatch Corporation in Brainerd, but he'd been raised on a farm and often lent his son a hand; otherwise Michael managed his operation single-handedly. They would have finished their work on Sunday had not a broken universal coupling of the Case's Power Take Off delayed them. Michael disassembled the device, drove into town to pick up replacement parts, then put it back together. That took half of Saturday. Then he and his father worked that afternoon and the following one, and most of Monday, Ray pulling the corn harvester with the Case 970 and Michael trucking the corn back to his barnyard, where he loaded it into the silo. They finished around four. Michael drove the last load to the silo and, when his dad didn't show up in the barnyard, drove back to the field where presumably Ray was cleaning and greasing the harvester, in preparation for storing it for the winter.

Michael entered the field and drove slowly over the uneven terrain to the far end, where Ray had parked the equipment. As Michael drove closer, he was surprised to hear the clangor of the harvester's rotating chopper blades, but he figured that Ray was running the machine on empty in order to clean out its residual grain and chaff. But then, where was Ray? Michael parked and got out of the cab. He caught sight of Ray kneeling down in the space between the tractor and the harvester. He was pitched forward at an odd angle and seemed to be rocking from side to side. Suddenly filled with terrible apprehension, Michael drew nearer, then froze in horror while he made sense of what he was seeing. Part of Ray's coat had become entangled in the unshielded PTO shaft and had drawn his face down onto the spinning universal coupling, which, Michael now saw, had eaten away half of his head. Blood and matter were spattered on the bin of the harvester. Panicked, Michael turned and ran stumbling from the field and across the road to the house of his neighbor, Daryl Moser, and pounded on his door.

While Mrs. Moser called 911, Daryl raced into the field. He took a glance at Ray's body, then sprang to the cab and stopped the tractor engine with a stroke of his hand. Soon the police arrived and then an ambulance. Daryl helped cut the body loose from the PTO shaft. After the police had observed the scene and left, he hosed down and cleaned the equipment. Emotionally, it was difficult work for him, although his relationship with the Tautges family had not been close—he'd simply rented the field to them. So despite the Tautges family's terrible loss, he had no particular grounds for siding with them during the following months in their dispute with the Case Corporation concerning the cause of Ray's death. The family wanted Daryl to affirm that he had found the PTO lever in the off position, whereas it seemed to him that the lever had been on. The more they pressed their point of view, the more Daryl resisted. The position of the lever was crucial. If Ray had turned on the PTO himself, say, to clean out the bin, then his accident was his own fault. If on the other hand, the PTO had somehow turned itself on and caught Ray by surprise, then he had died as the victim of a defective machine and the family had grounds to seek redress from Case. Whether Daryl had found the lever fully engaged or only slightly could matter greatly in the determination of responsibility.

Obviously it was difficult for Daryl to think his way back through the chaos of the moment and recall precisely the conditions in the cab. Eventually, he stated that to his best recollection the PTO lever had been far enough forward to suggest that Ray had deliberately put it there. He became more convinced of his position the more the Tautges family questioned it.

Why would he do such a thing? asked his son and widow, Ruby.

Unfortunately, the only evidence found at the scene, a grease gun lying close to the body, was open to diametrically opposed interpretations. To Daryl and eventually to the Case officials who inspected the tractor, it suggested that Ray had turned on the harvester in order to grease it, using the movement of the machinery to facilitate the diffusion of the lubricant. To the Tautges family, the grease gun supported the opposite inference—namely, that Ray had *turned off* the harvester in order to grease it. To everyone who knew him, this scenario made the most sense, for a workman as meticulous as Ray Tautges would never risk his life by greasing a running corn chopper with its whirling blades and revolving auger. It would make as much sense as trying to clean a running blender, not to mention that with the machine running, half the grease fittings could not be reached.

But Case maintained that, legally, the question could not be decided, so there was nothing the Tautges family could do. Without witnesses to Ray's death, whatever they proposed was simply conjecture. Also, Case pointed out, if anyone was at fault in Ray's death, it was Michael, who had removed the shield from the PTO shaft on Saturday morning, when he had replaced the universal coupling. Had the shield been in place, Ray's coat would never have become entangled. Shield or no shield, the Tautges family contended, the PTO should not have turned on.

And there the matter rested for about a year, and there it would have remained had not a friend of the family mentioned it to Leo Feeney, a product liability attorney, who was vacationing at his lake cottage outside of Brainerd. Feeney became interested when several of his friends told him about the case and attested to the careful work habits of Ray Tautges. In their view, Case was getting away with murder. Feeney agreed to meet with Michael and Ruby Tautges. They showed him around Ray's place, pointing out the meticulous condition of his garage, his tools, and his woodworking shop. Ray was always working around power tools and had never once had an accident, they said. How likely was it that he would decide to risk his life at the impossible task of greasing a running corn harvester?

In August 1991, Feeney filed a wrongful death claim against the Case Corporation. Case countered with a motion for summary judgment, which, if upheld, would end the case, in which it sought not to refute Feeney's claim but to neutralize it through legal logic. Case argued that since both its scenario, that Ray had turned on the PTO, and the Tautges family's, that the PTO had self-started, were equally plausible, they canceled each other out. In a memorandum attached to their motion they wrote:

> For purposes of this motion only, J. I. Case does not dispute that one could speculate that the accident occurred as Plaintiff alleges. However, the legal issue in this case is not whether the accident could have occurred as Plaintiff alleges, but whether "the entire evidence sustains with equal justification two or more inconsistent inferences so that one inference does not reasonably preponderate over the others. . . . It is J. I. Case's position that the evidence sustains with equal justification an inference that Plaintiff purposely and/or intentionally left the power-takeoff system on.

For Feeney, the question was whether the evidence was indeed complete. True enough, if the evidence consisted solely of the accident scene with its ambiguous grease gun and no witnesses, then it was impossible to decide between the two accounts. On the other hand, if something had caused the Tautges tractor to malfunction, perhaps other Case tractors might be found with the same flaw. Evidence might be accumulated that would tilt the balance in the Tautgeses' favor. Feeney asked Chris Olson, the investigator, to do some sleuthing about the Case 970. In the following days and weeks, Olson dropped in on Case equipment dealers around Minnesota. He discovered that there had been problems with the PTO of the Case 970 from the start—not self-starts, although there had been reports of these, but a high rate of PTO clutch burnouts. The basic mechanism inside the PTO consisted of two round disks or plates, one driven by the tractor engine, which was in constant rotation, and one that locked together with the first plate and then transmitted the drive to the attached equipment. The problems being reported to them, the Case dealers believed, were due to farmers not pushing the PTO levers far enough forward to lock the plates tightly together. Rather, they would push the lever until the PTO started to turn and then leave it there; but at that point, inside the PTO unit, what was driving the second disk was what the engineers call "viscous drag," the swirl of hot hydraulic oil, and not the full locked-together force of the plates. But when the plates spun in this loosely engaged fashion, the oil overheated, and the heat warped the plates, after which they would never lock solidly together again. Soon, they would burn out, often before the expiration of the warranty. Case found itself replacing so many PTO units at its own expense that it came up with a couple of retrofits for the PTO lever—two different ramps, one sloped and one in the form of a "top hat," that would force the operator to push the PTO lever all the way forward and lock it there.

Olson reported his findings to Feeney, who in turn contacted an engineer, Lee Sapetta, with whom he had worked on other cases. Feeney's guess was that if the PTO could turn on by force of the viscous drag, then perhaps that explained what had happened to the Tautges machine. Ray had been using it all day; the hydraulic oil in the PTO must have been extremely hot, consequently thin, circulating rapidly, capable of entraining the other plate at the least provocation—perhaps even without provocation, perhaps even with the PTO lever in the off position, since the driving plate would still be turning. Feeney sent Olson and Sapetta to Brainerd to see whether anything they could observe on the Tautges tractor bore it out.

The men spent a day experimenting with the tractor, running it at various speeds and hooking up various implements, but none of their efforts produced results.

Feeney was unwilling to give up. After what Olson had told him about the PTO clutch plate warpage and burnout, he was convinced that the PTO had turned on and killed Ray Tautges. Case's line of defense that he could not tip the scale of plausibility in his direction simply intensified his resolve. But time was slipping away. Feeney had another strategy session with Olson. "What we need," Feeney said, "is a bigger evidence pool. We need to find some self-starting Case 970s. I know they exist. I can feel it. Let's run a notice in some farm journals."

"What kind of notice?"

"Just a sentence or two. Very simple. Ask whether anyone has experienced a self-start with the PTO of a Case 970. Run it in four or five nationwide farm journals. No names. No explanations. We don't want to attract speculators. Just the question and your phone number."

In the week following the appearance of the ad, Olson's phone began to ring. Within the month he had a dossier of reports by two dozen farmers who had experienced self-starts with their Case tractors, one or two of whom had suffered serious harm. Notable among the latter was a farmer from Tennessee, Mickey Jones, who had nearly lost his arm in the process of replacing a belt in his baler in 1986.

Methodically, Feeney and Olson began visiting those who had responded. They found what they were looking for, 970s whose PTOs had turned on without human intervention, some quickly, some after lengthy delays, some rarely, some all the time. Feeney stood with the various farmers in front of their equipment, listened to their stories, and watched their PTOs turn on by themselves while Olson videotaped them. Armed with this evidence, Feeney wrote his brief against J. I. Case's appeal for a summary judgment.

When Case was informed of Feeney's investigations, the chief engineer of the agricultural machine unit, Max North, and his team decided to do a second inspection of the Tautges tractor, and notified Feeney. On a savagely cold Saturday in October 1992, Feeney and Sapetta drove up to Brainerd to be in attendance. They stood around stamping their feet, beating their hands or stuffing them into their coat pockets, while the Case team essentially did the same tests and maneuvers that Olson and Sapetta had tried earlier. The Case engineers came up with the same results they had recorded on the previous visit: no self-start. After several hours of inspection, the Case team got back into their cars and left.

Sapetta was ready to leave too, but Feeney was not ready to give up. "Lee," he said, "let's keep checking this thing. It's now or never. I *know* this thing self-started. We've seen lots of others do it. We've got to catch this one in the act. If we don't, we're sunk."

Despite the punishing cold, Feeney and Sapetta continued to experiment. They parked the tractor uphill, downhill, increased the load, lightened the load, revved the engine, idled the engine, all to no avail. It was getting later and soon they wouldn't be able to observe effectively. Their hands and feet felt frozen. At last, Feeney was ready to give in to the cold and frustration. But then Sapetta suddenly got the notion that something on the underside of the tractor might provide a clue. It was the only place they hadn't looked. Taking a flashlight, he got down on his back on the frozen ground and inched his way under the tractor. Feeney watched the beam wobble around. Then all at once, the corn harvester attached to the tractor began to operate.

"Lee, what did you do?" Feeney yelled.

"Nothing. I didn't touch anything."

"Unbelievable," Feeney said. "We finally caught it in the act. Now we can file our brief."

On March 20, 1992, United States District Court Judge Paul A. Magnuson denied J. I. Case's motion for summary judgment. Feeney prepared for trial.

Even with all of his gathered evidence, however, the prospect facing him was not an inviting one. It was one thing to convince a judge, preliminarily, to give marginally more weight to Feeney's hypothetical reconstruction of the accident; it was another to convince a jury that a tractor designed and built by the reputable J. I. Case Corporation, of which model there were many thousands both in good working order and in active use, was seriously defective. Feeney's law firm, Robins, Kaplan, Miller & Ciresi, was a large one with much experience in product liability cases, but arrayed against it would be the resources of a corporation that was no longer a local manufacturer with the strict ethical nineteenth-century standards of Jerome Increase Case, but a billion-dollar multinational with money to burn to win this important case. For if they lost this one, who knew how many other potential lawsuits might be waiting in the wings?

Presumably the prospect of additional suits led J. I. Case to offer to settle. It proposed paying $350,000 to the Tautges family to end the case with no admission of guilt or wrongdoing on the corporation's part. The family considered the offer, balanced it against the possibility of losing everything at trial, and accepted it. It was their check that had arrived in Minnesota in Feeney's mail.

IN THE CONFERENCE ROOM, Manning and Feeney, alerted by an odd tone in Olson's voice, began paying attention to his telephone conversation.

"Would you mind spelling your name?" Olson asked.

He wrote it down.

"And where are you calling from?"

He wrote down "Oregon."

"And your number?"

Olson gave them a glance that wavered between confusion and intense interest. He poised his hand to hit the mute button.

"Just one moment, sir," he said, "I'm going to put you on hold, so don't hang up."

"You guys aren't going to believe this," he said. "I've got a guy on the line here who says he's responding to that ad we ran about the Case PTO."

"That ad's three years old," Feeney said. "Something's fishy."

"I kid you not. This fellow says a friend just showed it to him, and that he's got a kid who's been badly injured by a Case 970 tractor."

"Hold on," Feeney said. "I think this is a setup."

"What do you mean?" Olson asked.

"It's somebody at Case. They're screwing with us."

"Case? Why?"

"Well, they send us the check, and then they call us up, pretend that they're calling in information that would have exactly served our purpose. It's a prank."

The men exchanged uncertain glances.

"On the other hand, Leo," Olson said, "what if it's for real? What if by some weird fluke . . . ?"

There was a moment of general indecision.

"Look, OK, tell him you'll call him back. You got his number, right?"

"Yeah. Why?"

"Because that way we'll see whether we're calling Oregon or Wisconsin."

Case was based in Racine, Wisconsin.

Olson returned to the caller. "OK, sir, we'd like to call you back on this, if you don't mind. That way we can have a longer conversation at our expense. So you hang up and I'll call you right back, OK?"

Olson hung up. He waited about thirty seconds. Then he redialed. "OK," he said, "I'm putting this on speakerphone."

They heard the amplified buzz on the line, the sound of the ring, and then the connection.

"Hello." It was a voice with a western drawl.

"Hello," said Olson. "Who am I talking to, please?"

"This is Randy Sharp. R. E. Sharp. Who am I talking to?"

"Mr. Sharp, my name is Chris Olson. You've reached a law firm in Minneapolis. You said you have a son who has been injured by a Case 970 tractor, is that right?"

"Yes, that's right. Steven."

And so, in this utterly implausible and unlikely manner, a connection was made between a law firm in Minnesota and the Sharp family of eastern Oregon, the tenuous link consisting of a one-sentence notice printed in the back pages of a farm journal that happened to catch the eye of a man who had no reason to retain it, since he was neither a farmer nor an owner of a Case tractor, but who had unaccountably stored the memory of it in his head and the journal in his barn, and then moved to Eagle Valley, where he happened to join a minuscule congregation and become a hunting companion and friend of R. E. Sharp. Little of this unlikely chain of events, of course, was apparent to Chris Olson as he sat scribbling on his pad, but enough to make him wonder.

"What do you think, Leo?" he asked, after hanging up the phone. "Worth looking into?"

The next day, Tuesday, they were on the morning flight to Boise, there to pick up a rental car for the drive to Eagle Valley.

CHAPTER THIRTEEN

OLSON AND FEENEY drove out of the Boise airport onto Highway 84 and headed west toward Oregon, a straight three-hour shot that led them, after some thirty miles of trailer courts, fast-food joints, bottle shops, and outlet stores, into a landscape that grew wider and more moonlike and more stripped of human signs as they went on. Rock, sand, and cactus encircled them within the wider circles and standing formations of talus, butte, mesa, and mountain. Tumbleweed and dust blew across the endless shoelace of highway ahead and behind. Early in the afternoon, they pulled off for a sandwich and coffee at the only gas and truck stop for seventy miles, then continued driving. They took it for granted that FM radio would stay with them all the way, but they lost it shortly after the turnoff by Baker City onto 86, a mile or two past the Oregon Trail Interpretative Center where the narrow road began climbing between gray, striated high rock walls. By the right roadside was a thin rocky stream that tumbled over itself in a green culvert. There were no road signs or billboards other than those warning them to beware of falling rocks or forbidding them to turn off onto unnamed ranch roads marked Private. About thirty-five miles into their ascent toward Richland, there was nothing in the rearview mirror and on the highway ahead except at roughly five-minute intervals, when barreling lumber trucks loaded with mountain pine and fir approached and disappeared, their massive back draft rocking even the rented Cherokee.

Where their map told them they should be entering Richland but obviously weren't, they pulled abreast of a cyclist in shorts, his feet flying around in low gear on the steep upgrade in a parody of speed. Feeney rolled down the window and asked him for directions. Breathing hard in the chilly air, the cyclist pointed toward the next ridge of mountain, in whose fold, he said, lay Eagle Valley. Detecting an accent, they asked him if he was from around there. No, he was a retired mailman from the former East Germany who was fond of biking the western mountains for his health.

In Richland, they pulled up at a single-pump gas station/fruit stand opposite The Shorthorn, and while Olson filled the tank Feeney called R. E. on an emergency phone affixed to a pole. As he spoke he peered around at a town so succinct his glance in each direction not only sailed through it but measured it against the desert. R. E. gave them instructions to the farm on Newbridge Road. They parked in the gravel pull-off, level with the bungalow roof, then took the wooden steps down to the plank bridge over the irrigation channel that ran along the property line. In the yard, to the left, they found a rose garden with a few late roses, and to the right, R. E.'s service truck beside a vegetable patch. There was no sound except for the barking of unseen hunting dogs. R. E., wearing jeans and a faded work shirt, stepped from the front door and approached the men in their suits and polished shoes. They gripped his slablike hand and introduced themselves, then stood for a moment as if disoriented after the long forward thrust of their trip by the standing block of autumn sunlight and the audible silence of the surrounding fields, until with some tentativeness R. E. asked them whether they would like to step inside.

They sat in the orderly pine-paneled family room, its walls decorated with family photos and Steven's paintings, and at Feeney's request R. E. gave them an account of his son's accident. He seemed relieved to do so, for in the valley there was no one, save for his son Ed and his friend Dick McNulty, to whom he could tell Steven's version and be met with other than polite disbelief. He spoke quietly, leaning forward in his chair with his feet squarely planted, his Adam's apple working, now and then interrupting himself to clear his throat with a constricted seal-like bark. The visitors felt the intensity of his emotion, which, to their surprise, seemed devoid of anger. In their line of work it was rare to encounter this much hurt without a corresponding need for payback.

When R. E. was done, Feeney gave his theory about the Case 970 that had injured Steven, and he briefly recounted his experiences with the Tautges family. R. E. listened with avid interest, but found the theory hard to credit. He had serviced the Case tractor for thirty years, had twice rebuilt the PTO, and was unaware of any tendency for it to self-start. Plus there were the Saunderses, who were using it day in, day out, and if they had noticed anything of the sort they would surely have mentioned it to him.

Feeney's heart sank a little at R. E.'s information.

"You rebuilt the PTO?" he asked. "Why?"

"The clutch burned out. Twice," he told them.

"Did you actually rebuild it or just replace the unit?"

"Just the unit."

"Which you got from a Case dealer?"

"Yes."

"And which you didn't modify or alter in any way?"

"Correct. I popped it in right off the shelf."

Feeney was relieved to hear that.

"You understand, Mr. Sharp, that we're not sure exactly why this PTO behaves as it does. Each tractor seems to be a little different. Some of them self-start and some of them don't. It seems the Saunderses' must be one that does."

"Well, why don't we run over there so you can take a look," R. E. said, getting to his feet.

They stopped for Dwight, then parked at Stan's. The elderly rancher emerged from his back door wearing large dark glasses and his wide cowboy hat and boots. He responded to the lawyers with reserve, wary about the implications of their visit. After the introductions, Feeney suggested that the quickest way to put them all on the same page would be to take a look at a video of Case 970s they had put together during the Tautges investigation, so Stan invited them inside. As the lawyers approached the paint-stripped house through a straggle of weeds and stepped onto the swaybacked porch with its ripped screen door, they exchanged a glance full of the understanding that the Saunders family, whatever their land and cattle holdings, apparently had a cash-flow problem.

"We think that the self-starts you're going to see on this video," Feeney explained, "will give you an idea of what might have happened to Steven." The Saunderses received this supposition with the polite air of people trying to keep an open mind and only partially succeeding. Or perhaps they were self-interested enough to wonder what the advantage to them would be to discover that their equipment had been responsible for Steven's accident. Steven had coverage from workmen's compensation, after all, but what did they have but some inadequate insurance? Feeney handed the video to Stan, who inserted it into the VCR.

Watching a blank screen, they heard the high-pitched clattering wheeze of a diesel engine trying to start, turning over three or four times under protest and then, with a clatter, catching. The name Raymond Tautges appeared on the screen, and the date, 10-31-91. The stationary camera presented a view from the vantage of the tractor cab of a forage harvester, a wide squat piece of equipment like a trough on wheels with two covered compartments, its paint a faded green. It sat unmoving as the sound of the diesel tractor steadied. Then the PTO shaft began to revolve, slowly at first, and then picking up speed until it reached a loud clatter. Fadeout.

Then a new date appeared, 8-6-92, and a rear view of the same equipment, this time with the bin covers opened and the immobile top half of the large auger visible. A full minute or even two went by until the auger screw began to turn with the same unhurried ease as before. With no increase in tractor engine rpms, the undulant ripples of the auger picked up speed and soon became a blur. It was an eerie demonstration, with no humans in view and no commentary, the tractor out of sight, and the message purely implicit.

Then the video showed a series of interviews of farmers Feeney had conducted at various farm sites in Minnesota, Indiana, Texas, and elsewhere. In each, the farmers stood beside their tractors and in response to Feeney's questions matter-of-factly recounted hazardous events that seemed out of keeping with the placid settings and benign appearance of their tractor. The Case 970, named the Agri-King, had the appearance of a comfortable, manageable machine—compact, sitting low to the ground on outsize tires with huge ground-gripping lugs, its engine cover often brightly painted and its roomy squared-off cab an easy step off the ground. Each of the farmers had a version of the same story to tell. Sometimes the tone was droll, as, for example, when a father and his son talked about the day they had gone in for lunch and left the tractor and manure spreader idling in front of the house, only to come out later and find that the spreader had unloaded itself on their front lawn. But more often the story had an edge to it, as when one farmer recalled greasing a sickle bar and becoming distracted by a slight noise, which caused him to look away and set down the grease gun, and in that instant the machine had turned on. "If there hadn't of been that little sound, if I hadn't stopped working at that particular instant, I would have lost my fingers. No question."

There were several such accounts of near escapes. The angriest of the farmers was John Pemberton, a middle-aged man, who recalled the outrage he had experienced when his corn chopper had turned on while he was sharpening the blades. He said he had called his local Case dealer, but had been given the runaround. Then he had contacted Case headquarters by phone and letter, eventually faxing the new CEO of the corporation, Jean-Pierre Rosso, which had only resulted in a form letter instructing him to contact his local dealer.

Pemberton was the exception, however. Most of the farmers responded to Feeney's questions in a businesslike manner, relating their episodes in the dispassionate tones of people for whom dangerous equipment was a fact of life. To Feeney's question of how, having discovered the danger, they dealt with it, several said that they used the PTO only under strictly controlled conditions, disconnecting it otherwise. One Texas farmer had rigged up a homemade clamp and cotter-pin device that held the shaft immobile when it wasn't in service. Oddly, none of these farmers mentioned the remedy of simply getting rid of the tractor. Even Michael Tautges was still using the one that had killed his father.

Then the film moved indoors and showed a middle-aged man in a short-sleeved shirt sitting at a desk in what was obviously a law office.

He had thinning dark hair, dark eyebrows, and large aviator-style glasses, through which he stared intently at the camera. Feeney, off camera, asked the man to state his name and where he lived.

"Mickey Jones," he said. "I'm a farmer from Clinch Mountain, Tennessee."

Feeney then asked him to describe what had happened to him while using a Case 970 in the fall of 1985. Jones replied that he had very nearly lost his arm when the PTO of his Case 970 turned on while he was installing a conveyor belt on his baler. After multiple surgeries and a long convalescence, he had sued J. I. Case, but had received only a small award, because the court found him partially negligent for having undertaken a repair with the tractor engine running. In telling his story, Jones's tone was quiet, matter-of-fact, emotion entering his voice only when he held up to view several photos of his arm, showing its condition both before and after surgery.

"And the condition of your arm today?" Feeney asked.

Jones lifted his arm, which until then he'd kept below the view of the camera. The wrist and elbow were bent at an odd angle, as if extra joints had been added and then frozen, but the full extent of the damage did not become apparent until he turned his arm over and showed the inside of it. The flesh and muscle had been chewed and lacerated, as if by sharks.

Feeney asked: "Did you contact the J. I. Case Company?"

"Yes, sir, I did," Jones answered with a slow drawl.

"And did they come down to inspect your tractor?"

"Yes, sir, they did."

"And what did they do?"

"They took it to the local equipment dealer and worked on it. They replaced the PTO, and then returned it to me."

"Did that fix the problem?"

"No, sir. Every now and then it would still turn on."

"Did they give you any explanation of why your tractor had malfunctioned?"

"No, sir."

"Did they warn you that it might happen again?"

"No, sir."

"Did it happen again?"

"Yes, sir. It kept on happening."

"So what did you do?"

"I sold it."

"You sold the tractor?"

"Yes, I did."

"Did you warn the new owner about its condition?"

"I did. Several times. I told him about my accident. I showed him my arm. I told him I was selling the tractor *as is*. And the day he came to pick it up, my wife and his wife talked about it and she warned his wife. So he knew."

"Thank you, Mr. Jones."

The film concluded by displaying the name of Raymond Tautges again, this time above the dates of his life, 4-18-30–4-28-87. Then followed the briefest of epilogues, several still photographs of Tautges—as a child with his 4-H lamb, as a teenager, as a grown-up riding a tractor, then a wedding photo, then with a granddaughter on his lap, and finally standing in his woodworking shop, smiling up from his lathe.

In the silence following the film, Dwight's agitation was evident.

"That was real interesting, Mr. Feeney. Obviously there was something out of whack with them other tractors, but, you know, we've run ours thirty years and never had it turn on once. That I'm aware of." The last comment was for R. E.'s benefit.

"Well, let's go take a look at it," Feeney replied.

The tractor was standing in the field below the house, the same field where Steven had been injured. Feeney asked Dwight if he minded having Chris turn it on. "He's been dealing with these tractors for a while and he knows their quirks."

"Sure, you go on ahead," Dwight replied.

With the ease of long practice Olson mounted the step and seated himself in the cab. With a glance at the controls, he manipulated the gear shift to make sure it was in neutral, checked the brake, then reached down to the right of the driver's seat and checked the play in the PTO lever, moving it fully forward and back. Finally he activated the starter. After a couple of protesting whines, the engine caught, blowing a dark puff of diesel exhaust from the upright pipe. Olson set the engine speed to a little faster than idle, then dismounted from the cab. The engine puttered smoothly, and nothing happened. The four men stood at the rear of the tractor, staring at the PTO shaft. A minute went by, then two. Dwight and Stan glanced at each other, then at Feeney and Olson, who stood with their eyes fixed. Another minute passed.

Olson said, "Remember, the engine's cold."

Feeney gave him a glance.

"Give it some time," Olson said.

They continued watching, Feeney recalling the endless hours he had spent with the Tautges tractor.

Then, with something like a sigh, as if drowsily stirring from a deep inertial sleep, the intake wheels on the baler stirred and slowly began to revolve; the belt and chains started to move.

"Son of a *bitch!*" Stan burst out.

"How'd you do that?" Dwight snapped, sounding irate and looking at Olson as if he were some sort of black magician.

"They *all* do it," Olson replied, unsurprised and tensely vindicated, "if you give them enough rope."

"Let me see you do that again," Stan demanded, "and this time I'm in the cab with you."

Olson remounted the cab and pushed the PTO lever into the full on position, then pulled it back to off. The baler ceased working.

"See," he said. "You see where the lever is, right?"

"Right."

"It's off?"

"Yeah, it's off," Stan confirmed.

"OK, let's get down and wait."

This time they waited longer than before, but when it caught, it did so abruptly. Without a transition, the baler sprang to life.

"It might have caught quicker if we had the motor turning over faster," Olson said, "but I wanted it running the way I'm guessing the way it was the day of the accident."

Dwight was still struggling with his disbelief. "How come it never did that for us?"

"Well, maybe it did," Olson replied, "but not at a time when it was hooked up, so you didn't notice. And of course, the heavier the load on the shaft, the harder it is to turn. Or maybe, in fact, Steven's accident was the first time. Who knows? It's possible. Maybe he was the first one to place that PTO lever in just that spot, just a hair away from the back of the ramp."

Dwight shook his head.

"Mr. Saunders," Feeney said, addressing himself to Stan, "now that I've seen your tractor, I'm fairly sure that my firm is going to want to take this case. We have some more talking to do with Mr. Sharp and with Steven, of course, but if that goes ahead OK, we'd like to start thinking about buying this tractor and baler."

"Buying them?"

"For the moment, I'd like to write you a check for the right of first refusal. If we decide to proceed, and we file against J. I. Case, I can promise you they're going to want to buy it too. But what I'd like to do is write you a check that gives us first dibs. We can talk about final figures later on. Would that be all right?"

Stan said that sounded fine. Dwight concurred. Feeney took out his checkbook.

"When's Steve coming home?" Dwight asked.

"Soon. He's just about done," R. E. replied.

"You tell him we're all thinking about him," Dwight said.

"I sure will."

IT WAS LATE in the afternoon before Feeney and Olson left Richland, heading for Portland. R. E. had signed a consent form. They would need his wife's as well, since Steven was still a minor. If Steven agreed, Feeney said, he would file a claim against J. I. Case on their behalf. Then, in all likelihood, there would be a trial, unless, of course, the company chose to settle. That was a possibility, given the precedent of the Tautges case. On the other hand, Tautges was a fatality. R. E. asked what the settlement had been to the Tautges family, and Feeney told him $350,000. "Would you be willing to settle for something in that ballpark?" Feeney asked.

"Well, I guess that would be Steve's decision," R. E. replied, "but I think he would. Money's been a concern, you know, with his medical expenses, which are considerable, but it hasn't been the main thing. There's workmen's comp, you know. I think more than anything Steve would like to sit down with those folks from Case and talk to them. Have them take a look at that tractor and fix it. And apologize. He'd appreciate an apology. If they did that, I think Steve would be fine with that."

"Well, Mr. Sharp, we can always present that option when the time comes."

It was after midnight when Olson and Feeney arrived in Portland and crashed at a motel near the Shriners Hospital. By nine the next morning they were sitting in a lounge talking to Betty Sharp while Steven completed his morning physical therapy. Initially, she had reservations about getting involved in a lawsuit; it seemed to her a thing that other people might do or have happen to them, like an exotic illness. When Feeney explained about the defective PTO, she wondered whether it couldn't serve as a point of negotiation between her family and J. I. Case. Feeney told her that thus far only a fatality had induced Case to talk. "It's not just about your son, Mrs. Sharp. There are approximately seventy-five thousand 70-series tractors still functioning out there, each a potentially serious hazard."

At that, her resistance vanished. She told Steven, when he joined them, that she thought it would be a good idea to cooperate with Feeney. When Steven heard what Feeney had discovered about the PTO on the Case tractor, the color went out of his face and he became very quiet. "So it really wasn't my fault," he said finally. "You know, I *knew* it wasn't. I told Stan that day that it happened all on its own. I don't think he believed me. Maybe in his shoes I wouldn't of believed me either. But now, this changes things." He paused. "You said you stood there with Dwight and Stan and you all saw the Case PTO kick on all by itself?"

"Yes, we did, Steve," Feeney replied.

"I wish I could of seen it."

"You will. You'll have plenty of opportunity."

"'Cause you know it's one thing to know something all on your own or think you do, but another thing when it's right out there and the people standing there have to accept it."

"Right."

"You think you can prove this in court?"

"That's the plan, Steven. But maybe we won't have to go that far." He explained about the Tautges settlement.

"Well, then, OK," Steven said, "I'm on board."

Feeney said he would get started on the paperwork with Betty. In the interim Steven showed Olson around the residential area of the Shriners Hospital. There he introduced him to a young woman who was a good friend of his. She was in the final phases of recovering from a near-fatal burn she had suffered when a lighter had blown up in her hand. She and Steven hung around together: danced, watched videos, and played pool. Olson took a picture of the two of them standing side by side, she with her arm around him, an attractive woman with long dark hair. For several years thereafter Olson kept the photo tucked into the blotter on his desk. "I was touched by the two of them," he said later to Feeney. "They seemed so . . ."—he hunted for the word— "happy together. Strange, wouldn't you say, under the circumstances?"

"He's a phenomenon, that kid."

"A nice guy, don't you think?"

"Sure, he is. A very nice guy. But there's something about him . . ."

"What?"

"I don't know. He's a little unnerving."

"Unnerving?" Olson asked.

"I'm sixty years old and he's what? Seventeen? Eighteen? And yet after I'd talked to him for about fifteen minutes and he'd told me about his accident, all very matter-of-fact, I got the weird feeling that in some ways he was way older than me. In a certain way. You understand?"

"In terms of experience, you're saying?"

"I don't know. Maybe. Let me put it this way: no fear. He seemed to have no fear, no anxiety. None that I could detect."

"Yeah, well, he's obviously a gutsy guy."

"Take you and me, Chris. We jog, we work out, we get checkups, we watch our diets, or at least I do." This last phrase was added because Olson was smiling at him. "All right, so I'm something of a fanatic in that respect, I admit it. But the point I'm making is that all this . . . carefulness . . . is, in a certain sense, a kind of fear."

"Prudence, maybe."

"Well, what's prudence? Looking over your shoulder, watching out, reading Jane Brody, taking vitamins. Which is fine, I'm not saying that. And who knows? Maybe Steven Sharp wears a seat belt and works out too, I hope he does, but if so, I don't think he does it in the same spirit I do."

"Could be he's on the other side of fear."

"Maybe that's it."

ON THE FLIGHT BACK to the Twin Cities, Feeney and Olson considered their next steps. As with Tautges, they had no witnesses, and this time not even something like a grease gun for circumstantial evidence. They would have the tractor, of course, but in itself it was of doubtful or ambiguous value. It was thirty years old, and as far as anyone could tell, the PTO had spontaneously engaged twice. How compelling was that?

How many defective 970s had they videotaped? Ten?

Olson said he thought that sounded right.

"I need more, Chris. Do you think you can get me some?"

"Sure, Leo. Don't worry. As many as you need."

CHAPTER FOURTEEN

THERE WERE MOMENTS during Steven's ordeal, that August day, when he lifted away from the scene and saw himself with the eyes of an observer. Perhaps he was on the point of fainting, perhaps his pain was causing him to dissociate. Whatever the explanation, he observed himself with the kind of dispassionate objectivity that can come to one caught in a traffic accident or falling downstairs, when everything starts to go by in slow motion. But those moments, however long they might feel, are usually fleeting. In Steven's case, though, they were not. Simply in order to stay alive, he had had to watch his every move until he reached Stan's house. Similarly, in the days and weeks thereafter, the need to keep assessing his situation, balancing its demands against his resources, paying rapt attention, be unremitting. Years would go by before everyday tasks could become routine for him, automatic, and never would he be able to encounter a stranger without seeing himself through the stranger's eyes.

Somehow he managed to accept this new duality, seeing himself as who he now was without attempting to measure himself against the Steven he had left behind. This allowed him to take the initiative in encounters with people, set the tone and preempt pity, which was the last thing he wanted. Indeed, he wanted it so little that in time he drove himself to such a degree of ease and competence with his single prosthesis that it was clear he was placing himself in a class of one rather than in the general ranks of the handicapped.

This was so even before he finished treatment at the Shriners Hospital. His medical team was sufficiently impressed with his progress to invite him to make a presentation to their board of governors. Accordingly, on February 23, 1993, about a week before the end of his final stay, he appeared onstage with Kristin and Mike, his prosthetist. In the video of the event, Mike greets the audience and then invites them to shut their eyes and imagine driving southeast of Portland, crossing the mountain range that transects the state, leaving the green half behind and continuing on through the high desert where the temperature rises as they speed onward toward the Idaho border, until it reaches a hundred degrees or better. He invites them next to contemplate the Snake River winding through its narrow gorge below the small town of Richland, and to observe a group of kids jumping from the tall bluffs that border it. One of those kids is Steven Sharp.

"Now open your eyes," he tells them. "Tragically, Steve lost both of his arms last summer in a farming accident. For the past five months he has been in the care of a medical/therapeutic team here at Shriners that has been attending to his injuries and training him in the use of his new prosthetic arm." Beside him on a table Mike had all the component parts of a prosthetic arm: the sock that covers the stump, the socket of the artificial limb, the plastic forearm, the hooks, the brackets, the straps and wires. With a technician's appreciation of detail, he explained how the arm was put together. Then Kristin made some remarks. And then Steven was invited onto the stage.

Only when he rose in the first row did it become apparent that he had been a spectator the whole time. He stepped onstage dressed in his standard garb: heavy black-framed glasses, red baseball cap, blue jeans, sport shirt, and cowboy boots. He greeted the audience with a smile. "Hello, my name is Steve Sharp." He stepped to the forward edge of the stage, and, speaking in a conversational tone, he offered a brief account of his accident. Sensing that even this might be emotionally taxing, he managed to evoke smiles when he described how he tried to use his phantom arms to climb back into the tractor cab, as if his failed attempt was an act of dumb clumsiness. Clearly, his audience was grateful for the smile.

At this point Mike took over and asked Steven to demonstrate his precision. He invited him to pick up some of the objects on the table beside him—a drinking glass, a pencil, a lightbulb, a dime—while he and Mike provided the technical commentary, describing how each object represents a different muscular and prosthetic strategy.

Kristin offered an overview of the steps in Steven's training, mentioning the hours it took simply to get the hooks to close on objects, the hours it took to raise or lower an object while maintaining the appropriate pressure, the hours of experimentation to conquer the sequence of, say, picking up a comb and running it through his hair. "But now," she concluded, "to give you an idea of the progress Steve has made, we would like to show you a short video of what he can do."

The auditorium darkened, and in a few moments the screen shows Steven lying in bed in his hospital room, family photos on his headboard. He sits up, his torso and stumps bare, wearing only boxer shorts. He seems unaware of the presence of the camera as he sits there, unself-conscious of the truncated winglike movements of his mangled stumps. He stands up and moves to the wall hook on which his left prosthesis is hanging. Ducking his head between the straps, he straightens and shrugs the apparatus around his neck, then inserts his left stump into the socket, and with several more shrugs snugs it into place. Now he can grasp things. He picks a T-shirt off a chair and after four or five tries gets it draped around his head in such a way that he can pull it on. Then he takes his glasses from the nightstand and begins the process of putting them on. For the first time he looks at the camera, content with his maneuver, and the audience broke into spontaneous applause.

Cut to the bathroom (now he's wearing blue jeans) and we watch him move a wet washcloth over his face. Cut to the kitchen, where he pours cereal into his bowl, then milk. He sits down, then grips a banana from a bowl and uses his teeth to open the stem end. (The audience made appreciative murmurs.) He inserts the spoon into the bowl without trouble, but as he raises it toward his mouth he must consciously adjust the angle, second by second, or he will dump its contents. Even when the spoon is right before his mouth, there are adjustments to be made. The second mouthful is equally demanding. On the third, he seems to make a slight miscalculation with his right shoulder, because the "wrist" is starting to flex away from, rather than toward, his mouth. There were some apprehensive murmurs from the audience. But Steven halts and corrects the movement; and then, for the second time, he gives the camera a direct glance, this time with a sly smile, as if to say, Thought I wouldn't make it, right? and proudly inserts the spoon in his mouth. The audience broke into applause as the video ended.

Mike asked for a volunteer to step onstage, and a man in a suit obliged, to whom Mike handed a beanbag. The man was asked to throw it to Steven, who missed the first toss. He bent down quickly and tossed it back. He caught the next toss and the one after that and the one after that, causing the audience to clap and cheer. Then Steven was handed a Shriners Hospital T-shirt on behalf of his entire medical team "because of the way he has touched our spirits and warmed our hearts."

"Thank you," he said.

Almost as an afterthought, Mike invited the audience to pose questions. At first no one did, then, coarsely, a male voice blurted out: "Why didn't you bleed to death?"

Steven squinted to locate the questioner, but the man did not identify himself, perhaps out of embarrassment at the almost accusatory sound of his question. "Well, first, the heat of the rollers kind of cauterized my stumps," Steven said. "And then, while I was waiting for the ambulance, I sat with them pressed hard against my thighs."

IT WAS NOT only on such public occasions that Steven was willing to expose himself to the view of people, for them to make of him what they would—he did so regularly. Part of seeing himself with an observer's eye led him to understand that his example might be useful to others, so he spent many hours sitting at the bedsides of frightened or depressed children during his five intermittent months at the hospital, listening to their stories and sharing his homely tips for warding off despair. "Remember that you're not less than anybody else, just because you're different. You're still you."

The mother of one of those kids sent a large bouquet to Leora the following summer. In the accompanying note, she asked Leora to give the flowers to Steven and to thank him for saving her son's life. "He would not have made it without him," she wrote.

"What did you tell her son?" Leora asked Steven.

"I don't know. I probably told him not to look back."

It was advice he himself took, honing his competence with his single prosthesis. He got so he could snap a dime in the air, or reach down and seize a rattler behind the head as easily as a fallen branch. He could also let a cigarette burn down to a column of ash, then lift it unbroken from one table to another, something none of his friends could accomplish.

"You could if you wanted to," he told them. "Just a question of focus."

CHAPTER FIFTEEN

THE SAME MONTH that Steven left Shriners Hospital, February 1993, Leo Feeney filed a summons and complaint against J. I. Case on four counts: *strict liability* because the company had manufactured a tractor that was unreasonably dangerous; *negligence* because the tractor had been poorly designed, tested, manufactured, and assembled; *breach of warranty* because the tractor had failed to live up to its guarantees; and, finally, *punitive damages* because Case had known its tractor could cause serious harm and rather than eliminating or minimizing its dangers had attempted to conceal them. In the words of the complaint, the company had behaved in a manner that was "willful, wanton, reckless, and in deliberate disregard of its obligations to society." A Case representative was duly summoned to appear in court in Milwaukee on April 12, 1993.

In its terse reply, Case requested, preliminarily, a shift of venue to Racine, Wisconsin, home of its corporate headquarters, along with a delay, both of which were granted. Case in turn charged that Steven had caused the accident himself by his own careless behavior. From Racine, it then requested a shift of venue to Oregon, the site of the accident and the state in which the Sharps were resident. Moving to Oregon would have put an end to the lawsuit because of that state's eight-year *statute of repose*. In this instance, the statute provided that a lawsuit involving defective equipment, like Steven's, had to be brought within eight years of the original delivery of the machine, regardless of when the defect was discovered. The Saunders tractor was more than twenty years old, well beyond the limit under Oregon law. Wisconsin, on the other hand, had no statute of repose. The judge ruled that Wisconsin would retain jurisdiction.

Little of this early legal maneuvering was known to Steven or his family. Feeney had come and gone in the space of twenty-four hours, and they were not to see him again until the following summer, when he returned along with his counterpart from Case, attorney Frank Scherkenbach, to begin taking depositions and gathering evidence. By then Steven had completed his junior year of high school and was concerned only with reconnecting with his group of friends and moving on with his life. On one of his return trips to Shriners Hospital, the prosthetics lab had outfitted him with a fishing pole holder that could be mounted on his prosthetic arm, and in this way he was able to begin revisiting the streams and lakes he had been haunting since childhood. It was a thrill once again to hear the whistle of the long line around his ears and feel the tug of a strike.

He dated various girls that spring and summer of 1993, but was even warier of romantic attachments than he'd been. "You could go out with Steven every night for a week," a girl from his high school class recalled, "and as far as you were concerned everything was just fine, and then you might happen to learn on Friday, say, that he'd been ticked off with you since Monday." He seemed to function best in groups of close friends, where he could be a little wilder than he used to be, readier to whoop it up at keggers and all-night parties. Since these involved the risk of an encounter with the deputy sheriff, during the warm summer months a dozen or so teenagers would pile into pickups and cars and head separately out of town (thereby not alerting the watchful deputy) to some agreed-upon, remote stretch of pasture or range. There they would clip an unlucky rancher's barbed wire, set boom boxes and cases of beer on the tailgates of the trucks, build a campfire, and then dance and drink and pair off in the mild dark of the long summer nights.

As that summer drew to a close, Steven could finally buy the pickup he'd been considering the day of his accident. This signified that his life was back on track and moving toward independence. Ed had bought his first truck at the same age. R. E. mounted a metal ring on the steering wheel so that Steven could turn it with his hook. He would get the key into the ignition by twisting sideways at the waist, leaning forward, and relaying it from his mouth. Now he could drive to school in Halfway on his own during his senior year or pick up friends. Or he could use the pickup to haul pig feed, harvested mushrooms, wild berries, or live rattlers he was taking to the taxidermist.

Not that he was ready to live on his own yet. He still required help in certain basic areas. One chilly day in August, for example, Betty helped him get into his boots and zip his heavy winter jacket as he headed out the door to visit his cousin and uncle at the latter's played-out gold mine in East Eagle. From his early childhood, Steven had been fascinated by the aura of gold that lingered from the gold rush days. Like everyone else, he'd heard stories of rich lodes dynamited shut for safekeeping by wary prospectors who had then spent the rest of their days hunting in vain for the fabulous wealth they had momentarily glimpsed. His uncle's mine supposedly had such a hidden entrance, but so far no one had found it. It made little difference to Steven. It was the hunt that stimulated him, the close reading of the familiar terrain, discovering its secrets. On their hikes in the high mountains, R. E. had taught him to scan the gravel and screen for the rare chunks of clear, transparent quartz, which, he said, were a sign of the presence of gold—clear quartz being a product of the same intense heat that had caused the gold to flow from the mountain eons ago. He had nuggets in his dresser drawer that he'd panned from Eagle Creek years ago.

All morning he and his cousin had clambered up and down the steep slopes around the mine, hunting for those water-clear stones. He had recovered his sense of balance, or had fashioned a new one. He could no longer use his upper body in the old way or grab hold of tree roots or sapling trunks, but his legs were becoming proportionately stronger. In his thick-soled boots, he tilted and swayed up and down the steep grades like a high-wire walker, doing his best to avoid a fall so as not to impact his hypersensitive upper arms.

Early in the afternoon his uncle lit a fire near the mouth of the mine and the three of them boiled coffee and ate lunch. The wind had continued chilly all morning, and before them in the open folds of the

gray, snowcapped mountains they could see skeins of rain come trawl-
ing in as if from a high, hidden fleet. The moist air carried a tang of pine
and fir. Each time Steven returned to these familiar sites, it felt like a
homecoming, as if all this rock and silence and piney raw weather were
handing him back to himself. Whenever he thought back on those
fruitless counseling sessions he'd been through in the hospital, it
became clear to him that the basic mistake of the psychologists had
been to assume that who he was was somehow locked away inside of
him like an animal in a burrow, whereas in fact it showed itself most
fully in places like this. The mountains set a kind of standard. If these
rocks, trees, peaks, and bluish vistas had not changed in his absence,
then neither had he, essentially.

Around four he told his uncle that he had to head back, that he'd
promised his mother he'd be home by supper. "Drive careful," his uncle
told him. "Looks like heavy rain coming."

Steven slung his hammer and sack of rock samples into the front
seat and took off. Sure enough, he was soon driving through rain, at
first a light shower but on the long upgrade to Newbridge, about five
miles from the turnoff, it started coming down in sheets. He slowed his
speed, turned on his headlights, and switched the wiper blades to high.
The rain pelting the cab roof was making a steady din, so he heard
nothing when the left front tire blew. Or perhaps the tire had gradually
lost air over a couple of miles. In any event, he felt a quiver in the steering wheel, which then began to shake erratically as the truck weaved
back and forth over the yellow line, and now he could hear as well as
feel the pounding of the rubber on the asphalt. He stepped on the
brake, guided the truck onto the shoulder, turned off the engine, and
pulled on the hand brake.

"Shit," he said aloud. "Ain't that a pain."

He had a spare, of course, but it was mounted under the rear bed
and held in place by a brace that probably hadn't been unbolted in
years. This was going to be interesting, he thought. In the last six
months he had learned to handle a pool cue or toss a beanbag again,
but changing a tire presented an entirely different prospect, especially
in a cold downpour. He stepped out of the cab, and at once his glasses
fogged and blurred. He took them off and set them inside on the dash.

His nearsightedness in the rain made the world feel flowing and eerie around him. Maybe some helpful motorist would stop.

He got the jack and tools from the bed, removed them from their canvas sack, then mounted the jack on the footplate. He inserted the tire iron into the ratchet and, using his foot, began jacking up the left front side of the truck. The cold rain had soaked him, sticking his clothes to his body. While he still had the flat tire firmly on the ground, he fitted the star wrench over the nuts and stomped to break each one loose. Then he jacked the tire off the ground and knelt to unscrew the nuts. About half an hour had gone by in the process. Then he walked to the rear of the truck and looked among his tools for a wrench he could use on the nut that held the tire bracket, but all he had was a crescent wrench. It would have to serve.

At the rear of the truck he lay down on his back on the gravel shoulder and worked himself under the bed by flexing his back and pushing with his heels, plowing gravel and grit with the back of his head, the nape of his neck, and his shoulders. The truck was parked facing the upgrade, so the cold rain ran like a river down his back and around him. His teeth were chattering with the cold. When he was positioned beneath the spare, he discovered, as he'd feared, that the nut securing the brace was badly rusted. He adjusted the wrench by placing it on the ground, pinning it with his shoulder and then pushing on the adjustment wheel with the tip of his hook. This he did a number of times, trying to get the jaws of the wrench to fit snugly. But because of the angle he couldn't seat the wrench squarely, so at each attempt he found that he was stripping the head. The rain had soaked the canvas straps that controlled his hooks, so he was finding it hard even to maintain the right degree of tension to hold the wrench in place. Working those straps was tricky enough when he was upright and dry, but to work a crescent wrench while lying on his back in the grit and running water under his truck was taxing his abilities to the limit.

Rust and flakes sifted into his eyes from the corroded metal. He had the taste of it in his mouth, sandy and sour. Repeatedly, his grip slipped on the wrench. If he continued stripping the nut, it would soon be immovable and the spare would stay where it was. He hunched himself over the wrench and adjusted it as precisely as he could, then fitted it back on the nut and, leaning up, gave a long steady push, hardly breathing. At last the nut gave. He breathed out in relief. Carefully he gave the nut several more partial turns, to the point where he was able to turn it with his hook. When he came to the end of the thread, he rolled quickly to the side so that the falling brace with the weight of the tire upon it wouldn't brain him. The tire crashed down beside him.

Half his job was done. About an hour and a half had gone by. No one had stopped. He turned and shoved the tire with his heels out from under the truck, then inched his way out. By now the light was fading. He got to his feet while quantities of water, gravel, and road grit sagged off him. He bent, hoisted the spare, and carried it to the front of the truck. He got to one knee and, lifting and balancing the spare with the aid of the other knee, mounted it on the wheel base. Once he had one nut in place, it was easier to thread the rest. He flipped the release on the jack and, reverse cranking with his foot, let the truck down. Then he removed the jack and tightened each nut by fitting the wrench to it and, for the final turn, stomping it with his foot.

Finally he was ready to stow his tools. He was bone cold. He climbed back into the cab and turned on the motor and let it run to get some heat in the cab. The ache in his shoulders and stumps where he'd scraped on the rough roadway was more intense than he could remember. On the day of his accident, a certain numbing had set in. In the hospital there had been pain medication. Now there was nothing. More than anything he wanted to hold himself for comfort and heat; instead, he sat upright in the freezing, baking kiln of his pain, and shook.

When he'd warmed a little, he turned his thoughts to the final task of the operation—remounting the arm of the spare tire bracket. If he failed to do that he would rip off the bracket arm as soon as he started driving and damage the undercarriage. And he had to do it before dark, which was rapidly approaching. But the nut that had secured the brace was too badly stripped to be rethreaded.

What would R. E. do?

He'd do something temporary, like tie it in place, so he could at least get home. But he had no string or twine in the truck. He thought for a while. Well, his boots had laces. Of course!

He reached down and pulled his laces to untie them. He kicked off his boots, then pulled out the laces. With the help of his teeth he tied them together with a square knot. Then he got out of the truck, barefoot, and again wiggled his way on his back beneath the frame. When he reached the brace he pushed it up and held it in place with his forehead, while he looped his laces around it and the frame, making a couple of turns to be sure. Then, using his teeth, he tied the laces with a simple slipknot. It wasn't a great job, but it would hold for the five miles between there and home.

HE WALKED THROUGH the front door, stammered a greeting, then stood dripping in the entry. Betty hurried from the kitchen. "My *Lord*, Stevie, where've you been? Look at you!"

"Yeah, where you been, son?" R. E. echoed. "Whoa, looks like you been through the war."

"Feels like it too. I had a flat coming home from East Eagle."

"And you changed it yourself?"

"Nobody else around," he replied. "I kept hoping somebody'd stop, but no one did."

"Why you're barefoot, Stevie. Where are your boots?" Betty asked.

"In the truck," he said, stuttering with chill.

"Here, let me help you out of those filthy wet clothes," she said. "I'll run a bath. You know, son, I really think it's too early for you to be doing this kind of stuff."

For once, he didn't disagree.

Later, when he was warm and clean, they sat with him while he ate dinner, and he recounted his exploit step-by-step. Betty was appalled, but R. E. said, "What else could the boy do?" When Steven got to the part about the shoelaces, R. E. was impressed. "That was good thinking, son. You'd of ripped that brace off otherwise."

Betty said nothing, but it occurred to her that she'd had a hand in that. The physical therapist at the hospital had cautioned her that Steven's cowboy boots were throwing off his gait. He preferred to wear them because they were easy to pull on and off. But that morning, for once, she had talked him into wearing his farm boots, which had laces, which she had bent down and tied for him.

CHAPTER SIXTEEN

I N THE SPRING OF 1993, Leo Feeney began making what would turn out to be numerous trips to Eagle Valley to conduct depositions and gather information. At the start, Feeney had had decent relations with Frank Scherkenbach since it was in the interests of both lawyers to accommodate each other's schedule and travel arrangements to this relatively inaccessible section of Oregon. Tension quickly developed between the two, however, when it came time to depose the Saunders family.

Apparently Scherkenbach had hoped that the ranchers might turn out to be friendly witnesses, based on their own self-interest, but they resisted his overtures and insisted on giving strictly factual, unopinionated answers to his leading questions about Steven, his work habits, and the events of the day of his accident. The Saunderses refused to venture an opinion about what had activated the PTO of their tractor, careful not to engage in speculation that might tilt blame in Steven's direction. Once their stance became clear, the deposition sessions devolved into grueling endurance contests as Scherkenbach tried to gain by dint of close and endlessly repetitious questioning what he was unable to obtain by innuendo. Dwight, Debbie, and Stan each in turn sat on uncomfortable chairs in worn courthouse offices beneath slowly turning ceiling fans or in the clammy currents of window air-conditioners, hour after hour, sometimes on video, trying to recall the exact wording of an answer given hours or days ago. Feeney offered what relief he could from tendentious or repetitious questions, and he did so with such frequency and such tenacity that relations between him and Scherkenbach cooled and then turned hostile.

The Saunderses grew resentful under the grilling as their words were picked over and combed through, cited back to them and finely sifted for contradictions. They were people whose word in the valley was as good as a contract, and they felt that both their honesty and their intelligence were being impugned. Stan, recovering from a heart operation, was too physically weakened and perhaps demoralized to register an objection, but Dwight, hot-tempered by nature and suffering from his recent back surgery, struggled to hold his anger in check. Privately, Feeney advised him to remain cool, telling him that Scherkenbach was trying to goad him into compromising statements. Dwight promised to do his best, but told Feeney that he resented Scherkenbach's condescending tone when he asked him questions such as whether they had running water and inside plumbing at the ranch, or whether they had a TV.

After the Saunderses, Feeney and Scherkenbach moved on to Steven and his parents, and then to Steven's co-worker, Barry Neal. Intermittently over the next twelve months they widened their nets and deposed a multitude of other witnesses with information relevant to the case, like OSHA inspector Gerald Beverage; Julie Garcher, Steven's high school counselor; and Norman Koopman, the instructor of the farm safety course Steven had taken in his sophomore year. It was a slow process, as both Feeney and Scherkenbach tried to amass sufficient details to paint a coherent picture not only of what had happened to Steven during the noon hour of August 22, but of the context—economic, social, and even psychological—in which it had occurred.

Relevant to both sides, for example, was whether Eagle Valley was close-knit. Was it a place where everyone would lock arms against an outsider like J. I. Case in order to protect one of its own? Were the Sharps well liked? Was Steven considered to be a reasonable and prudent individual? A careful worker? What about his habit of camping alone in the wilderness? What about him jumping off tall bluffs into the Snake River? What about the accident he'd had the year before he'd lost his arms, riding on the back of his friend Jason Blade's motorcycle, in which he'd nearly severed his left heel? In response to one of Scherkenbach's questions, Steven said that he guessed he was somewhat accident prone. Feeney later had to file a motion to have that remark banished from the trial as prejudicial. And what about his frequent absenteeism from school? It turned out that he had strained relations with at least one of his high school teachers. Why was that? And what about his run-ins with the deputy sheriff? Feeney and Scherkenbach probed into these matters, conducting their depositions now with a cold professionalism that occasionally cracked to reveal a bitter underlying antagonism. About a year into the process, Scherkenbach launched a surprise attack, filing a motion in the circuit court in Racine to bar Feeney from practicing law in Wisconsin as punishment for disrespectful remarks and behavior allegedly made by him during the depositions of the Saunders family. Had the motion been successful, it would, of course, have deprived Steven of his legal counsel and effectively ended the lawsuit. After examining the evidence during an entire day, Circuit Judge Dennis Barry denied the motion and gave both lawyers a stern talking-to about the necessity of upholding the dignity of the law. The judge was aware, he said, that the adversary system, to a certain extent, fostered confrontational behavior. "The adversary system presents a contest," he said, "and winning sometimes becomes the sole object of the proceeding, but if our system . . . is going to endure and if the rule of law is going to be meaningful, the rules of the contest must be followed and must include the requirement that attorneys be civil toward one another and reduce puffing and other such confrontational behavior."

Sometime after the motion was denied, Case now replaced Scherkenbach with a lawyer from Milwaukee, Ralph Weber, whose manner in deposition was more fine-grained and subtle, and whose array of legal maneuvers was wider than Scherkenbach's. He too tried to prevent the case from going to trial, filing for summary judgment on the grounds that the Saunderses' general negligence had been responsible for Steven's accident, a move Feeney successfully countered. Weber devoted much of his energy to the filing of motions designed to restrict the scope of the evidence Feeney could present at trial. Feeney found himself in the rather Sisyphean dilemma of gathering evidence on the one hand and struggling to keep Weber from barring it from trial on the other.

As one year rolled into the next, Feeney found himself under increasing strain from all the legal skirmishing. The case was taking a disproportionate amount of time relative to the seven or eight he routinely handled. He was spending his days filing and replying to motions, oppressed by the weight of legal minutiae as the trial date, tentatively set for December 1995, loomed closer. Even at this late date, Feeney was still wrestling with Case to gain access to basic technical information about its tractor. By the fall of 1995, he had filed over sixty interrogatories (requests for information), to many of which he had not received a reply. Balanced against this frustration was his sense of responsibility vis-à-vis Steven, the course of whose entire life would be altered, one way or the other, by the outcome of this trial.

One day in October, Terry Wade, one of Feeney's close friends and partners, dropped into Feeney's office and shut the door. He sat down and without preamble told Feeney that he looked as if he was under a lot of stress.

"I am under a lot of stress," said Feeney.

"How many cases are you working on right now, Leo?"

"Eight," he replied.

"That's too many. I want you to give me two."

Feeney said he would think about it. Wade recommended that he not think too long. "Suppose," he said, "you were to hand over two of your cases. Which would they be?"

Feeney thought a moment and then reluctantly stated that one of them would be the Sharp case. He told his partner that both because of all the work he had done and because of the Sharps themselves, the kind of people they were, he felt extremely attached to the case. On the other hand, precisely because of the importance of the case to the Sharp family, he would seriously consider handing it over. He had a bad feeling about it. He had won many skirmishes thus far, but the prospect of going to trial was taxing his endurance.

"What do you say," his partner asked, "that I talk to Bill Manning about it?"

Manning, a partner in the firm in his mid-forties with an extensive background in product liability work, was a good friend of Feeney's. Earlier, Feeney had been sufficiently impressed by his younger colleague's abilities that he had handed off a case or two to him.

"You can mention it to him," Feeney replied. "Let me know what he says."

"He said," his friend reported to him the following day, "Why don't the two of you go for a jog? I think it'd be a good idea, Leo."

MANNING HAD BEGUN jogging in high school, when he had run track and played basketball, then continued it in college as part of the strict regime entailed by his basketball scholarship, and later, intermittently, during law school, when it had allowed him to breathe some fresh air and clear his mind. It still did, although now its function had shifted to offsetting the effects of middle age and too much airline food and long hours of sedentary office work. He liked to lope along the tree-lined Mississippi Park Road not far from his house, preferably early in the morning. During the summer months, the sun would be rising as he stepped out of the front door, but on a chilly October morning like the present one, the streetlights were still contending with the dark and the morning fog. A large man, six feet three, about two hundred pounds, he paused to take a couple of deep breaths, then pulled his stocking cap over his ears and stretched. It helped that the first block was downhill. As he approached the river road, he merged with the usual flow of joggers, many of them students—the Minneapolis campus of the University of Minnesota is a couple of miles to the west—and the proximity of runners who had gotten up earlier and were training harder energized him. Below the steep bluff to his right lay the Mississippi, about an eighth of a mile wide at this point, its dark surface scattered with mist. Warming up, he headed east at a quicker pace, scanning the faces of the oncoming joggers in the glow of the streetlights for Leo Feeney's.

They met up on the approach to the Ford Avenue Bridge and fell into stride with each other, heading out onto its long open expanse where the early-morning traffic gave a hum to the open steel and where the cold wind off the river made them catch their breaths. They tucked their chins and hustled to the other bank. Here the path moved in long S curves between unlit houses and the river. Moving at a pace that permitted conversation, they began talking about the Sharp case. Manning asked Feeney if it was true he was thinking about handing it over, and Leo said that, after painful consideration, he was ready to do so—to Manning, if he was interested.

"It's one of the hardest decisions I've ever made, Bill."

"I can understand that," Manning replied. "I talked to Terry. He told me about the amount of work you've put in."

"It's not only that, Bill. It's the people. It's Steven Sharp. He's a special guy. And the family's special too; you'll see when you meet them, if you take this on. What's your workload like right now?"

"I could manage it."

"I know if you took it, you'd do a good job."

"Thanks, Leo. I'm honored that you thought of me."

"Well, I like your work. You know that. And I was thinking, maybe what this case needs right now is some fresh blood. I'm feeling overworked. I really am. I know you'd give it your best shot."

"Yeah, I would, Leo."

"Court date is coming up quick, you know."

"When?"

"About six weeks, end of December."

"Six weeks?" Manning replied, startled.

"I know it's short notice, Bill."

"How soon can you pull everything together for me?"

"Right away. I'll talk to Chris. He knows where everything is."

"I want everything in one place. Everything on this case and everything on Tautges, all together in one room." His tone had sharpened.

"That won't be a problem," said Feeney.

For the rest of the run, Feeney reviewed the main twists and turns the case had taken in its three-year history. "For one thing," he said, "you'll be trying this case in Racine, where Case has its headquarters. It's a company town. The only other large employer is the SC Johnson Wax company. Case has been there for a hundred years, so it has deep roots. The high school is named after J. I. Case."

Manning asked Feeney whom he had for his main expert. Feeney mentioned the name of an engineer who often gave plaintiff's testimony in product liability cases. "The only problem," Feeney reported, "is that he's been having some heart trouble. He's scheduled to go in the hospital for observation."

"Is it serious?"

"No, I don't think so. His doctor says he should be on his feet by the end of November."

In his mind, Manning made the decision not to use him.

"Were there any eyewitnesses to the accident?" Manning asked.

"No," said Feeney, "just like the Tautges case."

He said the Saunders family, who would testify for Steven, were close by, but they were not eyewitnesses.

"Well, one thing I would want to do," Manning said, "is to review Tautges and everything you gathered then. That's going to be important for negligence. There's no way Case can claim they weren't warned about this. A fatality sends a pretty clear signal."

"Talk to Chris," Feeney advised. "He'll tell you about the dozen or so farmers that we've got on tape talking about their self-starts."

Yes, Manning would do that. He'd get in touch with Olson as soon as he got to work that morning. Already he was engaging himself, strategizing. In his mind he was reviewing various technical experts he had worked with over the years in his many product liability cases, assessing their usefulness for this one. He needed somebody knowledgeable, somebody with great credentials, not a plaintiff's witness. Strange, he thought as they came to a halt close to where Feeney's car was parked, when he'd stepped out of his front door scarcely forty-five minutes before, he'd been curious to see whether Feeney would actually offer him this case, as Terry had intimated. And now he was already alone with it. The swiftness of the transfer and the imminence of the trial date gave him an uneasy rush, not unlike the onset of a fever.

The two of them did a couple of quick stretches to prevent their leg muscles from seizing up, vapor steaming from their sweatshirts and stocking caps. Then they faced each other, understanding that most of what was in their minds would remain unspoken.

"Bill, I appreciate this," Feeney said.

"Look, we help each other out."

"Yeah, I know we do," Feeney said with a small smile, mock punching his friend in the shoulder. Manning stood and watched his senior colleague walk stiffly up the embankment to his car.

IN THE MANNING KITCHEN, Ruth, Bill's wife, looked up from her coffee and morning paper as he sat down on the chair by the back door to tug off his sneakers and socks.

"What's up?" she asked.

"Up?" he asked with studied unconcern. "Is something necessarily up?"

"Come on," she said. "I know you. You've got that look."

"What look?"

"Like you're already out of here, like you're not even going to eat breakfast."

"Well, you know, honey, I'm not." He stood up. "I'll shower and dress, then I'll fill you in." Ruth was also an attorney, so he brought her up to speed quickly.

At work he appropriated a small, temporarily unallocated room down the hall from his office. It came to be known as the war room. Currently used for storage, it was about the size of two office cubicles, windowless and stuffy. He had it cleared out. Then he called Chris Olson and soon Feeney's materials were being moved in—the depositions, pleadings, machine parts, photographs, videotapes, the works. In the following days he continued to fill the room, wall to wall, floor to ceiling, with boxes in tall columns—Tautges materials to one side, Sharp materials on the other. They brought in a portable TV and VCR so that Manning could view the taped depositions and interviews with farmers. On a small table they spread out machine parts.

"What I want to see first," he told Olson, "is the PTO. Not the shaft or the lever, but the central hydraulic unit."

Olson handed him a chunky sealed unit about the size of a football.

"Has anybody ever looked inside this thing?"

"No. It's simply an on/off device, Bill. You push this lever forward [he pointed to a metal rod on the table] and it supplies power to the shaft. You pull it back, and it turns off."

"I'm going to get a cutaway. I want to see how this thing looks inside."

Manning put in a call to a machinist. Once he had the unit in pieces, he made another call to Bud Christopherson, an engineer who was a friend of his at the locally based Toro Company, well-known manufacturers of lawn and garden equipment. "Bud," he said, "I need to have you look at a piece of equipment for me that's come up in a case. It's a hydraulic Power Take Off control. The control unit. Could you do that?"

Manning dropped it off on his way home from work.

Several days later, he was sitting in Christopherson's office. "This is a strange setup, Bill," the engineer told him.

"Why?"

"This is a simple enough device. You see this little rod? That's called a spool. You see this notch on the end of it? That lets the pressurized hydraulic oil into the chamber when the control lever is moved forward. Clear?"

"Clear."

"OK. The spool moves forward, the oil enters, as I said, under great pressure, causes the two clutch plates to engage, and power is delivered from the engine to the shaft."

"I understand."

"Except, what is strange about this deal is that the notch on the spool is way too long."

"What difference does that make?"

"A great deal. That notch is long enough to start letting oil enter as soon as the spool just starts to move forward."

"How long should the notch be?"

"About half an inch shorter. That way the operator could move that lever about halfway forward before it would engage the plates. That would be the correct way to engineer this. But with this setup, it looks like if the spool is moved just that fraction of an inch, it could pressurize the system instantly."

Manning fought down his rising excitement. Perhaps this small but apparently important flaw would account for both the perennial clutch burnout problems and the spontaneous self-starts. "How come it doesn't always do that?"

"Bill, if all the units have spools that are notched like this, the potential will be there. Possibly on some machines, the cable that connects the lever to the spool might be a little looser, in which case there would be a little more play in the system."

"But basically it's on a hair trigger?"

"Hair trigger? I'd say so. It looks like a dangerous setup."

Manning thought. "What about vibration? If all the lever has to do is move forward a fraction of an inch, could motor vibration possibly do that?"

"Maybe. I don't know. Seems like it. We'd have to see it in action."

"Bud, would you be willing to run some tests? We've got the tractor in storage."

In posing the question, Manning knew that he was making a request beyond the ordinary, for if the tests corroborated what Christopherson was explaining to him, then his next request to Christopherson, as the other well understood, would be to ask him to serve as his expert witness—inviting him, in other words, to violate the unwritten code of solidarity among the employees of manufacturing companies that forbade them to testify against each other, particularly employees of large companies like Case and Toro. Christopherson hesitated before answering, obviously considering the various implications facing him.

"Hey, I realize it could be a hassle for you, Bud," Manning said, offering his friend a face-saving exit.

"Bill," Christopherson interrupted him, "I'm pretty sure I'm right about this, and if our tests bear it out, then I guess I'd be willing to say in court what I'd say here at Toro, if this was one of our machines."

"Which is?"

"That it should be recalled."

"You'd testify to that?"

"Yes."

"Bud, I know this takes guts. And I appreciate it."

"Well . . ." Christopherson began.

"But more than me, the person I'll be representing, a kid by the name of Steven Sharp, he'll appreciate it."

"Tell me about him," Christopherson said. "You have time for lunch?"

"Absolutely. I haven't met him yet, but I can tell you what I've heard."

CHAPTER SEVENTEEN

MANNING TOLD HIS SECRETARY, Sharon, that for the next couple of weeks he'd be working mainly at home. In the office his phone was constantly ringing, the e-mail blinking and chirping, people dropping by. What he needed were large blocks of uninterrupted time in which to read and take notes, to think and talk into his tape recorder, to start assembling his notebooks. Sharon was used to seeing him in this mode. Soon, she knew, tapes would start arriving on her desk for transcription. Manning took all the deposition transcripts and pleadings to his basement office at home, a finished room with a large, low table, a couple of comfortable chairs, and a couch. Down here there was a minimum of household traffic, the laundry room on one side and a spare bedroom on the other, which he'd converted into a small workout gym with his NordicTrack and a weight machine. When he found his eyes blurring from reading or his head getting fuzzy, he'd go in there and work up a sweat. Then he'd shower and go up to the kitchen and make a pot of coffee. Later he would come back down and resume working.

To a degree, this was his normal mode of trial preparation, only intensified by the tight time frame. Looking at the case objectively, he did not find it out of the ordinary. In the ten years he'd been with his firm, he had worked on larger cases with much more pain and suffering at issue, and much higher economic stakes. Yet, during those first weeks of November as he burrowed deeper into the materials, he felt himself getting hooked with a passion unusual even for him, for whom passion was a working fuel. Perhaps it was the tenor of the voices from Eagle Valley as they began speaking to him from the pages and video-tapes of their depositions, the plain talk, the understated manner, the obvious concern of most of the area residents for Steven. He was sur-prised at the lack of rancor from R. E. and Betty, who floored him with their gentleness and calm. Manning was the father of a five-year-old daughter, and he knew for a certainty that in Betty's and R. E.'s shoes he would have been incapable of such forbearance.

But mostly it was Steven's voice that got to him. He too spoke with a calm objectivity that seemed to be the prevailing tone of Eagle Valley. His deposition was one of the briefest and, if possible, even less tactical than his parents'. When describing the events of August 22, he spoke to the Case lawyers in an unguarded conversational tone, as if he were speaking to well-meaning or at least objective questioners. Of course he was aware that he and Case were in dispute, but nevertheless he seemed to take it for granted that the crux of their difference was not to be found in ordinary words. *Clog*, for example. He used the word *clog* to explain why he had climbed down from the tractor that day—to clear a clog from the baler—even though Feeney had clarified in his own ques-tioning that there had never been a true clog, in the sense of hay so tightly jammed between the rollers of the baler that it prevented them from turning. And yet every time Ralph Weber used the term in posing his question, Steven responded in kind. Manning chalked this up to the boy's inexperience while suspecting that it might also have had to do with a certain kind of Eagle Valley tact, as if for Steven to split hairs with Weber would have amounted to treating him not only as an oppo-nent, which he certainly was, but also as a person heedless of truth, which was not necessarily a given. Well, Manning mused ruefully, let Steven observe the local decorum, if that's what it is, but he has no idea what he's up against.

More than the depositions, however, it was one minor incident for-tuitously captured on video that cracked open Manning's heart to Steven. Sorting through the file boxes, he found a tape labeled simply "Steven Sharp, Shriners Hospital, January 1993," apparently shot by someone on Steven's medical team. Manning inserted the tape into his

VCR to see what it contained. It opens with Steven standing by the hospital swimming pool, a tall, skinny figure in blousy swimming trunks, his flesh pale, his skin-grafted stumps puckered and raw. He is staring toward the camera while the silvery water wobbles around him in the empty hall. At someone's muffled request, Steven steps into the pool at the shallow end and moves out to chest level, where he leans forward and slips into the water. The camera follows him making his way through the water with a flexing of his spine in an eellike motion, rotating his shoulders and lifting his head every three or four undulations to snatch a breath. After several minutes of this, he returns to the shallow end and stands up, breathing hard. The off-camera voice asks him to get out, and he mounts the steps. Then he is told to walk to the deep end and dive off the diving board. His face is flushed with exertion and, it seems, pleasure. He is enjoying himself. He trots down to the diving board, mounts it, takes three measured and springy steps, and dives in.

He makes it nearly to the shallow end entirely underwater, using the same rippling spinal movement to fuller effect with the force of the dive behind it. Submerged, his dim form is reminiscent of a seal's. Close to the steps he stands up and starts to mount. But halfway up it becomes clear to him, as well as to the camera's eye, that the momentum of his dive has dragged his baggy trunks halfway down his butt. He pauses, trying to blink the chlorinated water from his eyes, twisting around to glimpse his backside, perplexed. Then the screen goes blank, the record of his embarrassment lasting no more than a couple of seconds. Manning, meanwhile, sat on the couch with the VCR control in his lap, his mind momentarily blank as well.

Well, of course he can't pull up his swimming trunks or wipe the water out of his eyes, he thought. That's perfectly obvious.

Then he felt tears falling on his hands.

Manning had been a swimmer at Steven's age, and perhaps something in his own nerves and musculature had engaged as he had watched Steven exit the pool. It was such a small indignity in the context of so many larger ones, Manning thought, but on the other hand a permanent one. Never again would Steven give that little automatic swimmer's hike to his trunks as he left the water. And because the unforeseen detail was so specific, it hit Manning like a slap. Before he knew it, he was weeping in earnest as his mind set off like a lighted fuse to all the daily humiliations and impossibilities that a man without hands would have to put up with. He stood up. He stuffed his hands in his pockets. Let's take the next ten minutes without hands, he thought to himself. Then he mounted the stairs to the kitchen.

He was alone in the house. How, for starters, to get a glass of water? Answer: He couldn't. The best he could manage, after kicking off his shoes, was to balance awkwardly on one foot and prod the cold water handle with his toes, then lean forward and drink from the tap.

Suppose he was hungry? He opened the fridge by shoving the door with his shoulder, but inside nearly everything was wrapped, sealed, and contained in a way to make it ungraspable with his teeth. This was what it had been like those first weeks for Steven—near-total helplessness. Now, of course, he had his prosthesis, but as Manning continued his exploration in other rooms in his house, hands strictly out of commission, moving his eyes over the various textures and surfaces—upholstery cloth, wood, the covers of books, the flowers in vases, the logs beside the fireplace, the piano, his daughter's toys—he felt all these routinely touchable things suddenly as remote as museum exhibits. Slowly Manning sank down on his living room couch and his eyes wandered to the side table beside him where some framed photos stood: of Ruth, of his daughter, Sonja. They would be home soon, and he would get up and greet them with a hug. A hug that he would feel. The house grew quiet around him. Enough. He stood up and removed his hands from his pockets. He'd had enough. His throat and chest ached with anguish.

THURSDAY AFTERNOON, November 9, 1995, he flew to Milwaukee and drove a rented car to Racine, where he checked in at the Radisson, a newer hotel located on a rocky point jutting out into Lake Michigan. After dropping off his bag in his room, he walked down to the beach. Ice sheeted the shore rocks and boulders with sprays of aboriginal flora. He walked down to the water. There were miles of empty sand in either direction and the temperature was dropping. A late pewter sun balanced on the horizon while raucous seabirds rose up at his approach, squalling. The scene spoke to him deeply: bare and clear, primitive and open. There was an icy wind. He thought of a line from one of his favorite authors, Saul Bellow: "Beauty is not a human invention."

The following morning, he breakfasted early, then walked the seven blocks to the courthouse. He was on his way to the first hearing on preliminary motions, his first appearance in front of Judge Emily Mueller, and his first courtroom encounter with Ralph Weber. The judge was a petite woman in her mid-forties, sharp featured, attractive, warily pleasant. Weber was already known to Manning through their encounters at depositions and a by now ample correspondence. Manning anticipated a strenuous day as they would each try to shape the playing field. Weber, he had discovered, was bright, quick, and full of self-confidence. He presented his views with a disarmingly fluent conversational delivery, as if self-evident to any halfway intelligent and reasonable person. Six years younger than Manning, he approximated him in build, six feet–plus, and was similarly husky. Indeed, the resemblance between the two might have been striking had it not been that Weber's hair was sandy brown while Manning's was prematurely snowy white. Both dressed in expensive, well-tailored business suits. In manner, however, the contrast was marked. Weber was analytical, cool, insinuating; Manning was edgy and mercurial, full of heat, enthusiasm, and dismay. Instinctively, chemically, the two of them would likely have squared off in any setting that constrained them to take notice of each other, let alone a courtroom, where the effect was compounded.

This antipathy was conditioned by their educational and early career paths. Weber had graduated summa cum laude from Marquette University; five years later he had been admitted to the bar, having graduated Phi Beta Kappa from Columbia Law School, where he had been the recipient of several honors and had served as one of the editors of the prestigious *Columbia Law Review*. His was an impeccable launch into the practice of law, where he specialized in product liability defense.

Manning, on the other hand, had taken somewhat longer to decipher his vocation, working for a couple of years after college for an international holistic pharmaceutical company in New York. He had returned to St. Paul to attend Hamline Law School only when it became clear to him that his life was calling him elsewhere. He had pursued a regular meditation practice. He had read Thomas Merton in his spare time. With no savings or other means of support, he had worked two jobs while attending law school full-time, during the evenings as a downtown parking lot attendant, and three or four afternoons or mornings a week as a clerk in a food co-op, where he had used his employee discount to buy his groceries at wholesale prices. In the evenings he had sat in the attendant's cubicle of the underground parking lot and studied law, and then driven at midnight to his rent-controlled high-rise between Minneapolis and St. Paul, the "ghetto in the sky," as it was commonly called by its inhabitants, few of whom were American citizens. The elevators were often on the blink. Odors of cumin, red pepper, curry, and other less familiar spices stood in the hall. In mid-winter frost piled up like snow on the inside ledge of the closed windows. It was an austere and focused existence, not uncongenial to him, and that left its mark.

Judge Mueller greeted them and invited their opinions on the first order of business for the day, which was the substitution of Bud Christopherson for Leo Feeney's previous expert. Manning justified it by stating that the previous expert witness was still recovering from open-heart surgery, adding that Christopherson was already deeply involved in researching one of the three main areas of defect in the case—namely, the spring on the lever of the PTO. Case had added this spring a year or two into the production of the 970 in an attempt to solve the then newly discovered clutch plate burnout problem, hoping the spring would help force the lever back into an off position whenever the farmer released it. To date, Christopherson had examined seven 970 tractors and had found the spring broken on six of them. Most operators, Manning said, including the Saunderses, were unaware of the spring's existence.

What Manning was doing was not simply responding to the judge's invitation to discuss the relatively bureaucratic matter of the switch of experts; he was, like a horse out of the gate, already running the race—or, to drop the metaphor, he was already pleading his case.

Weber intervened to speak against the substitution of Christopherson. Here they were about two months away from trial, he complained, in a three-year-old case, and a new expert witness was being sprung on them, a new expert with new evidence. He hadn't heard Christopherson's name until the day before yesterday, nor had he ever heard anything about a PTO lever spring before this very moment. He said he thought the days when lawyers tried to blindside each other were in the past.

Christopherson was not really a new expert, Manning replied. He would, excepting this recent research, be offering the same testimony as the previous expert. And as for blindsiding, all opposing counsel had to do was get busy and depose Christopherson; then he would be aware of the exact nature of his investigations and of the evidence he intended to present at trial. Exasperated, Weber protested: "We keep getting jammed, judge. Plaintiffs bring up this new stuff, oh see, you have plenty of time to respond. We need time to get ready for trial. They wanted a new expert, had him do new work. They could have done it a month ago."

"This is not a new expert," Manning replied.

"Not a new expert?"

"This is not a new expert, you *know* that," Manning shot back. And you *know* that was a signature Manning counterpunch. If Weber was going to get personal with him, Manning was going to reply in kind. From her desk the judge observed the heated exchange, faintly bemused, and then instructed Weber that if he felt strongly enough about the matter he should offer the appropriate motion.

They then turned to the day's main item, which would remain central during all the pretrial hearings: determining the scope of admissible evidence. Again mixing argument with exposition, Manning declared that he planned to call ten witnesses who had experienced PTO self-starts with the tractor, and that he would have much supporting evidence. In addition to the tractor and baler themselves, which would arrive separately, he was going to bring down a large rental truck loaded with exhibits and supporting material. Among his witnesses would be Mickey Jones, who had been seriously wounded when his PTO had spontaneously started, and Michael Tautges, son of the fatally injured Raymond Tautges.

Weber's cocounsel, Sandra Botcher, argued strenuously against the appropriateness of these witnesses. Given the large number of 970s in operation and the relative dearth of incidents, each of these accidents had arguably been the result of operator error. What had happened in Steven's case, Botcher declared, was that his baler had clogged. The clog had stopped the PTO shaft from turning. This had led Steven to turn off the PTO only partially. He had gotten down from the tractor and removed the clog, with the result that the shaft had started turning again, activating the rollers, which had seized his hands. Steven had more or less endorsed this scenario, Botcher told the judge, so she urged her to exclude the other incidents Manning was attempting to put in evidence. Nothing indicated they were comparable to Steven's. If the judge admitted them, Botcher warned her, she would find herself presiding over many mini-trials, which would stretch out to inordinate length. In making this last argument, Botcher was targeting a possible weakness in Judge Mueller's judicial experience, which, while broad, had not been much concerned with product liability. Simply to deal with Steven's incident was going to be complicated enough, in terms of the technical testimony. The evidence would become unmanageable, defense counsel argued, if she allowed Manning to bring in all of his proposed material.

Not so, Manning replied. All the incidents he wished to introduce were automatically comparable because they had all been caused by the same defective PTO. There were many more incidents that could be cited, he assured the judge. The machine was defective, and that defect would in all likelihood cause more accidents in the future. That Case had done nothing about it after the Tautges fatality and the Jones incident he found incomprehensible. "It is willful and wanton and malicious indifference this company has shown to Steven Sharp. His arms should be on. This shouldn't have happened. "They knew for six years about this, prior to 1992," Manning argued, "and that they continued to run this risk, rather than change the design immediately, is deplorable."

The case had nothing to do with a defective machine, Botcher argued, but rather with a single operator, Steven, who had simply failed to turn off the PTO before dismounting from his tractor. In making this claim, the defense brought to light the underlying bone of contention, both of the day's debate and, to a certain extent, of the entire trial's: What did it mean to *turn off* the PTO?

Was it off when the lever had been pulled to the back of the ramp and the PTO shaft had stopped turning? Or was it off when the lever had been pulled *beyond* the back of the ramp and locked in place by a spring-mounted pin called a plunger? Further complicating this seemingly simple question was the fact that the metal of the ramp on old tractors like the Saunderses' was rough from decades of wear and tear, and tended to cause the lever to catch at the rear of the ramp, but not beyond it.

Weber moved to a mock-up of the PTO control that stood before the judge's bench, pointed to its lever and its plunger, and said: "This case is about Steven Sharp leaving this plunger up here, OK? [He was pointing to the back of the ramp.] Steven said, 'I know I've got to have the plunger down here' [behind the ramp]. And I said, 'And what happens if you leave it up—you leave it up on the ramp?' 'You can get hurt,' he said. I said to him in his examination—you will see it on videotape, perhaps—the look in his eyes when I said to him, 'Well, you were told, weren't you, that Stan found the pin up on the ramp?' And he claimed that he hadn't been told that, and then his eyes teared up, like 'Oh my God. I didn't shut it off.'

"That's what this case is about," Weber said. He said he had no interest in retrying the Mickey Jones or the Ray Tautges case or any of the other incidents Manning kept bringing up. He would try this case, focusing on a simple fact—namely, that Steven ought to have placed the pin behind the ramp, and he did not do that.

The judge turned to Manning for his comment. He strode to the mock-up in order to point out that the difference between what he and Weber were calling "off" was one- or two-sixteenths of an inch. He pointed to the back of the ramp. "I disagree with how Mr. Weber is presenting the facts," he said, "and about where the lever was. It was here." He pointed to the rear of the ramp. "The baler shut off. They will never be able to refute that. Steven didn't walk back when the baler was moving and put his arms in. It was off. He heard it turn off. It's a dramatic noise.

"You have to imagine this," he continued, appealing to the judge. "The PTO is off. There's a delay, sometimes a half minute. I've watched it. I've seen it on the accident machine, which we will bring down on a flatbed if need be. We're prepared to do that. On this machine, when you have that lever in that position, you get *off* and you go back and sometimes it's forty-five seconds and sometimes it's four minutes, but the hydraulic fluid gets by the spool that we don't see inside there and it self-starts, and it's defective, and it's happening all over the country."

He turned to face Weber.

"All of these arguments about clog: I understand Steven used the word *clog* in cross-examination. But a lawyer can do that to a witness. He can put words in his mouth. That's because he is putting together an argument. Well, let him. So be it. I know what Steven intended to say in response to counsel's question about the lever. He intended to say that when the lever got to this point, it was back, it was off. He heard that it was off, and he thought he had it all the way back. He never evaluated, 'Do I have to look back every time and see that the plunger is behind that point behind me on a control?' He didn't evaluate it that way. He evaluated by pulling it back, thought he had it all the way back, and everything he heard and everything in the operation of the machine confirmed it.

"And I have to say that he sure had it close, Your Honor. He had it two-sixteenths of an inch away from off, *two-sixteenths*. And because he didn't get it all the way, and because these other ten farmers didn't get it all the way, their machines started in that position, and Steven Sharp, well, you know what happened to him."

Judge Mueller made a note, then turned to Weber and advised him: "It's apparent to me that the testimony of Mr. Sharp is going to be somewhat different than it was at the discovery deposition. I mean, there's going to be real room for cross-examination, Mr. Weber, if your characterization of what he said . . ."

Weber jumped in: "It's repeated, Judge."

Manning listened to the exchange with some surprise. It was one thing for a lawyer to put the best possible spin on a witness's statement, but this seemed to him to go further. Manning had studied Steven's deposition with care, and he felt certain that Steven had never made the statement Weber was attributing to him.

"I—," Manning began to protest, but Weber peremptorily overrode him: "Please," he said. "It's repeated, Judge. I'd love to go and get the transcript cites for you," he hurried on, "if you thought that was important." But before she could reply, he shifted the topic from whether Steven had admitted to not turning off the PTO to whether he ought to have turned off the tractor engine. "You know what's *really* going on, Judge," he told her. "See, the manual and the sticker that was on the baler that had been removed by his employer says specifically and repeatedly: Shut off the engine before unclogging the baler. Mr. Sharp took a high school training course where a cartoon was shown of a man getting pulled into a baler because he let the engine run when he was unclogging it, so now we have a re-creation of history. They're going to say, Yeah, the warning says shut off the engine before unclogging, but Mr. Sharp wasn't unclogging the baler. That's what's going on here. It's Alice in Wonderland."

Manning stared at Weber as he carried out this elaborate feint and swerve. Suppose Judge Mueller had taken Weber's offer at face value and asked to see the citations of Steven's alleged remarks. What would Weber have done then? Manning drew a deep breath: "I'm going to stop . . . I'm just going to stop responding to some of the arguments."

The judge gave him a questioning look. He was not going to respond to Weber?

No, he had stated his view of the facts. They would not be settled by a debate in the judge's chambers. "I really look forward to the trial testimony, Your Honor. I look forward to Steven Sharp explaining to this court that what he meant by *off* was that he pushed the lever all the way back as he was supposed to do, and then the machine turned off. I look forward to hearing him say that. I look forward to the cross. I look forward to the interpretation of the jury on all these issues.

"And, by the way, to refer to my account of what took place on August 22 as Alice in Wonderland, it's just not accurate. I understand what counsel is doing, I've seen it done before. We'll watch it again in this case and see if it works." He gave Weber a steady look. "I think it will backfire."

THAT EVENING, back at the hotel, Manning went through Steven's deposition and found the passage Weber had been referring to that afternoon. It was as he remembered. There had been no tears, no appalled "Oh my God" . . . , no outcries of remorse. And definitely no multiple admissions. What Weber had asked him was whether he would be surprised to hear that when Stan had turned on the tractor, he had found the PTO engaged. Steven had replied: "Yeah. It'd surprise me a lot. Because I pushed it all the way back. It wouldn't go no farther." Then Weber had asked: "If Stan were right, and for whatever reason you had left the plunger up on the ramp and not pulled it down behind it, would you want to reconsider your lawsuit?" Feeney had vigorously objected to the question, but Steven had answered it. "Well, the way I look at her is, I pushed it all the way back, and the baler is off, what else is there to do?" Weber persisted: "Is it possible in your mind that you didn't push it all the way back?"

"No," Steven shot back. "It's not possible. I pushed that thing all the way back. You know, if you don't, you get hurt. I did it. That's all there was to it."

Manning looked up from the deposition, took his pen and marked the passage, then paper-clipped the page. He would get the passage blown up and copied, and mounted on poster board as an exhibit. He was confident that Weber would attempt the same kind of maneuver during the trial, and when he did, he wanted to be ready for him.

Altogether, it had been an instructive day. He had a much better sense of his opponent and his tactics. He was not naïve enough to think that catching Weber when he deviated from the record would carry all that much weight with the jury or even with the judge. Her primary concern was with the law and running a fair and procedurally correct trial. Weber had clearly engaged her attention when he warned her against admitting other incidents into evidence. In Manning's eyes, they were all arguably comparable, but that was exactly the hitch: They would each have to be argued over. What had Judge Mueller said at the end of the day? "I believe that some of these ten incidents may be relevant. On the other hand, I frankly would like nothing better than to pare this case down as much as we can." Then she had given Manning a warning look as she told him that for any of his proposed accidents or incidents to be admitted, they would have to be "very, very similar."

He would sacrifice the rest if he could at least keep the Raymond Tautges case. If anything would point up the menace of the Agri-King 970 and the indifference of J. I. Case to its hazards, it was that.

CHAPTER EIGHTEEN

ARLY IN NOVEMBER, Manning called the Sharps, whom he'd not yet met face-to-face, and invited them to fly to the Twin Cities. It was time for a talk. Betty and Steven arrived the first weekend in December. Manning drove to the Charles Lindbergh Airport through evening rush-hour traffic with a collage of images of Steven fresh in his mind, photographs from three-year-old newspaper stories and recent videos from the hospital and deposition rooms. He felt this composite image waver and adjust to fit the tall, lanky individual walking toward him, together with Betty, at the arrival gate. Steven looked older than Manning had expected, and not just in years; a little heavier, too. His eyes, surprisingly large and dark, were watchful until he smiled, and then he looked nearly boyish. He was wearing what Manning recognized as his standard outfit: jeans, riding boots, a sweatshirt, and a 49ers baseball cap. The right sleeve of his plaid hunting jacket was folded and pinned. He carried his suitcase with his hook.

Manning moved forward to greet them. Betty smiled as she shook his hand. "I'm Betty Sharp," she said, "I'm pleased to meet you." She was a slim, engaging woman of medium height who was wearing a fall coat over a wool skirt and sweater.

"Bill Manning. Pleased to meet you, too."

Setting down his carry-on bag, Steven extended his hook to Manning: "Steve Sharp." The hook prevented any sort of mutual clasp, even a pretend one, so Manning touched the heavy curved metal lightly, then placed his hand on Steven's shoulder. "I've been looking forward to meeting you both," he said, speaking the conventional phrase with a distinct sense of its inadequacy. As occasionally happened when he first met clients, Manning was feeling a split between the ordinariness of the encounter—three people orienting themselves in the bustle at an airport gate—and its momentousness. These people's lives were in his hands as much as in any doctor's. It made him a little breathless, which he overcame with a bustle of activity, seizing Betty's carry-on and guiding their little group toward the main terminal.

Manning knew from their itinerary that Steven and Betty had been traveling all afternoon, coming by way of Boise, and were presumably hungry. He had given the choice of restaurant careful thought and made reservations at a popular Italian bistro in St. Paul whose youthful clientele and animated atmosphere might provide an easy backdrop for their first conversation. Falling into step between them on the long walkway to the terminal, he asked if there were any good Italian restaurants in their area. "I suppose not . . ."

"Well, yes. In Baker City there's some," Betty said.

"Is Baker City close?"

"Oh, about an hour."

"That's quite a hike."

AT THE RESTAURANT, once they were seated, Manning asked whether Steven and Betty would like him to order. The menu was a foot and a half tall and five or six pages long.

"That would be fine," Betty said with a smile.

"Well, let's see," Manning said in response to the waiter's query. "How about some spaghetti and meatballs? Do you both like spaghetti and meatballs?" It was standard fare, and he knew from previous visits that it was a tasty dish here. Betty and Steven thought that was fine. And he ordered salads. Manning handed the menus back to the waiter, pleased to have that preliminary hurdle out of the way, and felt himself relax a little. He was more tense about this meeting than he'd realized, grateful that the Sharps were turning out to be easy people to talk to.

And yet, during the initial minutes of the conversation, he continued to feel a certain disjunction, especially in Steven's regard, which Manning had first registered at the airport. From some internal observation post he watched himself making typical get-acquainted remarks with his young client, whom, by way of the mountain of data he'd already combed through in his regard, he already felt he knew better than most human beings in his immediate circle. And more than that, in a deeper sense, he knew him by way of an empathy that not once but repeatedly had left him weeping as in his imagination he'd lived his way into Steven's circumstances. When Betty peeled a straw for her son and inserted it into his drinking glass, Manning watched Steven lean forward and drink. How does he peel a straw when he's by himself? he wondered.

"How is Mr. Sharp?" Manning asked.

"R. E.? Busy with work, as usual," Betty replied. "He and Stevie have had a couple of good hunting trips this fall."

"Really? You went hunting this fall?"

Steven replied they had both gotten their quota, each a buck.

This was unexpected information. He had heard about the fishing pole prosthesis, but hunting, he'd assumed, would have been beyond Steven's condition. "How do you go about holding and firing a rifle, Steve?"

"A friend of my dad's, Vaughan Mattson, he's a gunsmith. He rigged up my old 30-06 for me so I could fire it."

The gunsmith had mounted a spring-loaded mouthpiece on the stock, above the trigger, which, when Steven bit down on it, contracted a wire that in turn pulled the trigger.

Manning tried to visualize this. "So you hold the rifle . . . ?"

"Right. I set the rifle across my right stump. I hold the barrel like this, with my hook. Then I bring it up, line up the sights, and when I'm ready to fire, I bite down." Steven mimed the process, tilting his head to one side and putting his prosthesis in position.

"Wasn't that kind of hard to adjust to? I mean, since before you were right-handed?"

"Sure, it took a little getting used to at first. Then there were some kinks we had to work out."

"Like what?"

The first time they'd tried it out, they drove to the woods and set a pop can on a log. R. E. put a shell in the chamber and handed the rifle to Steven. Gingerly, Steven adopted the unfamiliar left-handed position, tilted his head, took aim, placed his lips and teeth around the two metal plates of the trigger device, and carefully bit down. The recoil startled him, jolting his sensitive shoulder and jarring his teeth. They were using R. E.'s home-loaded shells, which packed a wallop. "My ears were ringing," Steven laughed, "and the kick about knocked me down." The men tinkered with the device, adjusting the mouthpiece to the angle of Steven's head, as he took several more test shots. Eventually, the pop can exploded from its perch.

"Wow! That must have been great," Manning said.

"It was," Steven agreed. "I'd been worried that I wouldn't be able to shoot or hunt again. And I'll tell you, if anything would of depressed me, that would of done it."

"Really?"

"Yeah, hunting has been such a big part of my life. I've been doing it since I was a kid, you know. My dad hunts, my brother does, all my buddies do. We're always up in the mountains or over in Idaho, or somewheres, fishing and hunting. Do you hunt?"

"Me? No," said Manning.

"Well, you live in a big city. You gotta remember that in Eagle Valley, where I come from, there's not a whole heck of a lot else to do."

"But you love to be up in the mountains and out and around," Betty remarked. "You always have. You wouldn't want it any other way."

"That's true, Mom. But I'm just saying."

"And I suppose there's the meat angle to it," Manning said. "You eat what you hunt, right?"

"Sure do," Steven said. "Between Ed and my dad and me, we keep the freezer full."

They talked more about hunting. Steven delivered information in an instructive tone that suggested Manning might want to store it. When Manning came to know Steven better in the weeks ahead, he would often hear that level, patient tone when questioning him about his life in Eagle Valley. Steven gave explanations of procedures relating to almost any aspect of his unfamiliar life with the impersonal, self-effacing air of a guide handing on essential, or at least very useful, information. It dawned on Manning that Steven was not responding to the questions in a way that would help the lawyer plead his case in court; it was almost so that Manning might begin to orient himself should he ever find himself required to take care of himself with his hands and some tools and his immediate resources. From this, Manning got a whiff of how the men in Steven's family and circle spoke to each other—that is, when they weren't joking or gleefully "harassing" each other.

The waiter set their fragrant plates of pasta and meatballs in front of them.

"Then once you get the meat home?"

"Take it to the butcher shop. Some goes into sausage, but the better cuts, you keep those as is."

Manning said yes to grated Parmesan, no to freshly ground pepper, and the others followed suit. Then they picked up their utensils, Betty and Manning their fork and spoon, Steven his fork, and smiled at each other. Manning wound a forkful of pasta around his fork, savored the taste, and glanced inquiringly at his guests for their reactions. He then realized the serious miscalculation he had made. Steven was holding his fork between his hooks, but the pasta kept sliding off his fork. He was making ineffectual stabs at the slippery food, lifting it and losing it halfway to his mouth. Had Manning ordered almost anything else, meat or fish or pizza, Betty could have sliced it into manageable bites for him, but now what? As if stricken with embarrassment, Betty was twirling her spaghetti on her fork while Steven continued to push the food around on his plate.

With a rush of self-reproach, Manning stood up and moved his chair next to Steven's. "Here," he said, tucking a napkin into Steven's shirt, "we're going to do this together." And then he proceeded to feed Steven the pasta, alternating forkfuls between them. Steven accepted this without remark, occasionally mopping his mouth with the napkin, seemingly unembarrassed. Betty, too, seemed to find the arrangement entirely in order. A problem, a little one, had arisen in a new setting, like countless others in the past three years, and a simple solution had been found. Whatever the potential for embarrassment, it had been dispersed.

But Manning's self-reproach stayed with him during the rest of the meal, held at bay by the conversation. It emerged with full force as he drove home.

"How was your evening?" Ruth asked him when he walked through the door.

"It was fine," he said. But she could hear that something was wrong.

"But . . . ?"

He told her about his gaffe with the spaghetti. Ruth was relieved to hear that it had been so small a thing.

"That's a simple mistake, Bill. In fact, it's not even a mistake. It's the kind of oversight anybody might have made who wasn't used to being around Steven."

"But the thing of it was . . ."

"What?"

"I don't know. Does this sound strange to you? I've been going around here for weeks, now, thinking about Steven, reading his depositions, studying his medical history, and on and on, to the point that I was almost thinking I could think his thoughts, or at least see things from his viewpoint. And what happens? First time I meet him I make a stupid mistake that shows that for even such a basic thing like ordering a meal, I wasn't on his wavelength."

"Well, don't be so hard on yourself, Bill," Ruth advised. "Like I said, it was an oversight. As for knowing him, who knows anybody, I mean, from the inside? And, besides this way you had a chance to get closer to him. He was OK with you feeding him?"

"Fine. He seemed fine with it."

"Well, there you are, then. I'm sure he could sense how concerned you are about him."

"I guess," he said. Then, after a pause: "And you know what else?"

"What?"

"He skis. He told me all about it."

"He does? What, with one pole?"

"With no poles, Ruth. Skiing is a new thing for him, something he's taken up since losing his arms. He's learned to ski by balancing."

"Cross-country?"

"No. Not cross-country. Downhill. In the mountains. Sometimes alone."

"You're joking."

"You'd think so, wouldn't you? But no."

CHAPTER NINETEEN

IN DECEMBER, with the trial looming nearer, the pace and pressure of Manning's preparations increased. Chris Olson, who was now implementing some of Manning's requests, was startled at the resources Manning was pouring into the case. In two months he had spent more than Feeney had in three years.

Not content with the in-house videos shot by Olson and Feeney, Manning engaged two media firms to make two professional videos, each costing roughly $40,000, one a collage of scenes from a typical day in Steven's life and the other showing multiple PTO self-starts by the Saunders tractor. He was preparing exhibits and mock-ups of all the machinery. Feeney had been prepared to go to trial aided by one expert witness; Manning had four: Christopherson, a metallurgist, an expert in the interaction between humans and machines called a human factors expert, and a hydraulics engineer. Manning took various members of his team on outings to gather information. He and his partner on the case, David McKenna, along with their experts, flew to Minden, Nebraska, to spend a day at Pioneer Village, a museum of antique farm equipment, poring over hydraulic and PTO mechanisms on tractors built prior to the 1970s. Manning flew Christopherson to Tennessee to talk to Mickey Jones and examine his tractor; they both drove to Brainerd to interview the Tautges family.

Manning's most important exhibits right now were not for the trial but for the pretrial. They were several oversize charts showing in table form similarities and/or comparability between the Sharp accident and the Tautges accident, which he was attempting to get admitted to trial. Manning could see that Judge Mueller was paying close attention to Weber's arguments about the dissimilarity among the various tractors and the various incidents. Not all the tractors were 970s; some were 1070s. But to Manning the differences between the two models were moot since they had the identical PTO. Some of the tractors had the original level PTO ramp; some had been retrofitted with a square bracket-type ramp, some with a sloping ramp. The purpose of both of these ramps had been to lock the lever in the full forward position, but by slightly different mechanical means. Manning hoped to explain in simple graphic form that the differences among all the machines were inessential. Every tractor, every incident, involved the same PTO. And inside that PTO was the identical spool that allowed oil to seep prematurely into the chamber and cause the machine to self-start.

Meanwhile Manning continued to pore over both the Tautges documentation and the Sharp material, flagging anything of relevance for the trial. He assembled a separate notebook for each of the principal actors in the case. He combed through the depositions and color-coded passages according to their relevance for each point of law that would arise during trial. He brainstormed into his voice recorder. He conferred with Dave McKenna about their respective areas of responsibility during the trial: Manning opening and arguing the liability, or defect, aspects of the trial, McKenna handling the damages, or compensation, phase. Concurrently, Manning discussed with another colleague, Howard Orenstein, the point of law that Case had originally invoked in its appeal for summary judgment—namely, Oregon's statute of repose, which he had no doubt would surface either during the trial or during a possible appeal.

Manning had abandoned the routines that normally gave structure, support, and texture to his daily life, starting with dinner with Ruth and Sonja, and extending to working out, jogging, reading, and golf. He collapsed into bed in the early morning. His weeks of basement seclusion were over. He now spent all his waking hours on the road gathering information or fitting meetings, conferences, and strategy sessions into whatever slots he could find in his day. In mid-December, when he was riding his own gathering momentum like a wave, Judge Mueller ordered a final settlement conference with Case to see if an agreement might be reached. Manning thought it a waste of time and requested to be excused. Nothing he had heard from Weber or from Brian Cahill, head of litigation at the corporation, suggested Case was willing to make a reasonable settlement offer. Judge Mueller, intent on leaving no stone unturned, insisted. Manning countered with a compromise offer to attend the conference by speakerphone. The shortest trip to Racine would eat up two of his precious days.

"No," insisted Mueller, "I want you at the table."

Manning conferred with Steven and his parents. The Sharps would accept a settlement offer of no less than $2 million. Manning presented the figure to the Case officials and they promptly rejected it. Case offered $250,000. The chief court administrator, who was at the meeting and with whom Manning was on friendly terms, now spoke up.

"You might want to reconsider that offer, Bill," he advised.

"Oh? Why should I?" Manning asked.

"Because in the history of this courthouse, there has never been a trial award greater than the amount you were offered today. Remember, this is Case's hometown."

"Do me a favor," Manning replied, smiling. "Come to the courtroom the day of the verdict, would you do that?"

"I'll be there," the officer replied.

The settlement meeting now came to an abrupt halt. Everyone in the courthouse meeting room stood up—a half-dozen men in freshly laundered shirts and sober business suits recapped their pens, snapped shut their briefcases, and left.

ADDING TO THE INTENSITY of Manning's preparations was the palpable hostility between him and Weber. The hostility had a prehistory dating back to the early days when first Feeney and Scherkenbach, and then Feeney and Weber, had been contending with each other. Manning had a bad taste in his mouth from everything Cahill, Scherkenbach, and Weber had put his colleague Feeney through, and it was clear to him from this final settlement conference that Cahill and Weber had every confidence they could continue in the same vein and prevail. What did Manning have to threaten them with? A few vaguely similar incidents that they intended to have ruled inadmissible. Could Manning *prove* that Steven had turned off the PTO? Weber knew he couldn't. His own hackles had been raised by Manning's peremptory introduction of Bud Christopherson as his main expert witness. With that move Manning had gained an advantage, a well-placed engineer from a highly respected manufacturer who was willing to break ranks and stand up against a fellow manufacturer. Accordingly, the deposition that Weber conducted of Christopherson on December 7 in Manning's office had been notable for its acrimony.

Weber arrived twenty minutes late due to travel complications. Manning was irritated by that because scheduling had been a particularly sore point between Feeney and Scherkenbach.

Weber began by asking Christopherson about the amount of consulting and litigation work he was currently doing, which was about 25 percent, mostly for defense lawyers. Then Weber inquired whether Christopherson had gotten clearance from Toro to appear in this case. The engineer replied that it was not necessary, but that he had reviewed it with some people. Who in particular? Weber asked. Christopherson gave him the name Seiffert, spelling it out while Weber wrote it down.

Weber then inquired about the kind of warnings Toro posted on its machines, and whether these were meant to be strictly followed. Christopherson said they were, of course, but that the company's engineers had to expect that at times they would not be, and design accordingly.

Had Christopherson ever testified in suits where people had been injured by Toro's snowblowers? Yes, he had. People occasionally stuck their hands into the chute to clear it of snow while the motor was running. Some of these people then sued the company.

Removing clogs? Weber asked.

Yes, clearing impacted snow and ice.

Weber was obviously pursuing the analogy between a clogged snowblower and a clogged baler: "And so even though the impeller switch is in an on position it can appear to be shut off because it's not turning; is that fair?"

No, because if a snowblower stops because of a clog, the belt squeals, the snow thrower jumps around, the engine makes a horrible noise.

Perhaps because Christopherson appeared to be such a well-prepared witness, fending off Weber's questions with ease, the lawyer asked him whether any of the notes he was using had been produced as a result of conversations with Bill Manning.

Yes, replied Christopherson.

"Where was that discussion?"

Manning objected to the question and instructed Christopherson not to answer. Startled, Weber asked Manning for the basis of his instruction. He refused to give it and replied that if he hadn't heard the instruction, the reporter could read it back to him. The two lawyers gazed at each other across the conference table and the tension that had been pooling in the air since the moment Weber had walked through the door gelled. Weber pretended not to understand, and again asked for the basis of Manning's instruction.

"We're wasting time here, counsel. Let's move on."

"The basis for the instruction is what?" Weber asked again.

"The instruction is given. Let's move on, counsel."

"What is the basis for the instruction?" Weber persisted.

"Just ask the questions," Manning snapped. "Let's move on."

"So you won't tell me the basis for the instruction?"

"My work product. Move on." Manning was making clear such information was private and confidential.

Weber: "Let's take a break."

After the break, the mood was no better. Weber continued to be interested in the meeting that had taken place between Manning and Christopherson the previous day, and continued to pose questions about it. When he asked whether anything in that discussion was proving useful in today's deposition, Manning again instructed the engineer not to answer. The locking of horns was practically audible. This time Manning did not wait for Weber to protest. "Objection, instruct the witness not to answer the question. Just move on, counsel. You can ask him what his opinions are and what they are based on. That's what he is here for. If you want to play games, we may leave, because I'm not going to play games with you all day. We have been very cooperative.

We have given you his report. We were here at nine-thirty. You didn't show up until ten. That's fine. I don't have a complaint about it. We have given you ample opportunity to review everything here. Ask him what his opinions are. Let's move on. We are not here to play games, invade work product. I haven't done it to you, I don't expect you to do it to me, and I don't expect it to persist."

Weber declared himself unwilling to reply to Manning's many comments but noted for the record that he had arrived at 9:45, his slight delay having been caused by a late plane arrival. These preliminary skirmishes over, Weber asked Christopherson to give his understanding of Steven's accident.

Christopherson replied: "Steven Sharp, when he was running the baler on the day of the accident, I believe it was the second cutting, the hay was light, fluffy, and it didn't go into the baler, it pushed ahead of it, so he shut the PTO off. He disengaged it by pulling the lever back, got down, and wiped the hay from the front. The second time his hand or two hands were pulled into the two rollers, the rubber top and steel bottom ones, where he couldn't get them out. He struggled, pulled back, and they virtually wore or burned his arms away before he got out and he went to Mr. Saunders's house and got help after that. The baler was not running when he was trying to move the hay in front of it but it started up, apparently, suddenly, and it was certainly unexpected for him to get his hands drug [sic] into the two rollers, his hands and arms."

As the engineer continued, he spoke simply and unperturbedly, apparently unaffected by the tension between the attorneys. Indeed, from his sincere manner one might have thought that he was not without hope of actually instructing Weber. But Weber's mission was entirely tactical. Keying off of Christopherson's balanced tone, Weber posed the next set of questions in a mode designed to appeal to any equitably minded person.

"Do you think it's fair to say that Steven was trying to clear a clog from the baler?"

Christopherson was ready for this question: "No, it was not clogged. It was pushing hay ahead of it."

"Do you think it would be fair to say Steven got the baler plugged up?"

"I wouldn't use that terminology. I wouldn't say it was 'plugged up.' I would say hay was not being ingested into the baler, it was pushing it ahead of it."

"Do you think it would be fair to say that Steven was cleaning the machine?" Weber asked.

"He wasn't cleaning the machine. He was taking the hay out from the front so it could be fed into the machine. Once you have a ball in front of it, it just pushes it along rather than feeding into the rollers."

"Well, do you think it would be fair to say that the baler was jammed with hay?"

"I don't think it was jammed. I think it wasn't just being ingested and it was pushing along the front."

Seeing that Christopherson was not going to give him the satisfaction of speaking the word *clog*, Weber tried another tack. How had Steven described his situation? Christopherson replied that he would have to look through the deposition to see how it was meant in context.

"As you sit here today," Weber asked, "you don't recall how Steven described what he was doing at the time he got caught?"

Manning intervened: "Objection, asked and answered. He already told you he has read the deposition, he would have to look through it in detail. It's here. If you would like him to take the time to do it, he will. Your question is repetitive, asked and answered, and argumentative. He's already indicated his answer."

Ignoring Manning's objection, Weber asked: "Let me make sure I understand what you have told me, Mr. Christopherson. Without going back and looking through the deposition transcript, as you sit here today you don't recall how Steven described what he was doing immediately before he got caught in the baler?"

Again Manning protested: "Objection, argumentative, been asked and answered."

"I recall his description fits as I've stated," replied Christopherson.

Weber shifted to asking Christopherson whether Steven had acted negligently in approaching the baler. Christopherson said no, that Steven was acting in conformity with what he had been trained to do, and with the standard operating procedure for balers attached to diesel tractors. But suppose, Weber asked the engineer, that Dwight Saunders had specifically instructed Steven to turn off the tractor engine before approaching the baler, and suppose that Steven had not done so, would he *then* have been acting negligently?

Manning objected. His witness was not going to answer hypothetical questions. Weber could, Manning told him, represent that these were the facts of the case, to which the engineer would respond, but he was not going to engage in speculation. Weber gazed back at Manning full of surprise. "I'll advise you that in Wisconsin," he replied, "experts are permitted to be asked hypothetical questions. That's what I'm doing here now."

"Not in deposition," Manning shot back. "They may be permitted to do so at the time of trial. That will be, of course, up to the court. At this time you are taking the deposition of an expert to find out what his opinions are and what the bases of those opinions are. We are not here to question him about hypotheticals, so I object and instruct the witness not to answer that hypothetical question unless you are willing to make the representation, which it appears you are not."

"So what you are telling me is, you will not permit me to ask your expert witness hypothetical questions in this deposition?"

"Correct," Manning replied. "We have already wasted enough time."

Weber stood up from the table. "Let's get the court on the phone."

They took a recess.

TEN MINUTES LATER, Weber reported that he had been unable to reach Judge Mueller, but as he resumed his seat he warned Manning that if he persisted in blocking hypothetical questions, there would be an appeal for sanctions later, including striking the witness's testimony.

Manning shrugged.

Blocked from questioning Christopherson further about Steven's possible negligence, Weber eventually moved on to Steven's failure to turn off the tractor, a seemingly tougher issue for Manning, for the warnings posted in the cab stated clearly that the tractor engine should be turned off before the operator left the cab and approached an attached implement. This point had also been made in Steven's agricultural training course. Christopherson agreed that the instruction was a good one in the obvious sense that, had Steven followed it, he would not have been injured. On the other hand, turning off a diesel tractor during a working day for anything other than repair was not the standard practice in the industry. "There are many reasons why you would not shut the engine off and not be negligent."

Well, then, Weber wanted to know, what would be a good warning for Case to post in their tractors? Use your best judgment? Turn off the engine sometimes, sometimes not, before trying to unclog a baler. Christopherson said that Case essentially said so in their manual, but Weber, apparently unsatisfied, asked again what the expert thought the instuction should be.

But Manning was not about to allow his expert to be toyed with. "Objection," he said. "Again the question has been asked and answered. It's repetitive. He just answered that question, counsel. I don't know why you continue to try to harass the witness. Just get his opinions. If he has opinions that you disagree with, then put up with them. But in fact you've hardly asked this gentleman anything about his opinions. We are here, it's noon, it's past noon, we have been at it two hours, and I have serious problems with how you are taking this deposition." Weber continued to pursue the matter, and Christopherson admitted that the instruction to shut off the engine was appropriate but that it can't cover all the circumstances.

After the lunch break, the early hours of the afternoon were devoted to exploring whether Steven had been negligent in disregarding the posted warning and removing a *clog*—Weber was never to relent in his use of the term, neither then nor later—from the baler. The tone of the debate grew increasingly heated as Weber persisted in posing his questions in hypothetical form, generally inviting Christopherson to place himself in Steven's shoes and then respond to whether it would be negligent or not to disregard a warning. With equal persistence Manning raised his objections. Eventually, by way of wrangling and speculating about what Steven understood himself to be doing, and after an extended discussion of the modulation between on and off, they arrived at the question of what Steven might have considered to be the off position of the PTO lever.

"It's your belief that Steven did not have an understanding that if he left the plunger up on top of the ramp he could get hurt?" Weber asked.

"Not if it was off," Christopherson replied, adding, "same as Case used to believe but now they found out different."

Christopherson knew from discussions with Manning and from having read the Tautges material that only recently had Case begun to assert that the off position for the PTO lever was *behind* the ramp. From the record it was clear that earlier Case had never given thought to where exactly and officially off was to be found. Weber was therefore quick to pounce on Christopherson's implication. He requested that the final portion of Christopherson's answer be stricken as not responsive.

Manning gave a snort of laughter. Weber paused questioningly, waiting for Manning to explain himself.

"Frankly, I find that a laughable objection," Manning stated. "Given the way questions have been asked in this deposition, I find it an incredible charge that his response was nonresponsive. In fact, I find it amazing."

"We will take a break," Weber declared. "I'll again ask counsel to conform his conduct to basic rules of civility. If you can't do that, we will go see the judge."

The mention of civility pushed Manning beyond a limit. "Let me make a record here," he broke out, "because for counsel to make a comment about basic rules of civility when this witness has been doing everything he could to respond to every question and then counsel attempts to strike—responding with a motion to strike—is totally inappropriate, completely inappropriate based on the nature of the question, the open-ended questions that are asked, and the witness is doing his very best, and nothing uncivil about that objection. There was nothing in his response that was uncivil, nothing.

"And I find this deposition to be one of the worst-taken expert depositions I have ever experienced, and to me, at this stage, at twenty after two, when we have been going for four hours in deposition, three hours with a lunch break, and to be on the first page of this witness's opinions, is deplorable, and I want to make clear on the record that we will not be going beyond five o'clock with this deposition.

"You have an opportunity to ask this witness his opinions and what they are based on. We came in here prepared, we gave you a copy of his report, we have brought everything he has reviewed and relied on, and to be treated like this by counsel is worse than uncivil but is less than human. The way you in your pompous and obstructionist manner attempt to take a deposition and the way you treat people, and it's exactly what I referenced in my letter to you. I find your conduct to be both inappropriate and unprofessional."

Weber gazed calmly at Manning. "Are you done?" he asked.

They took another break.

IN THE FINAL SESSION of the day, Weber focused on Christopherson's opinions, most particularly on the PTO, including the items he knew were going to figure in his theory of defect: the PTO lever spring and the lever itself. Having only recently become aware of the spring, Weber questioned the engineer extensively about it. Its importance to Manning lay in the fact that it showed that Case had been aware of the tendency of the PTO lever to fail to return to the off position; in other words, to seem to be off and yet be on. This was part of the problem that was causing all the clutch burnouts, which Case had been aware of and trying to fix for years.

Christopherson explained all this to Weber in great detail. They also revisited Christopherson's views on Steven's conduct. At the end of his notes, Christopherson had a section entitled "My reaction." Weber asked him what that was all about.

"These are just my thoughts if you ask me what I would do or should do, and it's a brief description of what we've talked about." Christopherson replied. "I feel obviously the PTO controls are wrong. I am surprised that they haven't been changed, not only before production but afterward, for numerous reasons over numerous years. I feel that Case was notified time and time and time again of the wrong use and the accidents. I suspect there are others. I don't know that. I feel they should change it, they should have changed it, they should have corrected it, they should have recalled it, and they still should, fix it so this doesn't happen again. Because it is going to happen again, the way it is, positive. Given the severity of the consequence, meaning loss of life or limb, even if it happens infrequently, once every ten years, that's a hazard, it's so severe. It does happen occasionally and it's going to happen again. It's understandable why it happened to Steven Sharp.

"I think it's outrageous conduct by Case, and shows they don't care. They are waiting this out. They are not going to fix it. They have been notified time and time and time again but they are not doing anything about it. They are denying it."

Weber asked simply, "Anything else?"

"If I was involved," Christopherson said, "if I had anything to say, if I owned the company, I would suggest a recall."

CHAPTER TWENTY

MANNING FLEW to Milwaukee on December 21, a Thursday, the airports thronged with Christmas travelers, in order to spend the afternoon and all of Friday in Ralph Weber's office taking the deposition of Case's expert witness, Professor Bobby Clary from the University of Oklahoma. Clary owned an engineering company and often testified on behalf of industry. Self-confident in manner, Clary found the Case 970 to be a perfectly acceptable machine. Asked whether he was aware of the documented incidents when the PTO had self-started, Clary replied that he had read the record, but saw no connection among the various incidents. The problem, in his view, was that the farmers were dismounting from tractors that were running.

"Was that not a reasonable thing to expect?" Manning asked.

"No," Clary said.

"How do you know it's not?" Manning asked.

Clary answered warmly, "I have observed farmers all across this great nation of ours, throughout Oklahoma as well as many other states across the country. I have observed both farmer-owners and operators of equipment that were hired hands of this type of equipment. I have been involved in the training of young men and women to maintain and repair this kind of equipment as well as the training of engineers to design this kind of equipment. In addition, in addition to that, I have given numerous or a number of presentations to user groups across this country on all types of problems and it's a part of my professional background to . . ."

"Okay," Manning prompted.

". . . to work hard to try to understand those issues."

Manning grinned. "That's great. I love that."

"Wait, wait, wait, hold on," Weber broke in. "Again I'll ask counsel to keep his comments to himself and ask questions and the witness will answer them, and if you want to make commentary, just keep it to yourself and not put it on the record."

The deposition ran late and took the whole of the following day. Manning insisted on questioning Clary on every document in his voluminous file, which was contained in a multitude of large boxes. Around five, Weber suggested the remaining documents might be copied and delivered to Manning's office, in view of the lateness of the hour. Manning turned down the offer and continued his meticulous search, scrutinizing every piece of paper. Around eight-thirty that evening, his persistence paid off. Attached to a miscellaneous yellow legal pad was a note bearing a rough sketch of the PTO with the E (engagement) and D (disengagement) points marked as standing side by side at the *off* end of the ramp. Manning studied the note with immense satisfaction. He sensed that blown up and mounted, it would be a crucial trial exhibit, for it was the single piece of concrete and dated evidence garnered thus far that showed beyond question that Case understood that the PTO would engage when the lever was a fraction of an inch from off. This tiny scrap of paper had been worth the trip and the two days of searching.

He called home. "Good news, Ruth. I'll be able to make Christmas Eve after all."

Then he called Chris Olson and the two of them whooped with delight.

ON JANUARY 16, via a conference call to both attorneys, Judge Mueller set the definitive opening date for the trial (it had been rescheduled several times) as February 20, 1996. During the intervening weeks she scheduled two final hearings to determine the final scope of the admissible evidence. The first would be in two weeks, January 30.

Weber showed up that morning in an agitated state, requesting permission to bring an urgent matter before the court before the business of the day got under way. In a voice resonant with indignation, he told the court how difficult it was to convey the depth of his outrage over a complaint that Manning had just filed, in which he accused the Case lawyer of trying to bring undue pressure to bear on Christopherson "to alter his testimony or to decline to testify altogether." Weber found this an absolutely outrageous charge.

Judge Mueller asked Weber to explain the matter in more detail.

While it was indeed true, Weber said, that someone from his firm had recently called a Mr. Byers, a paralegal at Toro headquarters, the call had nothing to do with objecting to Christopherson serving as an expert witness in the upcoming trial, as Manning's complaint alleged. Weber explained that his firm was representing Toro in another matter involving Christopherson and that his colleague had called Toro about a potential conflict of interest, indicating that Christopherson had been deposed by Weber in Steven's case. As proof of his innocence, Weber submitted affidavits from Byers and from the attorney at Weber's firm who had made the call. He also pointed to the fact that Manning had not filed any affidavits to back up his scurrilous charge.

Gravely, Judge Mueller asked Manning to explain the charge. Manning explained that Byers had called his law firm requesting to review Christopherson's recent deposition. Rather than comply with this request or refuse to comply, Manning had called Byers's boss, Mr. Seiffert, the person whose name Christopherson had given to Weber as the officer he had consulted about his participation in the Sharp case, and whose name Weber had carefully noted.

"How could the call come from Mr. Byers to my office requesting the deposition of Mr. Christopherson for their review if it wasn't discussed?" Manning asked. He knew the deposition had been discussed at Toro because Seiffert had told him. As for not filing affidavits, Manning said he had thought it best not to put them in the public record. On the other hand, he would be happy to do so if instructed.

Weber was appalled at this response. "Your Honor, if I may," he exclaimed. "I find it incredible that counsel would suggest that out of *concern*, out of some sort of *respect*, he makes these allegations a part of the public record without any supporting affidavits, since we have provided an affidavit from parties to the phone call specifically denying the allegations. I would ask the court that if the plaintiffs cannot substantiate these allegations of improper pressure through affidavits, that their *pro hac vice* status [right to practice law in Wisconsin] be revoked as a result of this serious breach of professional responsibility."

Manning explained that his conversation with Seiffert had given him a clear indication that the call from Weber's firm had amounted to a pressure tactic. He was willing to say so under oath.

To this, Weber quickly replied that Manning, however he chose to interpret this string of events, could not *prove* his charge. "To draw the inference that we were trying to get Mr. Christopherson not to testify or to change his testimony is outrageous."

Judge Mueller stated she was shelving this disturbing matter until later. For the moment, she said, she was going to retain the matter in a separate part of the file. And there it stayed for the duration, thanks to her overriding intent to focus narrowly on the impending trial and to treat Manning's and Weber's skirmishes as of secondary importance. She did, however, choose to address the larger issue of which this most recent clash was a symptom—that is, the extraordinary acrimony she had noted between the two opposing attorneys.

"Gentlemen," she began, "throughout this litigation, it has become apparent to me, first of all, that this is a fascinating case in which every lawyer involved has done some superb legal work. I have read your many briefs during the last few weeks, and you have done great work.

"It's also become apparent to me as we have gone through the last several months that there is extraordinary pressure between these two law firms. Now, I know that there are lots of things that have gone on between you that have not occurred in this courtroom, and I don't want to know about them. I also know that we are all going to be together for probably a good month during February and March, and with the difficulty of the issues in this lawsuit, it's going to be tough enough for us all to try this case, and have you try it well, and have you convey to the jury what you believe should go to the jury, and have this be a relatively clean case that goes in as quickly as we can make it go in, so that we can have a decent trial for both of you."

She paused to underline her point.

"I hope I need not despair that we are going to get into a trial which not only is going to be difficult in itself, but is going to be extraordinarily difficult between counsel as well. I'm sure that for you it will be, but I want to make damn sure that that is not the case for the jury once we get a jury here, and frankly for this court. If there are disputes that I have to determine, I'll certainly do that, and I know that some of them may be legal and some of them apparently personal or ethical, but to the extent that we can, I want to focus on the legal factual issues here because we have got to do that, and those are tough enough."

ADMONISHED, Manning and Weber settled in to the work of the two-day hearing, which was to make final arguments concerning the scope of admissible evidence. Day one concerned the immediate actors and materials of the case: Steven, the Saunderses, the tractor and its component parts, the OSHA report, and the farm safety course Steven had taken in his sophomore year. Judge Mueller extended something of a protective hand over Steven. She agreed with McKenna that Steven's remarks about being accident prone and fond of risks were not relevant to considerations of his accident. Nor could Weber mention Steven's fondness for jumping off high bluffs. On the other hand, she warned, if Manning and McKenna attempted to present Steven as a particularly safety-minded individual, they would be opening the door to whatever evidence of recklessness Weber wished to present.

The following day, January 31, was spent on the unwieldy but crucial matter of what other incidents Manning would be allowed to present in evidence. Feeling some wind in his sails from the relatively favorable treatment he had received from Judge Mueller on the previous day, Manning threw himself with great vigor into arguing for all ten of his supporting cases. These represented about a third of the farmers who had responded to his firm's single ad. More farmers could be found, he assured the judge. And as time went on, he promised her, basing his claim on the professional opinion of Bud Christopherson, more accidents would certainly occur. How many people needed to be injured or killed before J. I. Case did something about its dangerous machine? What was its response every time an incident occurred? Operator error. That was its sole response, he charged. Never once had it been willing to look at its own machine. All it ever did was blame the operator. Now it was blaming Steven. So now was the time to bring in a representative selection of essentially identical self-start incidents, and put Steven's injury in its proper context. In conclusion, Manning requested that the jury be allowed to consider punitive damages during the trial.

In response, Weber invited the judge to take a look at the Case Corporation and its excellent reputation. The 970 tractor was a good machine that had been serving people well for decades. Manning was playing games with the evidence. He warned the judge above all not to admit the Tautges material until Manning could prove that it was a defect in the machine that had injured Steven. There was a compelling logic to Weber's argument. If the judge admitted material relating to Tautges, she would be allowing an unknown to be used to prove an unknown, for no one knew with certainty what had caused Tautges's death. There was a fifty-fifty chance that his fatality had been caused by an operator error—*just like Steven's.*

Whether it was this argument that convinced Judge Mueller, or whether it was the "mini-trials" argument, or any number of others that Weber passionately advanced in the course of the long afternoon, the result was, at the end of the day, that she excluded Tautges. She made the pronouncement so quietly and unemphatically that Weber was not sure he understood her. Manning was hoping with all his energy that he had not heard her correctly. Weber paused in the rush of his argument and asked the judge to clarify what she had just said.

"Tautges is out," she said simply.

"Tautges is out as to what, Your Honor?" Manning asked quietly, the way one does so as not to jostle bad news into disaster.

"Tautges is out," she repeated.

"Entirely?" Manning asked, the color draining from his face.

"Yes," she replied.

She explained that in her view, the two incidents presented too many dissimilarities to be strictly comparable. Manning could, if he chose, file a brief making the counterargument, she said, but her tone gave him minimal hope.

It was a devastating blow. As he sat there, Manning felt the ground fall away under months of preparation and strategy. He and his team had counted on the persuasiveness of the argument that it was the identical flaw in all the machines that had caused all the incidents. But, as Weber had very logically pointed out, that was precisely what remained to be proved. And to prove that would require a different trial, or series of trials, than the one directly impending.

But what about the suffering? Manning asked. The essential similarity of at least Tautges and Jones to Sharp lay in their injuries, on the one hand, and the callous disregard of J. I. Case on the other. For Manning, the comparability of these incidents lay as much in the moral and ethical realm as in the strictly mechanical details. "I have," he said, "no comprehension factually or legally how the Jones case is not admissible in this case. Nor can I comprehend how Tautges is not admissible for notice. It told J. I. Case what was going on. I think this is a miscarriage. I am very, very concerned that a young man in 1992 had his arms taken off, and they claim they investigated these accidents, and then callously say nothing was wrong *when they never looked at the machines.* They never came back and looked at these machines in any way, shape, or form. And that I can't talk about that when I have that testimony explicitly in the record from all of these witnesses, I find that devastating, and I am upset about it. I mean, and I hope respectfully so, that we are making a mistake here, which redounds to the negative benefit of Steven Sharp.

"This company, in short, is really being allowed to get away with murder."

With his body language Manning was confronting the judge, insisting on eye contact, his voice filled with passion. That Steven Sharp was being put at a great and unfair disadvantage was clear to him. Was he, as Steven's lawyer, going to have to stand in front of a jury and present this accident as if it were unique? As if Case had not received ample notice that the 970 had a great potential to do damage to its operators? Standing there, he felt the wrongness of this in his chest, his heart, his muscles.

His outspokenness had hit a nerve in Judge Mueller. Roused but cool, she leaned forward on her bench and spoke to him very directly.

"You know," she said, "every time we get to what turns out to be a difficult ruling, I don't want to hear about what serious consequences there are to Mr. Sharp. I know that. This is an extraordinarily serious case, and I know that probably I'm going to have the same reaction that the jurors are going to have when your client walks in having had two arms severed in a horrible, horrible accident. I have read your trial brief. I understand what happened. I assure you, there is no need to remind me of the horror of this accident.

"But what we are doing during these two days of motions is trying to decide the legal issues and the liability issues, and I can tell you that there are times when I have difficulty separating them out because this was such a horrible accident, but that's what needs to happen here. So I would appreciate with both counsel, although I understand what an emotional case this is for the plaintiffs, and for the defendants for that matter, to try to stick to the legal issues."

Having proclaimed her function as the voice of reason and sound jurisprudence before these hotly engaged contestants, she continued in a softer tone. "If there are places where you think I may have erred and you want to submit further offers of proof, certainly you may do that, and it might be important to do that, both for my understanding and to make certain that the correct, or what I believe to be the correct, rulings have been made here. I want to make sure that I understand what's going on, to the extent I can when I make these rulings, but also so that you have your record so that if at a later time another court reviews these rulings or reviews the whole case, you have a full record here."

Turning toward Manning again, she continued: "I'm saying this because several times in the course of these two days your fallback position has been to remind us of how horrible this is for your poor client, and I have no doubt about that, and I have deep sympathy, but I'm trying to stick to the liability issues that I have an obligation to rule on at this time."

Manning nodded. "Thank you, Your Honor," he said, knowing that he would seize her offer and submit a lengthy brief arguing for the admissibility of both the Tautges and Jones material on the grounds of substantial similarity—forty pages of tightly reasoned argument. Apropos, forty pages of tightly reasoned argument on this point, on February

16, brought him to stand before the judge once again, to take his final, best shot. But she held firm, finding as before that the threshold of substantial similarity was lacking. The Tautges accident was out. Mickey Jones's accident was in, as well as the testimony of four additional farmers whose equipment was identical to the Saunderses'.

That was all he had. Judge Mueller had deprived him of one of his strongest arguments. Now Case could present the 970 as a machine with an essentially unblemished record, 67,000 of them presumably still in use. The Jones accident gave him something, to be sure, but since it had been ruled to be partly attributable to operator error, it was not particularly compelling.

Mickey Jones and four close calls. It was not much, but it would have to do.

The trial was one week away.

CHAPTER TWENTY-ONE

A HEFTY TRUCK from Minneapolis pulled up in front of the Racine Radisson on the frigid morning of February 16, a Friday, easing its way along the narrow approach to the hotel. Soon workmen were trundling office equipment—computers, a fax machine, filing cabinets—across the lobby to a large empty conference room on the first floor. Then they brought in all the machine parts and exhibits that had formed the contents of Manning's war room in Minneapolis. He stood by, monitoring the installation of the office where he would be spending most of his evenings and some of his early mornings for the next weeks.

The following day, he drove to Milwaukee and picked up Betty and Steven at the airport. In Racine, he parked the car in the open garage a hundred paces from Lake Michigan, now a frozen tundra where a few shoreline gulls battled the wind like enraged shuttlecocks. A gas fire log, apples in bowls, a thick burgundy rug, and large wingback chairs created a certain coziness in the lobby. Manning had secured a first-floor room for himself at the end of a hall where traffic was light, far from the restaurant and the pool, thereby eliminating the possibility of ever finding himself in the small brass elevator facing Ralph Weber or any of Weber's colleagues, all equally uncongenial people as far as Manning was concerned. In some trials it made sense to fraternize a little with the opposing counsel, but there would be no chitchat here. Manning needed to keep his anger fresh and bright.

On those weekends when Ruth and Sonja flew down, they stayed in the room next to his, with the door open. Such visits would be a welcome break from the steady pressure of the trial and the strict regime to which he adhered in an effort to counterbalance it. He set up his NordicTrack along one wall and worked out most days before dinner. After dinner he would settle in for a few hours of work, to strategize with McKenna, to fax memos on points of law to his colleagues in Minneapolis. Around eleven he would call it a day. Weather permitting, he would take a turn around the block or head down to the beach to clear his head and breathe the cold. In the early mornings, he would seat himself on a straight-backed chair before the lake-facing window and meditate for about thirty minutes, steadying his mind.

That first Saturday afternoon, he and Betty and Steven drove to a mall, where they bought Steven some clothes appropriate for the trial, two pairs of Dockers and three or four short-sleeve sport shirts. Betty and Manning tried to convince Steven to wear loafers, but he insisted on his cowboy boots. He was willing to move a certain distance toward Wisconsin normal but not lose himself entirely. As for his 49ers cap, they negotiated that he could wear it in the hotel coffee shop and restaurant, like any other male of his home circle, but not in the courtroom. Manning's goal was to present Steven in such a way that jury members could look over at him and feel that he could have been a son or a brother, a nephew or a grandson of theirs.

On Sunday, Manning drove Betty to the nearby Church of the Nazarene that he had located for her, where she quickly found friends. Every Sunday during her stay in Racine she would attend services there, and when R. E. arrived midway through the trial, he would attend as well.

Tuesday, Manning brought Steven and Betty to the courtroom before the jury pool arrived. "These are the people who are potentially going to decide your case," he told them. "Look at them, study them, listen to them. Get a feeling for them. I'll ask your opinion on each one before I either try to keep or dismiss them."

On the basis of a questionnaire the large pool of potential members had been narrowed to approximately thirty, a mix of working people, housewives, retired people, and the unemployed. They were questioned to determine their suitability first by Manning, then by Weber. "Have any of you ever been involved in a lawsuit in a way which might compromise your objectivity?" Manning asked all of them. Manning let several potential jurors go in quick order. One man had been involved in a bitter struggle with workmen's comp. Another had been injured in a train accident and felt that he had been mishandled by the attorneys. Still another simply disliked lawyers on principle.

"Why?" Manning asked.

"Because I got shafted in my divorce," he replied.

Steven and Betty followed the screening with great interest. Their family had never brushed up against the law, nor were lawsuits the standard mode of dealing with misfortune in Eagle Valley. Here it seemed that most of this random sampling of Racine citizens had tangled with the law or had turned to it.

Several potential jurors were let go by Manning because they had already made up their mind that Steven's accident had been his own fault. They felt he should have turned off the tractor. Another three or four were eliminated due to their negative views of damage awards, citing the notorious McDonald's–hot coffee award in which a woman who had been burned after spilling hot coffee in her lap had received a huge settlement. Then there was a crane operator who had been injured in an industrial accident and was totally in favor of the award process because it had paid his medical bills. Manning sought to keep him on the jury but Weber objected on the grounds that he had heard the man discussing his case with members of the pool, thereby contaminating it. Weber prevailed.

Several potential jurors were eliminated because of close and friendly ties with Case, men and women with grandfathers, uncles, and fathers who had worked for the company. Conversely, others were eliminated because of hostility to Case, which had been downsizing during the eighties.

Finally, one man asked to be excused because he could not bear to look at Steven.

"Why not?" Manning asked.

"Well, I find what's happened to him, you know, just kind of a little too rough."

The potential juror was excused by the judge.

During Weber's examination of the jury pool, he asked them to consider sympathy for a moment. "Sympathy," he told them, "is what makes us human. Not to feel sympathy for Steven would be less than human. And yet," he continued, "the judge is going to instruct you to empty your mind of all prejudice, all bias, and all sympathy, so that you can focus on questions of truth and the law. Now, do you think that you would be able to set aside your quite perfectly appropriate feelings of sympathy and understand that they are not to be part of your deliberations, so that you decide the liability side of this case—that is, Case's responsibility, as if the plaintiff had a broken leg? Do you think you could do that?"

Several people didn't think so.

Well, when they went through trial, Weber asked them, would they at least be able to understand when their sympathy was kicking in?

Again they were unsure.

"There's going to be some pretty tough evidence in this case," Weber warned. "It was a horrible accident. You're going to hear evidence that Mr. Sharp was caught in a big round hay baler for some period of time. And you're going to hear him describe how horrible it was to go through that. When you hear that evidence, is there anyone who thinks they won't be able to put it into its appropriate context as one aspect of the case, of course on the damages side, but not let it go to other aspects of the case? In other words, can you feel sympathy for what happened to Steven Sharp without necessarily blaming Case? Will you be able to draw that distinction in the face of very powerful testimony?"

A number of people could not and were dismissed at Weber's request.

Weber asked whether for any reason the potential jurors might not be able to participate in this trial with an open mind. At this, one man asked to be excused because he felt that Case's enormous financial resources ensured that Steven would not be able to get a fair shake. Weber seconded his request and the judge excused him.

Around four, jury screening was completed and Manning huddled with Betty and Steven, reviewing the notes Betty had taken. Then they made their choices. Both attorneys executed their peremptory strikes until sixteen jurors remained. The judge foresaw a lengthy trial and took the precaution of asking for four alternates. Twelve men and four women were sworn in, fourteen of them white and two black. Five men were in their twenties or thirties, two or three in their late sixties, the others middle-aged. Four of the jurors held college degrees. With the exception of the five retirees and the two unemployed, all were working people, wage earners or self-employed—two electricians and one plumber—generally low- to medium-income people. Most of the jurors had openly revealed their opinions and biases during the selection process, but one or two, as eventually became clear, had not.

While the judge was giving the jury members detailed instructions, Manning quickly drew a chart showing the name and location of each juror, along with a keyword or two, like "industrial background" or "pro farmer." While he was doing this, moving his eyes back and forth from his legal pad to the jury box, he found his gaze repeatedly meeting that of a short, gray-haired woman in the front row, apparently in her sixties, who returned his glance with an odd insistence. At each new encounter, the intensity increased, as if the woman was trying to send him some sort of message. When he had completed his chart, Manning gave her a questioning look. She stared back, then slowly shook her head from side to side reprovingly. I see, Manning said to himself, turning aside his glance, the trial's not even under way and already I've got a hostile juror.

FOLLOWING THE NEWLY empaneled jury's departure, Weber and Manning met in Judge Mueller's chambers to hear a request by Weber concerning Manning's opening statement. Weber's major drive throughout the pretrial hearings had been to put his opponent into as tight a box as possible by seeking to impose strict limits on the number of accidents or self-start incidents Manning could refer to. Except for the case of Mickey Jones, he had largely succeeded. Weber had also sought to prevent Manning from bringing up claims having to do with Case's responsibility to warn its customers about the 970—in legal terms, its so-called post-sale duty to warn. Mueller had not ruled on this last point, so it remained a serious battleground between the two attorneys. Earlier in the day, Manning had said that he intended in his opening to present Jones's accident as an instance when Case had been given crystal-clear notice that something was seriously wrong with its 970 tractor. Now Weber, bent on preventing it, said that if Manning referred to the Jones material in this way, Weber would call for a mistrial.

Manning gave him an incredulous look. He was allowed to refer to Jones any way he wanted to, he said.

No, argued Weber. He could use Jones for *comparability*, not for post-sale duty to warn.

Judge Mueller cut short the argument by telling Manning that she had not yet made up her mind about the post-sale duty to warn issue. For the moment, he could not refer to it.

But that's when the company was put on notice about the defect, Manning replied. "I mean, Jones happens. They send down their safety officer, Hartman. They investigate and say, nope, it isn't there, and they wait and try to wash their hands of it. *And it was there, it was there in spades*, it was hitting them in the face, but they have a pattern of conduct that we're going to talk about."

"I'm still having a hard time with it," the judge replied. "The conduct of the investigation of the defect, I still don't see the relevance to the issues in this case. There is a strict liability claim and a negligence claim. I mean, does this go to the negligence?"

"It goes to both, Your Honor. Defect and negligence are somewhat merged in Wisconsin."

Irked to hear Manning expounding on Wisconsin law, Weber assured the judge that Case had a responsibility to prevent the defect prior to 1972, when the tractor had left the factory, but that once the tractor was out the door, the company's responsibility had ceased. "We don't have anything to do with the tractor in 1986."

"What are you talking about?" Manning exclaimed. "Of course it's still your tractor."

"No," said Weber. "It's the Saunderses' tractor."

"But the duty goes all the way back. You mean all we can talk about is '69 to '72, and never say that Case had any responsibility after that? Is that what you mean?"

"Exactly," replied Weber, as if congratulating a dim student for having finally caught on to a self-evident truth. "That's exactly right."

"No, that's wrong," said Manning.

Mueller remained undecided on the issue. She told Manning to keep post-sale duty to warn out of his opening. Later she would listen to additional arguments on the subject.

Manning thanked her, eyeing this narrow opening with every intention of driving through it, although the ultimate usefulness of post-sale duty to warn, frankly, was still unclear to him. It would be a lot easier to drop it, he thought, as he walked back to the hotel, because it would require research and writing during the busy opening phase of the trial. Still, his instinct told him to wrestle it away from Weber, who so clearly was trying to withhold it from him.

He advised Betty and Steven to rest up for the long day tomorrow, what would be the first of many. He ate a quick supper in his room and sat down to work on his opening. He estimated it would run about three hours. He wanted to have it more or less memorized.

CHAPTER TWENTY-TWO

O N THE OPENING DAY of the trial, February 21, Manning asked McKenna to bring Betty and Steven to the courtroom in time to be seated before the jury entered. It was part of his strategy throughout the trial to have the Sharps sitting in the courtroom whenever the jury entered or exited, even at lunch breaks. He wanted their silent presence, seemingly constant, to say to the jury: Here we are, patiently awaiting your decision. Nothing is more important to us than that.

Manning, however, followed his standard practice of walking over to the courthouse around seven-thirty in the morning. Over the years he had often found it useful to stroll through courthouse halls early in the morning when the local staff was arriving, some chatting with coffee cups in hand. Occasionally he would stop and introduce himself and strike up a casual conversation, thereby picking up a feeling for the place and its personalities, as well as the odd piece of information.

On this particular morning, however, Manning stamped the snow from his shoes and headed directly to Judge Mueller's third-floor courtroom. He wanted to make sure his staff had correctly arranged his exhibits, including the mock-ups of the 970 controls. He also wanted to glance at Weber's exhibits. He stepped off the elevator, located the courtroom, then paused abruptly at the threshold. Beneath an actual 970 cab that Weber had had brought to the courtroom, a man in overalls was lying on his back, some tools beside him, busily applying some fluid to the underside of the PTO ramp with a brush. Cautiously, Manning stepped nearer. The man appeared to be about sixty. Manning craned his neck to get a view of his face, but at that moment the worker rolled out from under the cab and stood up. Startled, Manning recognized Wayne Hartman, the engineer who had investigated 970 accidents over the years. Still unaware of Manning's presence, Hartman began applying fluid to the top of the PTO ramp.

"Good morning, Mr. Hartman," Manning called in a hearty voice. "What do you say?"

The man started and faced the doorway.

"Oh," he said. "Morning."

"You're up kinda early," Manning said, stepping nearer. "Mind if I ask what you're doing?"

"Oh, just getting things ready," Hartman replied curtly.

"Uh huh, I see," said Manning.

Hartman finished applying the fluid to the ramp, took a handkerchief from his pocket, and wiped his hands. He was clearly in no mood for conversation. Manning cast a glance around at his exhibits, noted that they were correctly placed, then glanced at Weber's. His inspection completed, he turned to leave. "See you in a little while," Manning said to Hartman, who was gathering his tools. "Right," Hartman replied, sounding unenthusiastic at the prospect. He was the second witness Manning had scheduled to call to the stand.

Shortly before nine, Manning cranked himself around in his counsel's seat and checked the courtroom, where he saw a scattering of visitors, most of them unknown to him. He recognized Max North, his first witness, and Brian Cahill, and, of course, Hartman, now wearing slacks, sport shirt, and jacket. Their glances touched for the briefest of instants.

At nine, the judge entered. She called in the jury and gave them the order of the day's events: opening statements, first by Manning, then, after lunch, by Weber. What the jury would hear today, she cautioned, was not evidence but rather something like opinion. Evidence would come later, in the form of oral testimony, documents, or exhibits. She requested that during the trial the jurors not make any inferences from her facial expressions or from her rulings or from the tone in which she delivered them. "Rely on your own experience and common sense," she said, "when trying to determine the reliability of a witness. And bear in mind that the burden of proof is on the plaintiff, on Steven Sharp, not on J. I. Case."

What the judge deliberately did not tell the jury was how, at the end of the trial, they would deliver their verdict. They would be asked to allocate responsibility for Steven's accident on a percentage basis, so much for Steven, so much for the Saunderses, so much for Case. Theoretically, they could decide that any one of these three was 100 percent responsible, though that was an unlikely outcome. What they would not know when they set about their deliberations was that if they found Case's share of responsibility less than Steven's, even by one point, the company would walk away without owing him a dime. The law required the jurors to render their decision uninfluenced by its practical result. It was not required that the decision be unanimous.

Of course Manning and Weber were aware of these provisions and planned their strategies accordingly. Manning would chase the machine flaw down into its finest tributaries and then back to its single corporate source, while Weber would work to distribute the responsibility for Steven's accident among as many people and factors as possible: to the negligent Saunderses and their ill-kept equipment; to R. E., who had tampered with it; to the texture of the hay that had massed into a tight clog; even to the principles of physics and mechanics; but primarily to Steven, who could not read an instructional manual, who had paid no attention to posted warnings, who had been in a hurry, who had not used common sense, and who had even more or less admitted his error. And since none of Weber's charges was inherently implausible, indeed, since all of them might be entertained by reasonable people, Manning understood that Weber's odds were somewhat better than his own.

"MAY IT PLEASE THE COURT, counsel, members of the jury, it is an honor for me and my partner David McKenna to stand in the shoes of Steven Sharp and represent him in front of you," Manning began, using his standard opening, but meaning it more than ever. He gener-

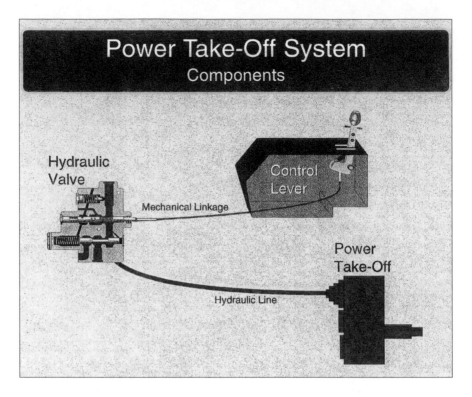

Power Take-Off System
Components

Hydraulic Valve

Control Lever

Mechanical Linkage

Power Take-Off

Hydraulic Line

The plaintiff's exhibit showing the relations of the hydraulic valve to the control lever and Power Take Off, the unit that provides power to any attached equipment.

ally identified with his clients, but Steven's case was special. Manning felt linked to him in ways he did not fully understand, but the simple realization that his own performance in front of the jury, today and in the coming weeks, would be the determining factor in all the remaining years of Steven's life was enough to fill him with an extraordinary sense of urgency. He spoke for the next three hours with only one ten-minute break, his voice passionate but controlled, his manner steady as he moved about among his exhibits. Knowing that juries, like everyone else, paid most attention during the first half hour, he used that time to review the equipment. With the help of slide projections and exhibits, he explained the alleged faults of the PTO. The first had to do with the ramp on which the PTO lever moved backward and forward. Because of the shape of the ramp and the metal of which it was composed, the

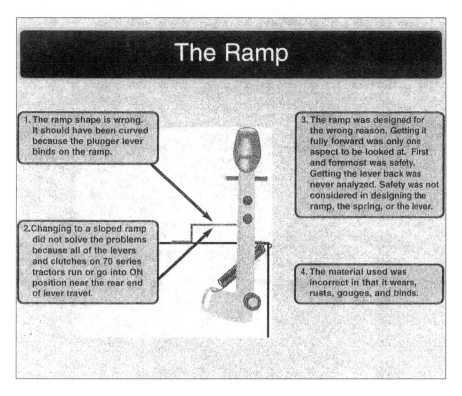

The plaintiff's exhibit illustrating the alleged inappropriate shape and unsuitable quality of the metal of the PTO ramp.

control lever tended to get stuck before reaching the off position. The second flaw, Manning explained, was the misleading impression given by the PTO control lever. It looked as if it should move at least halfway forward before engagement, while in fact it engaged at one-sixteenth of an inch from the off position. The third faulty element of the system was a spring added by Case two or three years into production, when it had discovered that the PTO lever tended to get stuck before reaching the off position. Case had added a spring designed to pull the lever back, but used a weak one and mounted it incorrectly. The most serious flaw was in the valve inside the PTO clutch. As Christopherson had earlier explained to Manning, the valve was notched by an overly long slot that allowed pressurized oil to enter the chamber prematurely when the PTO lever was nearly in the off position.

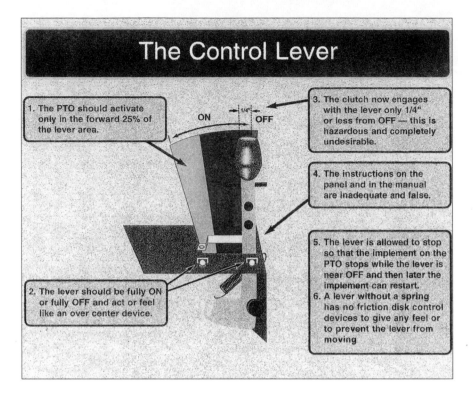

The plaintiff's exhibit showing the alleged faults of the PTO control lever. According to the plaintiff, the lever both engages attached equipment prematurely and tends to stick before reaching the full off position.

Each of these flaws was serious, he said, but what had brought them together in a nearly fatal manner was a bureaucratic failure, for the engineers who had designed and built the PTO had never conferred with the designer of the lever that controlled it. The latter had fashioned and even patented the PTO control lever without ever knowing specifically where on or off, in terms of the workings of the spool, happened to be.

"You will hear Mr. Johnson," he said, "designer of the controls, admit as much on this stand."

After Manning had been speaking for about forty-five minutes, he paused, having reached a transitional point in his presentation. In the silence a slight stir could be heard in the small courtroom. Manning glanced back and saw Cahill get to his feet and move toward the exit,

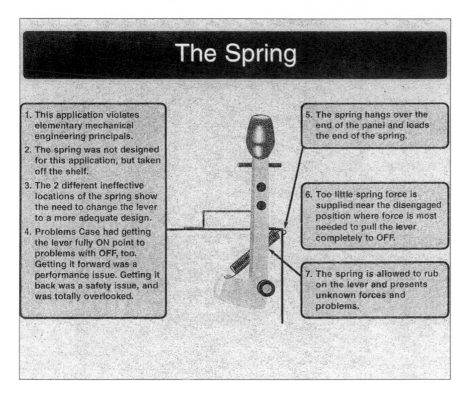

The Spring

1. This application violates elementary mechanical engineering principals.

2. The spring was not designed for this application, but taken off the shelf.

3. The 2 different ineffective locations of the spring show the need to change the lever to a more adequate design.

4. Problems Case had getting the lever fully ON point to problems with OFF, too. Getting it forward was a performance issue. Getting it back was a safety issue, and was totally overlooked.

5. The spring hangs over the end of the panel and loads the end of the spring.

6. Too little spring force is supplied near the disengaged position where force is most needed to pull the lever completely to OFF.

7. The spring is allowed to rub on the lever and presents unknown forces and problems.

The plaintiff's exhibit showing the alleged defects of the spring designed to pull the PTO lever to the off position.

pausing at the door to glance back at Manning with an unworried smile. After the briefest of twitches, Manning returned his attention to the jury.

He named his witnesses and the order in which they would appear. First, there would be Max North, chief engineer when the 970 tractor was released, and at one time in charge of safety for the Ag division, now a consultant; then Wayne Hartman, engine designer of the 70-series tractors; then Don Johnson, designer of the PTO controls; and finally Edwin Heys, senior technical specialist for product safety and regulations at Case and the only defense witness still actively employed by the company. After these, Manning would call Bud Christopherson, who would explain in greater detail the flaws of the PTO, and then other experts in more specialized areas.

"Our focus during the first part of the trial," he said, "will be on lia-

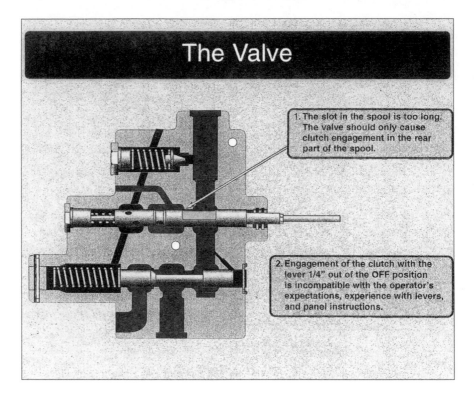

The Valve

1. The slot in the spool is too long. The valve should only cause clutch engagement in the rear part of the spool.

2. Engagement of the clutch with the lever 1/4" out of the OFF position is incompatible with the operator's expectations, experience with levers, and panel instructions.

The plaintiff's exhibit showing the valve inside the Power Take Off hydraulic. The plaintiff claimed that the slot in the spool is too long, allowing pressurized oil to enter the hydraulic chamber prematurely and cause self-starts by the attached equipment.

bility, which means Case's responsibility; in the second half, on damages, or on the reparations Case will be called upon to make to Steven Sharp." At the center of the trial was, of course, Steven, so the next step in Manning's presentation of evidence would be testimony by Steven, preceded by that of Dwight Saunders and Steven's parents. Manning gave the jury a brief overview of what they would hear from Steven. "Steven will tell you what happened that day, step-by-step, from the moment he climbed into the tractor cab on the morning of August 22 until he managed to make it to Stan Saunders's door. I won't give you that account now, because it is not mine to give. It's Steven's. For the moment, I'll simply make one or two points quite clear. First, that Steven shut off the PTO before leaving the cab in exactly the same manner as he had done a thousand times earlier that summer. Second, that it was this action of shutting off the PTO that stopped the baler from working. It was not a clog that stopped the baler, because there was no clog, not in the sense of anything substantial enough to stop the rollers of a baler driven by a 95-horsepower tractor.

"Let me sum up by saying that if any of the components of the PTO mentioned earlier had not been defective, Steven Sharp would have his arms today. In support of this claim, I am going to bring a farmer from Tennessee to the witness stand, Mickey Jones, who will talk to you about the accident he suffered in 1986, which in essential ways was similar to Steven's. And when you have heard this and all the other evidence, I am going to ask you to assess appropriate damages against the J. I. Case Company for its outrageous conduct and disregard of human life.

"Earlier today," he concluded, "you heard the judge define the term *burden of proof,* and tell you that the burden was on Steven's side. It is a burden that I and my partner feel privileged to assume."

AFTER AN HOUR lunch break, Weber gave his opening. Like Manning, he was dressed in a sober blue suit. His manner was brisker than Manning's. He spoke easily and confidently, his delivery periodically tinged by indignation at the way in which Manning had misled the jury. He would speak to them about Steven's accident, he said, but wanted to start by naming those who had acted responsibly with regard to the 970 tractor and those who had not. Taking the latter group first, Weber listed Norman Koopman, Steven's high school agricultural and farm safety instructor, who had not educated Steven well; then Dwight Saunders, who had given him inadequate training, and who had failed to maintain his equipment properly; then there was R. E. Sharp, Steven's father, the mechanic who had tampered with and inadequately cared for the tractor and baler; and, finally and mainly, Steven himself, who had injured himself out of carelessness. Steven had failed to turn off the PTO. He had violated the most elementary principle of machine safety by performing maintenance on an engaged machine. It was as simple as that. On the other hand, those who had done their jobs well, Weber said, were Max North, Wayne Hartman, Edwin Heys, and Don Johnson, all good Case employees. Weber gave brief synopses of their careers at Case, mentioning their long years of service and their various courses of upward advancement. As an expert witness, Weber would call Dr. Bobby Clary, emeritus professor in the engineering department at Oklahoma State University. Dr. Clary would testify that J. I. Case had designed a good tractor in the 970, and that it was "not defective nor unreasonably dangerous and certainly met the reasonable expectations of normal users."

Having thus preliminarily apportioned blame and worth, Weber gave a brief history of tractor engineering at Case insofar as it formed a background for the 970. He described the design and lengthy field testing that had gone into that model, both by farmers and by the company. Turning to the PTO, he explained some basic principles of hydraulics and the function of the clutch, which was, he said, to engage and disengage the plates. When the plates were apart, the PTO was disengaged; when the plates were together, it was engaged. Now, in between those two states, Weber said, was a very important modulation phase, the "feathering in" phase, when the clutch was in the process of becoming engaged. What the plaintiffs were calling premature engagement of the clutch was simply *modulation,* a necessary in-between phase that brought the plates together smoothly, so that they did not abruptly lock together and jerk the attached implement into activity. The jury would hear testimony from Max North, hydraulics expert, to that effect.

After much additional technical detail, Weber gave his version of Steven's accident, which, the attorney said, Steven would corroborate when he took the stand. "What Mr. Sharp will tell us," Weber said, "is that when he cleaned out the baler, he first removed the hay that was in front of the rollers, then he had to reach way down into the intake and take hold of hay that was stuck in there. He will tell us there was hay actually jammed tight between the rollers. He will say that he was trying to pull it. It was when he removed that tightly stuck clog on August 22 that the accident happened.

"We know the plunger of the control lever was left up on top of the ramp. We know the engine was not shut off, so there was pressure in the system. The evidence will be that when Steven got off that tractor and left that lever in a place where the clutches were still getting pressure, it was like stopping a car on a hill that was being partially held in place by an attached trailer.

"If you add a trailer to this equation, it takes more force to hold those plates together, takes more force to keep it from pulling back down the hill, more force being transmitted from the engine back to the drive wheels. And the evidence will be that when that clog was released, when that hay that was jammed between the rollers was removed, it was like cutting the trailer loose from the car [Weber snapped his fingers to dramatize his point]. Suddenly you don't have that resistance and the car is going to shoot forward."

Moving on to the machine parts, Weber asserted that, contrary to what Manning had been telling them, they had been performing exactly as they had been intended to. Both accidents, Steven's and Mickey Jones's, had been the fault of the operators. Clearly Jones had been injured because he was using his tractor improperly and violating safety rules, working on an attached implement while the tractor engine was running, contrary to both the tractor's manual and posted warnings. The same, of course, applied to Steven Sharp.

"Why," Weber asked with sudden regret, pointing to an exhibit displaying direct quotations from Steven's deposition, "did he not shut off the engine?" Weber gestured toward Steven's words as he quoted them. "He will testify, 'If I had only been warned to shut off the tractor engine before unclogging the baler, I would have done it.' He's not going to testify that he wouldn't do it. He's not going to testify that he's confused about what he was doing or why. He will tell you, 'If I only had been warned to shut off the engine, I would have done it, and I wouldn't be here today.' I ask you to bear in mind when you evaluate that claim, that Steven's words were: 'If I had only been warned, I would have shut off the engine.' "

Regret was audible in Weber's voice as he intoned the *if onlys*.

"But he had been warned," he went on in a sharper tone. "That was the point, he'd been warned repeatedly. Warned by the stickers posted in the cab and by the slides that had been shown in Mr. Koopman's sophomore farm safety class. Both clearly emphasized the specific danger of what he did that day: He did not turn off the tractor engine when working on an attached implement.

"So, in sum, we have two accidents where both operators worked on attached machines without shutting the tractor engine off even though, the evidence will show, both knew better. The evidence will show that Case is not responsible for Mr. Sharp's choice to ignore his training and safety knowledge on August 22, 1992, but that it built and delivered a tractor that was not defective and not unreasonably dangerous in its control of the Power Take Off system."

WEBER HAD SPOKEN for about an hour and a half. He had presented a view that was not only plausible but in certain respects irrefutably true. Had Steven turned off the tractor engine before approaching the baler, he would not have been injured. The judge announced a half-hour break.

In the cafeteria, where Manning and Steven had gone for a soda, they sat by themselves. Steven had been surprised and more than a little upset by what Weber had said about him. "Half of what that guy said was a lie, the rest of it was slanted. I don't mean to be harsh, Bill, but that Weber's a fatmouth. That stuff about 'if I'd only known,' those words he had blown up on his exhibit, next to my picture, that's not what I said. I mean, maybe I said them if they're written down somewheres but that sure as heck ain't what I meant."

"Steve, I know," Manning repeated in a tone showing that he too was irritated. He was particularly annoyed because Weber had been expressly ordered by Judge Mueller not to display any excerpts from Steven's deposition during his opening. Manning chewed the ice in his soft drink.

"Don't worry, Steve, we'll call him on that."

"But now the jury has a first impression."

"Don't worry. It's not serious. It's correctable. Besides, we're going to go back in there and give the jury something that'll make 'em sit up and take notice."

"What's that?"

"You remember I said that the first witnesses I was going to call were four officials from Case? North and Hartman, Johnson and Heys?"

"Yeah."

"Well, that's not the normal thing. The normal procedure would be for me to present my view of the tractor and accident, then call my expert witnesses to back me up. Then Ralph would do the same for his side, and it would all be pretty technical and tame. The jury'd be snoozing half the time. Well, what I'm going to do is take Ralph's witnesses from Case and force them to testify for our side. I am going to force them to answer questions that will present evidence favorable to us."

"How are you going to do that?"

"By forcing them to stick to testimony they've given earlier under oath. If they deviate by a hair, I'll jump on them."

"Great."

CHAPTER TWENTY-THREE

THAT AFTERNOON, Manning called Max North to the stand. North had retired from Case in 1986 but still did frequent consulting work for the company. He would testify the next day as well. A calm, heavyset man in his mid-sixties, he sat down in the witness stand with a certain wariness. Manning set a quick tempo with his opening questions, trying to deprive North of the security of his reserve. He soon established North as the person responsible for the evolution of the PTO lever on the Case 970. Later, pursuing the topic of safety testing, Manning bombarded North with precise questions designed either to elicit damning admissions or to call into question his credibility. North shifted uneasily on the stand.

Weber had blocked Manning from referring to the Tautges accident or case by name. On the other hand, all of the technical data relative to the 970 that Feeney, Sapetta, and Olson had brought to light were open and available to Manning. After four or five answers that failed to match up with his earlier depositions in late 1995, North began to claim forgetfulness rather than incomprehension, but this served Manning's purposes equally well, for it allowed him to deliver the information to the jury in a way that revealed North as a now very uncomfortable and perhaps unreliable witness.

Not that North was a pushover. As a highly trained engineer with loyalty to Case, he was able to resist Manning inch by inch, and when he was finally forced to concede a point, he did so with an air suggesting the point was of minimal importance. Even when forced to reverse his earlier testimony, he refused to become flustered. Periodically Weber rose to his client's aid by demanding that Manning give the context for the deposition passage he was citing, whereupon Manning would accommodate him with a show of easy compliance. "Happy to do that," he would reply, or "No problem," for he understood the importance of not appearing to be bullying North lest he lose points on sportsmanship with the jury. Picking on a solid former employee of a pillar-of-the-community company like J. I. Case had its obvious perils. At each memory lapse of North's, Manning would invite him to "refresh" his memory or, slightly stronger, "to check the accuracy" of his reply. If North could not recall a date or an event, Manning provided it with an air of helpfulness, never raising his voice, never betraying impatience, always addressing his opponent as Sir and Mister.

Over the course of the two days, patient and relentless, Manning elicited replies from North that suggested that safety had not been an explicit priority in the planning and manufacturing of the 970. During North's tenure at the company, J. I. Case had had no office of safety, no manuals of its own concerned with safety, and no specific procedures for evaluating safety when a piece of equipment was being designed. North conceded these points but implied in each instance that no such oversight had been necessary since the company knew what it was doing. Specifically in the case of the 970, he said, they had had hundreds of hours of field testing by their own engineers and selected farmers.

Even so, Manning countered, the first consideration in the field testing had been function, right, not safety? The company had been checking how the machine worked, how its controls felt to the operator, and had never explored whether any aspect of the device posed a hazard. North could not deny this. And when problems began to appear, Manning pressed on, that is, when the clutch plates in the PTO began to overheat and warp and burn out, the company did not consider revising the not entirely effective warning posted in the cab: To engage the PTO the lever must be fully forward. North further conceded that the remedies they had devised, the top hat ramp and spring, had been for the purpose of cutting down on clutch burnout, not safety.

As for the spring, while it was a commonly used part and Case had done some general testing of its effectiveness, including in the field, it had been subject to no specific investigation to determine its adequacy to keep the lever in the off position. Manning turned to the retrofitted PTO spring, designed to keep the lever in the off position. It routinely broke, right? There were reports to that effect, conceded North. What was wrong, Manning suggested, was that the spring, even before it broke, exerted very little pull, right? But North was unwilling to concede the point.

Manning was eliciting the information he needed but felt hampered by the constraint of not being able to place it in the larger context of the other accident cases. During one of the breaks in the judge's chambers, he protested against the limits she had imposed on him. "I feel," he said, "that by not being allowed in our opening statement to refer to recall, by not being allowed to refer to post-sale duty to warn, by not being allowed to refer to a full contention of the Jones investigation, by not being allowed to refer to the Tautges accident itself and that investigation, and, finally, by not being allowed to refer to the other farmers upon which we have submitted affidavits . . . prejudice has occurred to Steven Sharp."

"Fine," Judge Mueller replied dryly. "That objection is noted, and I will consider as the offer of proof what you have previously submitted."

Back with the witness, Manning shifted his focus to the sort of investigation Case had done of complaints about self-starts from farmers, working through them until he came to Mickey Jones. He wanted to know whether Jones's accident had suggested to Case that it had a serious problem. What sort of investigation and follow-up action had it taken?

Here Manning was venturing back into the disputed terrain of post-sale duty to warn. He had asked no more than a couple of questions in this vein when Weber was on his feet and approaching the bench to call for a mistrial. The judge called for a break and the attorneys moved to her chambers, where Weber promptly repeated his demand. Manning was trying to impugn the company, he said, implying that it cared little about the safety of its customers and had been derelict in its ethical duties. He reminded the judge that she had placed "very strict limits" on questions concerning Case's actions after the

Jones accident, permitting questions only related to the existence of a defect. Clearly Manning's questions were suggesting that there might have been other incidents and accidents that the jury was not hearing about, and in this way arousing their suspicions.

Judge Mueller turned to Steven's lawyers for a response. This time it was Manning's partner David McKenna who stepped up.

McKenna brushed off Weber's concerns by making a simple point: Since the company was asserting that its investigation of the Jones accident—and others—had found that there was no defect in the equipment, didn't he and Manning have the right to question them about the investigation and the follow-up, including what they *didn't* do and should have done? Otherwise, the court, the jury, and the plaintiffs would be forced to believe that Case had done all that was necessary.

"Now, Mr. North is going to say there's nothing wrong with the Jones tractor [or the other tractors] that has anything to do with defect, and it is the inadequacy of his investigation to form a basis for that conclusion and for that testimony that we feel we are entitled to explore." To explore these areas was not to impugn the company, but to ask a foundational question. Indeed, McKenna was asking this question for the purpose of inviting the judge to revisit the question of post-sale duty to warn.

"Oh, no," Weber protested. "The examination is very narrowly constrained by what happened to Mickey Jones . . . not what happened to people we have never heard of. So if they think they can prove defect to Mickey Jones, let them do it in Mickey Jones, not in things we have never heard about." Weber argued that criticizing the investigation into and follow-up of the Jones accident was not only irrelevant to determining the existence of a defect, but also unfairly prejudicing the jury against Case.

Mueller took a moment to think. "There's a fine line, and I'm trying to figure out a ruling that will do what I have already done, unless or until we get post-sale duty to warn, but [that will] also allow adequate cross-examination."

Manning kept silent, careful not to reveal his delight that the door Weber had been so eager to keep shut was now more than slightly ajar.

To close the first witness's testimony, Manning decided to focus on a point that would be plain and clear to a jury whose energy, due to the amount of technical questioning they had heard, was perhaps fading. He invited North to step down from the witness stand and mount the 970 tractor that had been brought to the courtroom by the defense. Once North was seated, Manning leaned over and lifted the plunger on the PTO lever, taking it out of the off position, and the lever, on its own, moved a fraction of an inch.

"If you just gently lift it up, don't move it at all. . . ."

"Just lift it out of adjustment?" asked North.

"I won't move it at all. I just lift it up and it pops a little forward, doesn't it?"

"That just means that we didn't adjust that quite right," North replied.

"That's one of the things I was going to ask you about. When I came in to get ready to make my opening statement the other day, it was early, seven-thirty, and Mr. Hartman was lying down here on the ground with a bunch of tools doing a bunch of adjustments. Did you ask him to do that?"

Manning was standing directly in front of North, holding his eyes with his own. "No, I asked . . . ," North began, pointing to the base of the lever. "There's a pointer down here to tell us where the spool is, and I asked him to put that pointer on so you could see the spool move when I move this lever. There's a pointer under the lever. Do you see it move?"

Manning looked down at the pointer and confirmed North's point.

"That's the only thing you asked him to do?"

"That I recall."

"Well, that's interesting, because I saw him making a bunch of adjustments up here," referring to the ramp. "You didn't ask him to do any of those?"

"He may have had to readjust it some to make it fit. I don't really know."

Fiddling with the lever again, leaning close to North, Manning asked, "Prior to the opening statements, did this pop forward a little more than that? Just a little more?"

"I can't answer that," North replied.

"Like a quarter of an inch?"

"I don't know that."

"You didn't address that issue?"

"Physically on this unit right here? I can't . . . I can't answer that."

Manning questioned North about the tractor, becoming increasingly intrigued by the lever and the ramp. He leaned in even closer. He asked North where the top hat had come from.

"We had to make one," North replied. "We couldn't buy one."

This interested Manning. "Had to make one? Couldn't buy one anymore?"

"No, sir."

"Couldn't get parts in the company?"

"No, sir."

"So you made that up and painted it black. Was the slope that is on there [a used one], was it rusted in sixty-five hours of service? What did it look like?"

"No, I recall, it looked like this."

Manning peered at it, then took a piece of paper from his notebook and ran it over the ramp.

"If we take this piece of paper and just wipe it over the top hat, what is that? Why is that grease coming off there?"

"I told you we painted it," North replied.

Puzzled, Manning asked, "You think that's paint?"

"I assume so. What do you think it is?"

Rather than reply to North's question, Manning shot back, "Did you grease that up? Did you grease that top hat?"

"I didn't," North replied.

"Do you know if *anybody* did?"

North repeated: "I assume it's paint."

But in so doing, he opened himself to an empirical test.

"You think that's *paint?*" Manning continued, incredulity straining his voice as he held the stained piece of paper under North's nose. But North refused to budge. He sniffed the paper and said, "Smells more like paint than grease to me."

"Is that right? It smells like black paint to you?" Manning asked, as if it could be a question of percentages. "Do you think paint would still be wet like that, come off like that?"

"I don't know whether they painted it up sometime the last week, last week they painted it."

Manning knew that the following day, Friday, he would have Hartman sitting where North was sitting now, so for the moment he was willing to settle for simply prolonging North's ordeal, forcing him to repeat the claim that the greasy smear on the paper in his hand was paint that had been applied a week ago. And yet, glancing at the jury, he could not resist asking a final time, "You think that's still wet paint, then?"

Carefully North replied, "It appears to me to be."

Glancing at North's hands, Manning pounced again. "Look, there on your thumb. You show that to the members of the jury."

North held up his hand.

"You don't think that's grease? You think that's *paint?*"

"Uh hum," North muttered, but in a tone so low that Judge Mueller asked both of them to please speak up. So in a loud, clear voice Manning asked, as he marked the stained piece of paper as exhibit 451, whether North still considered the substance to be black paint.

"It appears to be," the engineer replied stolidly, but then added, "I haven't made no specific evaluation of it, just a smell test."

"Yeah, smells like paint, too, to you?"

A slight hesitation.

"I think so."

Weeks later, in the jury room, the greasy swab on exhibit 451 would circulate around the room and be sniffed by each juror in turn.

IF ANYONE WAS in a position to know whether the substance applied was paint or grease, it was Wayne Hartman, who had done the job. Manning called him to the stand first thing the following morning and asked him about the substance in question. If Hartman was willing to equivocate about something as straightforward as whether a substance was paint or grease, it would offer the jury a useful marker for judging the rest of his responses. Manning invited him, like North, to climb aboard the defense's model tractor and asked him who had instructed him to fiddle with the equipment on the opening day of the trial.

"Max North."

While describing the adjustments he had made, Hartman mentioned the "white grease" he had applied.

"If I were to take this paper here and just rub that on that latch," Manning asked, "is that the white grease that I'm getting off that you sprayed on there, do you think?"

"You're getting something black," Hartman conceded. "I don't know what that is. Did somebody put something on? You're getting off paint."

Incredulous, Manning asked, "Do you think I just rubbed *paint* off that latch on that piece of paper?"

"Yes, I do."

"You do. You think that paint is still wet from yesterday?"

"Maybe the grease dissolved some of it or something. I don't know what it is."

"You believe that's paint as well?"

Just as North had done, Hartman handled the question not as subject to a yes-or-no answer, but rather to one of percentages. "It's more paint than grease, yes."

"Okay," Manning replied. As Hartman returned to the witness stand, Manning requested permission to enter the can containing the grease in evidence, along with the swab of paper.

Now that the jury had heard the kind of response the witness was willing to give, Manning asked Hartman about the investigations he had carried out on tractors belonging to Mickey Jones and Dwight Saunders. Hartman admitted that, basically, his "investigation" had consisted of running the tractor at different speeds while pushing the PTO lever fully forward and fully rearward repeatedly both with the tractor alone and with a baler attached, and not detecting any anomalies or any self-engagement. Manning had Hartman confirm repeatedly that the engineer had not placed the lever at any of the intermediate positions between fully rearward and fully forward. As Hartman explained, "That wasn't part of the claim."

Manning exhaled audibly, shrugged, and said that he had no further questions.

WEBER QUICKLY FOCUSED his examination of Hartman on the Mickey Jones accident, perhaps with a view to impugning Jones's own account of his injury. Jones had admitted to turning on the PTO when he had removed the belt from his baler, but had said that the PTO switch was in the fully rearward position when he remounted the belt the following day. Weber took Hartman step-by-step through Jones's claims and the subsequent investigation by Case, successfully raising questions about where fault for that accident should lie.

Weber finished his examination of Hartman around ten o'clock that Friday, which Judge Mueller had declared a short day.

Manning closed by once again asking Hartman to confirm whether the greasy substance on the ramp was or was not grease. Hartman stuck by his story.

CHAPTER TWENTY-FOUR

THREE OR FOUR nights a week Steven and Betty had dinner with Manning, McKenna, and their staff. Manning tended to be affable but absorbed, eating rapidly and generally disappearing to his room as soon as the meal was done. Steven and Betty would take long walks through the city in the early evening, bundling up against the cold, often returning by way of the video store. Back in Betty's room they would wait until around 9 p.m., 7 p.m. in Oregon, and call R. E. to report on the day's events. It was difficult for them to tell how the trial was faring. Long days of dogged testimony had produced no sense of progress. Manning had instructed them not to scan the jury, who in any event rarely betrayed their reactions. "A trial from the perspective of the plaintiffs can often be just tedium and tension," Manning told them. "There will be days when you feel like screaming from both."

Each night Manning answered their questions about his sense of the trial with cautious optimism, but his very caution made them uneasy. In Betty's hotel room, she and Steven played hearts or watched videos. After Steven went to his own room, Betty would say her prayers and go to bed. Steven, however, often tired but unable to rest, would put on his cap and coat and go out for another walk along the shore. He would fill his mind with the wind and the snow, trying to drive the tension from his mind and the physical lassitude from his body. When at last he felt some fatigue, he would head back to the hotel. As often as not, coming up the boardwalk, he would spot Manning's lighted shoreward-facing window and, through the parted curtains, glimpse Manning working at his desk.

THE MOST revealing witness to appear during the second week of trial was Donald Johnson, the retired mechanical designer from Case who had engineered both the controls for the PTO on the 70 series and the retrofitted "top hat" lever bracket and spring. Alone of the four Case witnesses, he made no attempt to deny, cover up, or explain away the mechanical flaws in the 970's PTO, perhaps because he was the only one no longer on the Case payroll as an employee or consultant. A heavyset, gray-haired man in his late sixties, somewhat physically impaired, he moved about in a motorized cart. He had begun his career at Case in 1957 as a draftsman and moved up to the rank of designer II by 1988, the year he had been laid off in the downsizing following the purchase of J. I. Case by International Harvester. Prior to Case, he had worked for the Simmons Company, drawing plans for Hide-A-Beds. He was a high school graduate with some night school, but no college coursework or formal training as an engineer.

Manning felt a certain sympathy for Johnson because of his candor and slightly forlorn, defenseless air. Nevertheless, Manning had virtually shaken him like a rag doll during his deposition, which had taken place in November, pressing him exhaustively on every point of vulnerability. He had finally admitted the lack of coordination between the lever and the valve and the inefficaciousness of the lever spring and the "top hat" retrofitted ramp. At the start of the deposition he had shied away from Manning's terms like *botch* and *failure,* but by the end it seemed to matter little to him. Now, several months later, when he took the witness stand, despite the presence in the courtroom of his former Case peers and superiors, Johnson again rapidly settled into an attitude of quiet compliance.

In quick succession he admitted that he was not an engineer, that he knew nothing about hydraulics, that he had never designed a hydraulic valve of any sort, that he had no knowledge of the kind of pressure generated by oil flows inside the machine, that, when designing his controls, he had not referred to any existing controls on other models of Case tractors—that he had started "at ground zero." Moreover, once he had fashioned the lever, he had never followed the cable down into the hydraulic chamber or looked at a cutaway of the chamber to measure its effect.

After Manning finished his questions about the design of the lever, spring, and ramp, and turned to the safety oversight that had taken place at the Case Corporation. Here, too, Johnson was utterly forthcoming that safety had never been a concern of his when designing the control, nor of anyone else at Case, either, as far as he was aware. Moving back and forth between Johnson and the machinery exhibits, Manning kept up a relentless stream of questions, interrupting it only when Johnson appeared to have trouble speaking, inviting him to take a drink of water or asking if he wished a pause. Johnson's lips were gray and his forehead damp with sweat, but he persevered for several hours with only one short pause.

After the lunch break, during the cross-examination, Weber attempted in part to establish that Johnson's responsibilities had been narrow and that he hadn't had to know about all the things Manning had inquired about. Asked, for example, whether he had gone into the field to talk to farmers and check out the performance of the 970, Johnson replied that North had done all the fieldwork.

Weber asked whether Johnson knew of any testing of the lever spring by the company.

No, Johnson was unaware of any testing.

Turning to the hydraulic valve, Weber offered Johnson the chance to modify or qualify the blanket statements Manning had drawn from him, but Johnson calmly stuck to his assertion that he was totally ignorant of hydraulics. Johnson did add, however, that he had consulted with the engine division and the hydraulic division while he had been designing—he hadn't been totally on his own.

Manning listened to these exchanges with satisfaction, of course, but also with more than a little surprise. Had Weber never seriously conferred with Johnson before putting him on the witness stand? Had he no idea what Johnson's answers would be?

"Mr. Johnson," Weber asked, "do you know how much resistance a clogged piece of power-take-off-driven implement could have in resisting the power of the tractor engine?"

"No," said Johnson.

Weber finished soon after; then Manning and he took brief additional turns. When Manning's final pass at Johnson came, Manning, rising energetically to his feet, said that he had just one brief question. What he yearned to ask Johnson in the light of everything he had just conceded was why neither he nor the company had ever done a responsible investigation of the PTO. But since post-sale duty questions were off limits, Manning had to satisfy himself with a personal question about Johnson's own feeling of responsibility. "When you take that lever," Manning began, "and you put it right there, one quarter inch out of off. As designer of this panel, it would surprise you. And you would not want it to start an implement at that point. That is not the way it was designed, correct, sir?"

Manning's quiet voice and manner were meant to appeal to the decency in Johnson, the former Case employee. As Weber's objection was rebuffed, the judge invited the witness to answer. Johnson gave an audible sigh and glanced down at his hands. "No," he said quietly, "I would not like that."

HEARTENED BY his success with Johnson, which occurred early in the week, Manning appealed to the judge for permission to show to the jury the video he had had produced of self-starting PTOs. Weber reviewed the film and strongly objected to it as misleading. Judge Mueller ruled the film could be shown as long as Manning made clear to the jury exactly what it was seeing.

Then the judge balanced that decision with one equally important to Weber. Weber had been pressing for permission to have the jury visit the tractor and baler, which were being stored in a large machinery shed on a nearby farmer's property. The prospect of this visit so alarmed Manning that if he had known the judge was going to balance his request against Weber's and grant both in a spirit of evenhandedness, he probably would have dropped his request to show the video. For he knew exactly why Weber wished the jury to visit the machinery. It was not to obtain technical information, all of which was present in the courtroom in abundance in the form of machine parts, slides, charts, and drawings. Rather, it was so the jury members would recreate the scene of Steven's accident. The normal human reaction for a jury member faced with the equipment would be to climb down from the cab, walk up to the baler and lean over it, and then say to him- or herself that never under any circumstances would he or she put a hand into that intake; nor could any juror see how anyone else in his right mind could do so either.

Manning felt the visit could be nothing but prejudicial to Steven's case, that it would shift the focus onto Steven's behavior and away from what he wanted the trial's focus to be—namely, the PTO of the tractor.

Despite Manning's objection, Mueller ruled that the visit would provide useful information. Manning was shaken. It was the first moment during the trial when he felt something like fear. A long, hard glance into the intake of the baler might be enough to swing who knew how many jurors. Furiously, he set about thinking and conferring with McKenna about how to counteract the effect of the visit. If Weber was going to fix the spotlight on Steven, they had to react quickly by putting maximum pressure on Mueller to admit arguments concerning Case's post-sale duty to warn. This would show the jury that the fault was not Steven's; it was endemic to the machine. They had to show the jury that Case had known about the flaw for years and had failed to do anything about it.

From the start of the trial, at every opportunity in the judge's chambers, Manning had been making use of a tactic called "an offer of proof," which is a statement by an attorney to a judge in chambers, out of earshot of the jury, concerning what a witness would have said if the attorney had been allowed to pose the question. An offer of proof can be nothing more serious than an attorney's best guess as to what a witness would say if questioned on a certain topic and, as such, easily dismissible by a judge, but Manning's consisted exclusively of verbatim material from the record. For more than a week, he had been trying to convince the judge that she had too narrowly confined the limits of the admissible evidence. For twenty minutes at a stretch he would read his proposed questions and then give the relevant verbatim replies from the Tautges case and from the depositions taken in Steven's case, always pounding away at the fact that Case had deliberately neglected to take responsibility for its dangerous machine. The offer of proof Manning made following the judge's concession to Weber of the machinery visit lasted over an hour. Judge Mueller conceded later that she had never experienced a comparable one.

The following afternoon, Thursday of the second week of the trial, she made her ruling. The threshold standard for evidence on the question of post-sale duty to warn had been met, she said. Manning and McKenna were now at liberty to recall and elicit testimony from Case witnesses on when and how the company had become aware of the flaw in the 970, and what it had done. This permission did not allow Manning and McKenna to mention the Tautges fatality explicitly, nor any other accident or incident excluded during the pretrial hearings, but they could use any relevant data from those events to pursue the question of whether Case had shown a consistent and deliberate disregard of customer safety with respect to the 970 tractor.

Manning and McKenna glanced at each other as the judge made her ruling. It felt like a turning point.

CHAPTER TWENTY-FIVE

I T WAS TIME, Manning now decided, to turn more of his attention to Steven. Soon he would take the stand to tell his story and face cross-questioning by Weber, and he was not yet ready for either of these tasks. Manning had to bring him to the point where he would be willing to talk more openly about his accident than he had ever done before, at least to strangers, and drill him in the possible approaches Weber might take with him. Over the weeks, a friendly rapport had developed between the two of them. Manning had been impressed by Steven's clarity and forthrightness, his utter absence of self-pity, but he understood that these very qualities could be used against him by Weber. It would not be enough, Manning realized, to sit down and instruct Steven about how to respond to his own and Weber's questions. Steven would absorb the instructions superficially, but then might follow his own naïve instincts under pressure. What Manning had to do, he realized, was to win Steven's confidence at a deep level so that he might first gather Steven's complete sense of his accident. Once he had accomplished this, he would be able to shape his own courtroom questions accordingly. And, just as important, he would then be able to prepare Steven for any questions Weber might throw at him. The best way to accomplish all this, Manning decided, would be casually, in friendly conversations. He proposed that the two of them start having dinner together in his room. "We'll get together around six, order from room service, and chew the fat for a while." Steven thought that was a great idea.

Given the disparity in their ages, backgrounds, and circumstances, it helped at the start that they had sports in common, not so much as a current interest but as a shaping factor in their teenage years—Manning's primarily in basketball and Steven's in baseball. From these, both had imbibed a passion for winning along with a necessary fatalism about losing. To Steven it made perfect sense that from a college career supported by a basketball scholarship Manning would have gravitated toward the cerebral contact sport of trial law. He asked Manning about that.

"No," said Manning. "No, in high school and college I had no idea of becoming a lawyer. To tell you the truth, it would have been pretty far down on my list."

"What did you want to be?"

"You ready? A monk. I wanted to be a Trappist monk. You know what that is?"

"Not really."

"A celibate priest who lives in a monastery, takes a vow of silence, eats vegetarian food, spends most of his time working and studying. And praying."

"*Lord,* Bill, why *ever* in the world . . . ?"

"Well, I'll tell you. When I was in high school, one of my biggest heroes was a Trappist monk named Thomas Merton, who was living down in Kentucky at a monastery called Gethsemane. I'd read a bunch of his books, his autobiography, and one in particular that really spoke to me, called *Confessions of a Guilty Bystander,* which, by the way, is a book I still reread. At the time, in the midst of the crazy sixties, it impressed me so much that one day at the end of my junior year in high school, I decided I'd drive down to Kentucky and talk to Merton, and from this conversation see if I should become a monk like he was. That was how much I admired him."

"Wow."

"You gotta remember, Steve, I was a serious Catholic kid from a serious Catholic school, and all around me was Vietnam and all the other uproar of the sixties."

"Still, it seems to me you could of admired him without wanting to live like he did."

Steven Sharp at age sixteen

Main Street in Richland, Oregon,
Steven's hometown

The home of Randolph and Leora Sharp, Steven's grandparents

A view of Eagle Valley, Oregon

Church of the Nazarene, where Leora Sharp was pastor

The house of Stan Saunders seen from the field where Steven was injured. *(Photo courtesy of Dwight and Debbie Saunders)*

The Case 970 tractor and Heston baler that injured Steven Sharp.

The Power Take Off lever in the Case 970, with the instructions: "Important. To engage PTO lever must be fully forward in slot. To disengage PTO lever must be fully rearward in slot."

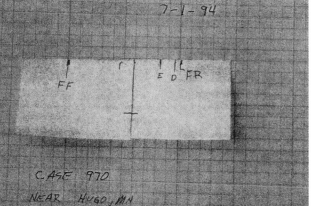

A crucial piece of evidence, the sketch by a defense witness showing the major points of the Power Take Off ramp: FF (fully forward), halfway point, E (engagement), D (disengagement), FR (fully rearward).

Steven firing his rifle using a specially built mouth-trigger device.

Above: Hidden Lake in the mountains above Eagle Valley, a favorite campsite of Steven and his father, R. E. Sharp

Below: Steven and R. E.

Steven, Al Gore, Steven's mother Betty Sharp, and Steven's lawyer Bill Manning at a Democratic fundraiser in the summer of 1997

Steven with his favorite dog

"Well, Steve, at the time I didn't have all that sorted out. I was full of enthusiasm. So a friend and I got in the car and drove down to Gethsemane, Kentucky. We'd called ahead, of course, and reserved some rooms in their guest house."

"So what did this monk tell you?" Steven asked.

"Not so fast, Steve," Manning replied. "Merton, whose name in the monastery was Father Louis, was nowhere around. Very important people made reservations well in advance to talk to him, something I hadn't done. It turned out he lived by himself in a cabin somewhere on the premises, but nobody would tell me where. So from the visitors' area I started wandering into the enclosed part of the monastery where visitors weren't allowed, and whenever anyone would stop me I'd act surprised and ask them where Father Louis was, and they would very nicely kick me out. This went on for a day or two."

"Did you ever get to meet him?"

"In a sense. On the third morning, I wandered back into the enclosure again and this time headed down toward the lake, where an older priest was sitting. We chatted about one thing and another. I told him a little about myself and he told me a little about life in the leper colony where he spent the last thirty years of his life, and time went by, maybe an hour, and then I mentioned how much I admired Father Louis, and he said he did too. And I asked him, 'Is it true that Merton is a hermit?' 'Yes,' he said. 'Where?' I asked. 'Oh,' he said, 'over there,' and he gestured across the lake toward a slope and some trees. Then he said, 'I guess I shouldn't have told you that.' And I said nothing."

"So now at least you knew where he was."

"Right."

"So what did you do?"

"I waited until it was dark, maybe nine o'clock. It was a hot, sticky June night in Kentucky with thousands of peepers making a big racket and I headed out around the lake toward those trees on that slope the monk had pointed to, and after a while I came to a clearing, and there was his cabin. It had a screened-in porch lighted by a lantern, and there sat Merton in a pair of shorts, at a table, writing. I moved closer and called his name, startling him, of course, and he jumped up, all pissed off. 'Who in the *hell*'s there?' he shouted, looking out into the darkness.

So I went closer so he could see me and I told him my name, and that I wanted to talk to him. He came to the door and started to open it. He was over being startled, but he still wasn't particularly friendly. He said it was officially past his bedtime, that he was working late, but that if I really needed to talk to him, he'd talk to me.

"But then all at once it hit me how much I'd intruded on his space, and that from being this sort of disembodied spiritual consciousness—you know what I mean?—he was instead this specific busy man in shorts and no shirt who would let me talk to him if I insisted, but that wasn't at all the way I'd imagined it. So I said that I really didn't want to bother him, and he looked at me like: Well, then, what was I doing there? While what I was hoping he would say was: No, look, that's OK, come on in, have a beer. But since he just stood there waiting for me to make up my mind, I . . . Now I really didn't know what to do. All I could think of was to repeat that I didn't want to bother him. 'Well, then, don't,' he said, and sat down again. Boom, the end. And I walked back to the guest house, pretty much in a muddle."

"So you never did get to talk to him?"

"No, I didn't. But in another way I did. As soon as I got back to the monastery, I sat down and wrote him a letter. I tried to explain why I'd showed up there that night, that it was because he was such a hero for me. And about a week or so later, when I got home, there was a letter from him, waiting for me, short but friendly, in which he apologized for being short with me, that it had been a long hot day, and that he was trying to cut off all appointments for the rest of the summer. Later I found out he was preparing to leave for Asia. He closed with the lines: 'There's no point in being an image anyway. Blessings, Tom.' "

"How old were you, Bill?"

"That was in '68. I was seventeen years old, just the same age you were when you had your accident. Like you, I was between my junior and senior year."

"I guess at least it straightened you out about being a monk."

"It did do that." Manning smiled. "Just from that visit and brief encounter, I could see there was no refuge, even in Gethsemane, for what was bothering me. Only a few months later, Merton was dead, electrocuted in Bangkok after grabbing the cord of a portable fan with wet hands."

On a subsequent evening Manning decided to ask Steven about a friend of his, Jim Fisher, who had died a year after Steven's accident. His name had come up in depositions, so Weber might pose questions about him. Given the sensitivity of the topic, Manning approached it by telling Steven about one of his best friends from college, Walter Middleton, who had died some years after leaving school. Middleton was a black basketball player who had grown up in Harlem and, like Manning, had come to Creighton on a basketball scholarship. By chance, he had wound up being Manning's roommate freshman year.

"Let me tell you, Steve, that guy could play basketball. He was a magician. A smart guy, too, loved to read. We became friends, both of us outsiders in Omaha, neither of us into fraternities, though obviously in many other ways we were very unlike. Our backgrounds were radically different, me from a white Minneapolis suburb and Walter from Harlem, which, until he arrived in Nebraska, I don't think he'd ever stepped outside of. It was something else to go out driving with him, a bunch of us, and he'd look out the window and ask, 'What *is* that stuff?' And we'd say, 'Chey'—that was his nickname—'that's corn'. Or 'that's wheat,' or whatever it was, and he simply could not believe it.

"Spring break of sophomore year he invited me home to Harlem. We pulled up to his place at 159th and Amsterdam. It seems like the largest drug corner in the world. Windows go up, people happy that Walter's home. 'As-Salaam Alaikum,' 'As-Salaam Alaikum,' people are yelling from all the windows. On each corner is a candy store, fronts for drug deals. I remember seeing a baby blue Lincoln get converged on by about seven cop cars. And they started pulling it apart, ripping drugs out of it, busting it. We're sitting there with Walter's mom in her apartment, and there's this big police lock on her door, you know, one of those big pole locks. She was a Baptist. She cooked us a wonderful Easter meal, corn bread and all. We ate a ton and it was great.

"And then we went into a side room after dinner and his friends came over, and there was one small lamp in there and I could hardly make out some of these guys' faces. We're sitting around and somebody pulled out cocaine, and I had never seen the stuff before. I mean, I had seen marijuana by that time in my life, but not cocaine. People started passing it around in the clip of a Bic pen. You know, on the cap, the clip like a little spoon? About six guys in the room. And it came to me.

Some music is on. And this guy comes over to me, and he stops, stares at me. He's to pass it to me and he stops and looks at me, this huge, long pause, I mean, minutes go by. Finally he says, 'Are you prejudiced?' 'Yeah,' I say, 'sure.' 'Good,' he says. ''Cause so'm I.' All his buddies laugh. So then he passes me the Bic, and I pass it on; I wasn't exactly in the frame of mind to experiment. And the mood in the room definitely gets better."

"Did you stay friends after that first year?" Steven asked.

"Yeah, we did, through the first three years of college. It was a whole new world for me, living on the edge of a black ghetto in Omaha, interacting daily with black athletes. It widened my world considerably.

"At the end of junior year, I quit basketball. I dropped my scholarship, switched to science courses so I could get some real education before I graduated. So I saw a lot less of Walter then. By that time he was pretty seriously addicted. Last time I saw him in Omaha was during spring break of senior year. He called from the county jail for help. Turns out he'd been picked up for writing bad checks. Had been in jail a long time and wasn't doing well. It was the first I'd heard. I told him I'd be right down."

"So what did you do?"

"I walked down to the jail to see him, about ten blocks. Once I got there I told the guard I was a friend, and he let me go up on the elevator. The door opens on a large cell crowded with prisoners, mostly black guys along with one very freaked-out white guy who was literally climbing the bars. They put Walter and me in a small room with a steel table. 'How long have you been here?' I asked him. 'Three weeks,' he says. 'You had a hearing?' I ask him. 'No,' he says. Then he says, 'I don't feel so good, Bill. I think I'm sick.' 'Hang on, Walter,' I told him. 'I'll be back as soon as I can.'

"So I walked back to school and went to see this Jesuit, a friend of mine, a young guy not yet a priest; he walked with a limp, as I recall. I borrowed a Roman collar from him and a vest, and went to the district attorney's office and asked to speak with him. He asked me why I was there. I'll never forget the look on the guy's face when I asked him for Walter's file. I said, 'I want to talk to you about Walter Middleton. May I see his file?' He starts looking for it, but he can't find it. So I ask, 'How long has he been up there?' He didn't know. I told him: 'Three weeks. That's wrong. You know it's wrong.' He had no information. So many black people had no representation at that time in that state. He kept hunting, repeating, 'It's around here somewhere.' So I made conversation with him. I was polite and deferential. Finally he said to me, 'OK, Father, you guarantee me one thing. You get the money and you guarantee me that he's got a one-way plane ticket, paid for, I'll let him out. To your custody. As long as you also guarantee me, Father, that you drive him to the airport and put him on the plane. You give me your word?' I said, 'Yeah, you got it. No problem.' I shook his hand. Then I went back to the jail and told Walter he'd be out in the morning. Going home. I got the money, I don't know where from. Three hundred bucks or so, one-way ticket. Next day, as agreed, I took him to the airport, put him on the plane. Waved good-bye."

"And that's the last you saw of him?"

"No, Steve, last time was about two years later. I was in New York, and I called him. Earl "the Pearl" Monroe, his hero, was playing with the Knicks. Walter came downtown to the Garden to meet me, and when he got out of the cab he was running toward me. I asked him what that was all about. He said, 'Oh, it's nothing, I just had to beat the cabbie out of the fare.' He had three or four guys with him. He looked terrible. At twenty-five he looked fifty. He wasn't walking so well, so I said, 'Walter, what the hell's wrong with your leg?' 'Oh, I got a bullet in it.' I said, 'How'd you get a bullet in it?' 'Oh, there was a gunfight. I was in a gunfight.'

"That night after the game, we parted on the sidewalk. I told him to take care and watched him limp away with his pals, the whole time with a strong feeling I'd never see him again."

"And did you?"

"No, Steve. He died soon after that."

"You wonder why some guys make it and some guys don't," Steven said, "although with your friend Walter the odds seem to have been pretty poor from the start."

"Yeah, maybe," Manning replied. "The friends you make in those years, you don't replace them."

"Tell me about it," Steven replied with some sadness in his voice.

"Why don't you tell me about your friend Jim," Manning suggested. "I don't mean to pry, but just air the topic a little in case it comes up."

"Well, Jim, let's see. He was like a brother. His family moved to Richland when I was in the seventh grade, he joined my class. We played sports together, wrestled, played basketball, baseball, and football. His mom was like my mom. I'll bet I watched more *Monday Night Football* at his house than I did at mine."

"Would you say he was your closest friend?"

"One of 'em, that's for sure. He helped me a lot."

"How?"

"Jim was one of the smartest kids in our class. He was one of my friends who took notes for me, and the one who read to me most in the evenings.

"On my side, I taught him how to hunt. Before coming to Richland, he'd been a city kid and didn't know much about hunting and fishing."

"Temperamentally, the two of you pretty similar?"

"Not really. Jim was higher strung, almost an overachiever, in school, in athletics. He could have had a scholarship to college either way, sports or academics. But he had a significant medical problem."

"What was that?"

"As a kid, he had some sort of seizures. Not many people knew about that, outside of his family and a few friends. But in high school he thought those seizures were behind him."

"Weren't they?"

"I'm not sure. In senior year he had a car accident that was maybe related."

"How?"

"Well, he said he'd been driving too fast and run off the road on a turn. Hit a tree, and his car was totaled. That's what he told me when I visited him in the hospital, that he'd just been careless; but something seemed fishy. So I decided I'd run out there and take a look at where it happened. And I found that it wasn't on a turn but on a straightaway. The tracks ran straight off the road and then twenty yards straight into a tree."

"So, you thought . . . ?"

"Yeah, that he'd had a seizure. That his illness was coming back. I knew that he'd stopped taking his medication at the start of high school. He thought he was cured. He hoped he was. He hated the medication, its side effects. But why else would a guy run off a straight road like that on a clear day?"

"I don't know. Sounds like you might be right."

"It's just a guess. He never did talk about it or about the accident to me again. And I stopped thinking about it, because as soon as he was out of the hospital he seemed fine again. His old self."

"The two of you got to be friends again?"

"We'd always been friends."

"Yeah, but didn't you say that you wondered why he never visited you when you were recovering?"

"That's true, I did wonder about that. But I didn't take it as unfriendliness. Jim was always kind of sensitive. I thought maybe seeing me like that, before I was really back on my feet again, bothered him. But once I showed up back at school, we were pretty much like before, goofing off and joking around. And in the fall, we started going hunting again."

"That was around the time he died, right?"

"Yeah."

"How did he die?"

Steven gave Manning a long look. "Didn't you know? He shot himself."

Manning looked startled.

"That day, it was during Christmas break, we went hunting together, he and I and another friend, Brad. Brad was driving. We hunted in the morning, then after lunch we drove to the quarry and shot some clay pigeons. Brad and Jim took turns pulling. Brad was hitting stuff and so was I, and Jim too, but less. He was getting pretty frustrated. That was clear.

"So I watched a little closer, and I could see it was from how he was holding his shotgun. Just a little off. I told him, and he tried to correct his grip, but it didn't help. I explained it a couple of more times, but nothing helped. We were losing the light, it was getting late, and it was cold. Starting to snow. So we called it a day.

"Brad drove us home, first Jim and then me. Jim went upstairs, wrote a note to his family, took his shotgun and shot himself."

"Jesus," Manning breathed. "That doesn't make sense. At least to me. Was there nothing else that day?"

Steven remained silent for a moment. "Well, there was one thing."

"If you don't want to talk about it . . ."

"Bill, I've thought about this a lot. 'Cause Jim's death messed me up pretty bad, you know, and I've gone back over that day a thousand times. Right at the end, when I was trying to help him get a better grip on his rifle, I finally just looked at him and I said, 'Jim, I don't know what more to tell you. I can't explain it any better. If I just had my arms I could show you.'

"Now, Bill, you gotta understand, I wasn't saying this like I was feeling sorry for myself. I just meant what I said, that if I'd had my arms, I would have been able to reach out and put his arms in such and such a position. But when he heard me say that, he heard something entirely different, because he gave me a strange look and he got this really weird expression on his face, like he was sick or something, and he said, 'Hey, Steve, I don't know if I can handle that.'

" 'Handle what?' I asked. But he just looked away, and in a second or two he seemed back to normal and it was like nothing had happened."

"But you think he took what you said . . . ?"

"Bill, I don't know what to think. I'm just telling you what he said."

A sense of the scene formed itself in Manning's mind: three teenagers with their rifles and a pickup in a stone quarry on a fading December afternoon, a few flakes falling, each locked in a dense solitude—a kid for whom it was just a normal day, a kid who had lost his arms, and a kid on whom his friend's loss posed too heavy a weight. Manning had come to understand that there are people for whom others' disasters are a sign of their own health and invincibility and others for whom such disasters are signs, read not only in the mind, of a deep, incurable flaw in things, a confirmation of a terrible foreknowledge. Apparently Jim had been one of the latter.

"You don't know what he wrote in that note?"

"No, the family never revealed that, other than he'd written that it wasn't their fault, and that he loved them. They were not responsible."

Manning continued to study Steven in the ensuing pause.

"You're not either, Steve," he said. "You know that, don't you?"

"Not what?"

"Responsible for Jim's death. Just like I'm not responsible for Walter's."

"Yeah, I guess I understand that, Bill. I think I got that worked out. But that don't change nothing."

HAD JIM'S DEATH been a factor in some of the wild behavior Steven had engaged in during the first year or two following his graduation from high school? Manning wondered. When questioned, R. E. and Betty told Manning that Steven had spent at least one night in the local jail after a run-in with the sheriff's deputy. There were other incidents, in time a kind of running feud with the deputy. Manning suggested that the unruly behavior might have been due to all the emotional and physical pain Steven had been through, not least the loss of his friend, and R. E. granted that these might have been factors. "But Steve always was an ornery bugger," he added. "He never did take orders well. I mean, well enough if he was interested in the job, but never if he thought you was just trying to boss him around. He also had some run-ins with a couple of his teachers in high school because of that, one in particular who seemed to resent the attention everybody was paying to Steve after his accident. Thought he was getting cocky. I think maybe some of that was going on with the deputy, too, that he resented Steve because he'd talk back to him while most of the other kids were smart enough to just shut up. Particularly if the deputy was busting up a beer party like the kids was always having. Maybe Steve got sassy with him."

For her part, Betty saw no deep psychological connection between Steven's losses, physical and emotional, and his insubordinate behavior. "He was just being a boy," she said, "being headstrong, like a lot of boys are at that age."

"I'm getting some conflicting information about you, Steve," Manning said one evening. "Is it true that you did a lot of partying and fighting after high school and then when you were attending business school in Ontario [Oregon]?"

"Well, yeah, I guess I did my share." He smiled. "But as far as the fighting was concerned, Bill, I never started anything. Mostly I was just defending myself."

"How do you mean, defending yourself?"

"Well, the first fight I got into in Ontario happened late one Saturday night, not long after I moved there. I was buying some beer at a little convenience store in the part of town where my friend Barry and I were living, which was kind of rough. And I come out of the store holding my stuff, along with my wallet and change, all in a paper bag, and these two guys were waiting for me outside, they must of watched and seen how I carried my money. One of them was standing off to the side, and I saw he had a knife in his hand. I noticed that. I didn't see the other one. He snuck up behind me and smashed a beer bottle on my head. But lucky for me, I was wearing my cap. I didn't get cut, but I went down on one knee, and I was kind of woozy for a second, but I never let go of the bag. This guy must have been looking around for something else to hit me with, because he wasn't right on top of me as I started to get up. I was still kind of half bent over when he started coming at me, I guess to punch me or kick me or something, and so I just stood up real quick and as I did I drew my left arm up across my body, so I had a lot of swing in it, and I connected with this guy's chin. Well, this hook of mine is as heavy as a good-sized hammer. The guy's knees just sagged and he flopped down in the street and he was gone. The other guy saw that and took off running as fast as he could. I stood there and I just laughed.

"Those kind of things happened a couple of times. Not exactly that way, but like, for example, at a county fair that fall. That year or the following."

"Somebody tried to rob you?"

"No. This was just a cowboy acting up. Me and a couple of my friends were walking down the midway, and he was walking down the midway with his girlfriend. He'd been drinking, walking with his arm around her, deliberately not paying attention to where he was going, you know, swaggering along, and he rammed into me with his shoulder. Well, I rammed him right back. That annoyed him, so he started coming at me. Then he saw my hook. 'Oh, *excuse* me,' he said in this nasty sweet kind of tone, 'I didn't know you was a *cripple*.' So I knocked him out. His girlfriend started screaming to beat the band. All his buddies come running."

"What happened?"

"Barry was with me. I guess you haven't met Barry. He's about six foot seven, weighs about two thirty—he's an ironworker—and he just loves to fight and brawl. He goes to bars and does it for fun on the weekends. So pretty soon we're all talking together, his friends and us, and the cowboy's back on his feet and conscious again and he apologized for calling me a cripple, and we all went drinking together. Had a great time."

AFTER PERHAPS four or five such conversations, Manning suggested to Steven one night after dinner that it was time they begin preparing in earnest for his oral testimony.

"OK, Bill," Steven said, "how do you want to do that?"

"I want you to tell me step-by-step what happened to you after you climbed out of the cab and approached the baler. That's what I need to know in order to determine what questions to ask you in court. Then, a little later on, we'll run through those questions and answers. We'll do that a couple times."

"Well, first I walked back there and kicked the hay from in front of it."

"OK. Then what?"

"Then, you know, I reached in to pull out the loose hay."

"Leaned over the bar to do that?"

"Yes. And for balance, I put my left hand on the lower roller, the metal one."

"They weren't both metal?"

"No. The upper one was rubber. Hard black rubber. Bottom one steel."

"And while you were leaning in like that, that's when it turned on?"

"Right. All of a sudden."

"And grabbed your hands."

"Well, yeah, first one went in, instantly, then when I grabbed it and tried to yank it out, the other."

"So then you were caught. And then you struggled."

"Yes, then I struggled."

"And eventually you got free . . ."

"Right."

"But how did you do that, exactly? You've never told me that."

"Well, actually, that's because it kind of bothers me to go over it, but I can if you want to."

"I do."

"Well, first I just pulled and pulled and screamed for help."

"How long, do you think?"

"I don't know. Until I was hoarse and couldn't yell anymore."

"Then what?"

"Then I noticed that whenever I jerked from side to side, I nicked off some flesh from the underside of my arms on this sharp ridge in front of the roller. A little cut."

"And so . . . ?" Manning prompted.

Steven breathed a long sigh. "And so, at the point where I figured I was either going to pass out and die—I was fading in and out already—or I had to do something different, I decided to cut off my arms. That was my only chance."

"And you did that by . . ."

"Like I said, by sawing my arms back and forth across that ridge. First one and then the other."

"I see," Manning said softly.

"The bones had already gone through, you see, Bill, so all that was left on my side was real thin, just some flesh and muscle and hide."

With some difficulty, Manning asked, "How long did it take you to do that?"

"I'm guessing about fifteen minutes. Each arm. I got one free and this wave of happiness went through me, 'cause then I knew I could do the other one and get free."

Manning exhaled audibly. "But weren't you losing a lot of blood?"

"Yeah, but I cauterized my stump on the roller, the rubber one. It was burning hot. It was smoking."

"OK, Steve, thanks, man. Thanks. That's enough for tonight."

Steven agreed. "Wears you out, don't it, talking about this stuff? What do you say we get us a beer?"

———

ONCE MANNING had broken through Steven's reluctance to talk about the details of his accident, he returned to the topic repeatedly, working it to the point of routine. And then, when he felt that Steven's accident held no more surprises, Steven surprised him. "You know, Bill," he said in a pause, "there's one thing I've never told you about my accident."

"Oh?" said Manning with studied calm, feeling a nervous tightening in his stomach at the thought of some important withheld detail. "What's that?"

"I want to tell you about a dream."

"A dream?" This from Steven, who rarely talked about his inner states.

"Yeah. A nightmare. One that I've been having since I was a kid. I thought you might want to hear about it."

Intrigued, Manning said, "Tell me about it."

Then Steven proceeded to tell him, as years ago he had told Betty, about his recurrent nightmare in which a baler broke through the back wall of the church while his grandmother Leora preached to a rapt congregation. "They could hear her, but I couldn't," he said. Then he described his feeling of panic and isolation when the nightmare carried him outside the church and planted him as a helpless bystander to the destruction within.

"Have you had that dream since?"

"No, never." He paused. "I thought I would tell you about the dream, because the other day, you asked me why when I was stuck in the baler I just didn't give up and die."

"Right."

"Part of it had to do with this dream."

"How?"

"Well, there was a point when I was woozy and fading in and out, and then I remembered my dream. Not like an ordinary memory, but like I was in it. And I thought to myself, Oh, right, here I am in my dream. This is the thing I always knew was coming. And now it's here. It was like I caught up with myself. You understand?"

"I think so," Manning replied.

"Then, in some kind of way, I was watching myself struggle from inside the dream. And while the struggling part of me was still terrified, the part of me that was watching was quiet and calm."

"Why do you think that was?"

"Well, like I said, because part of me had always known this was coming. And it wasn't surprised. Or even afraid. And that helped me."

"How?"

"It showed me that this wasn't just some random thing. It had been in my life from the start. So there was some kind of logic to it, and so maybe a way out, if I could just figure it out."

"Which you did."

Steven smiled. "Yeah, which I did."

Manning took a moment to consider Steven's account, temporarily stymied by the complexity of the response he felt stirring within him. On the one hand, he wanted to pose further questions about the uncanny event, explore its every nuance, while on the other he felt that not only did he grasp its essence already, but saw in it dimensions and aspects made evident to him by his decades of meditation and spiritual inquiry. In his own way, he'd had experiences analogous to Steven's, moments in meditation when his everyday self had fallen away and he'd connected to an aspect unrelated to, or outside of, time. They had marked his life, in their way, with a depth comparable to Steven's dream. They had shaped his life, presided over its choices. And they had also brought him here, it now occurred to him, to this present moment, to sit facing this specific individual, by a network of pathways that on one level was sheer happenstance, but on another was as inevitable as the intersection of highways when viewed from the air. From that vantage, as reported by Merton and other spiritual seekers whom Manning had studied, and confirmed as well by his own practice, time took on the characteristics of space, full of pattern and potential meaning. Wasn't that the reason, Manning suddenly asked himself, why he and Steven were presently working together?

How much of this strange hunch could he convey to Steven? Could he suggest that while on one level Steven had, of course, been utterly and completely alone in the field that day, prey to chance and a flawed machine, on another level he had been standing as a kind of node in an immense network of patterned events?

Tentatively, that night, he opened the topic with Steven, and in the days and weeks ahead he occasionally returned to it, trying not to lay his grid upon Steven's experience, but to probe gently and ask questions based on his own experience in order to see whether they might find an echo in Steven's. As it turned out, they had much to discuss.

"My grandma and me, Bill, we've often talked about this sort of thing, especially when I was younger and she would tell me stories about her dad. These kind of connections you're talking about, she knows all about them."

CHAPTER TWENTY-SIX

S O EAGER was Manning to recall the Case witnesses and question them on the company's long-term knowledge of the 970's defect that he decided to modify his strategic plan and not call Mickey Jones or the other four farmers he had fought so hard during the pretrial hearings to have admitted to testify. He rationalized this change to the judge on the grounds of efficiency and economy.

Weber, asked for his reaction, protested. At this point he was just as adamant that Manning call the farmers as before he had been opposed. Indeed, if Manning refused to call his promised witnesses, Weber said, he would call for a mistrial. He was now counting on those witnesses, Weber said, to rebut Manning's claim that their testimony would point to a single underlying defect. What their testimony would show, Weber promised, was that each of the incidents represented a unique and specific act of negligence on the farmer's part, just like Steven's.

These were serious considerations, of course, and Judge Mueller ordered Manning to produce his witnesses. On Friday of the second week they duly began to arrive, along with R. E., ready to be prepped for his testimony later in the week. Overnight the lobby and restaurant of the hotel felt more congenial to Steven and Betty with the addition of the Minnesota farmers, whose manner of speaking, clothes, and attitude identified them as kindred spirits. And since each of the farmers had brushed up against what had taken Steven's arms, they in turn felt a sympathy and rapport with the Sharps from the moment they said hello.

That weekend, the temperature warmed after weeks of cold, a late-winter shift with a fragile promise of spring. To celebrate the arrival of R. E. and give the Sharps a chance to become acquainted with the farmers, Manning and McKenna took the group out for dinner at one of Racine's better steakhouses. As the evening wore on and the conversation became more animated, the attorneys began to feel that it might have been a good development, after all, to have been ordered to call these men to the stand—they were clearly warming to Steven and his family. Thanks to the sharing of stories and information within the group, the farmers would be confirmed in their own sense of the danger posed by their 970 tractors. At the end of the evening they all agreed to meet the following morning for breakfast. It would become a ritual for the duration of their stay in Racine.

During one of these informal morning get-togethers, after Steven had gone back to his room, one of the farmers asked R. E. whether Steven was able to take care of himself, not only in daily situations, as was obvious, but out in the woods and up in the mountains, which seemed to hold such significance for him. In reply, R. E. related an incident that had occurred the previous fall on one of their hunting trips.

As usual, they had set out at dawn into the high mountains on muleback. After a pause for lunch, Steven had felt like doing some rock prospecting on his own and had asked R. E. to go ahead with the mules and the gear while he hiked over to Box Canyon on the other side of Hidden Lake. They would rendezvous around supper time. The hike would take Steven over difficult terrain, but he had regained his lower-body strength and was eager for the climb. R. E. was concerned about Steven's safety and told him to fire his rifle twice in quick succession if he got into trouble. Then R. E. hitched the mules together and went on alone. Mid-afternoon, he arrived at their familiar campsite by the lake, tethered the mules, and set up their tent. Then he walked down to the lake and caught some fish for supper. At early dusk, he heard a rifle shot. He stood listening, but no second shot followed. As the cool autumn afternoon deepened to night, he built a fire and kept an uneasy eye out for Steven. Just when he had decided to walk to the other side of the lake in search of Steven before it was completely dark, the mules began to make a fierce commotion, tearing and rearing and braying from a menace obviously close at hand. R. E. stood and peered into the dusk beyond the campfire. He glimpsed a figure coming closer. Then he saw Steven, hardly recognizable, his face, hair, and clothes matted and soaked with blood. He was gripping his rifle with his hook and on his back he had a freshly skinned bear pelt. Moving into the circle of firelight, he set down his rifle, and with a twist of his shoulders he dropped the pelt to the ground.

R. E. was startled. "I didn't know you was aiming to get yourself a bear, son," he said.

"I wasn't," Steven replied. "I was taking a rest, sitting on a stump over in the canyon, eating a sandwich, when this little cub come out of the trees. I guess it smelled my sandwich, 'cause pretty soon it was heading in my direction. So I got down on one knee and was coaxing it over, which was more than half stupid, I guess, 'cause then I heard branches and brush crackling behind me. I turned around and there was the mama, and she was heading hard at me. Fast."

"Never a good idea to get between a sow and her cub, Steve. You know that," R. E. admonished.

Well, sure, Steven knew that, but he'd been momentarily charmed by the cub, and then everything had happened so quick. He'd just had the time to scramble, snag his rifle, and squeeze off one shot before the sow reached him, and luckily that's all it had taken.

"You mean to tell me," one of the breakfasting farmers asked, "that he shot that bear and then skinned it all on his own?"

"Yeah, he did," R. E. replied, "which took some doing, because all he had was his hook and a pocketknife, an Old Timer, with a blade for gutting fish."

Manning had not heard about this incident. Naturally he was startled by it, but not surprised. He could well imagine Steven in the situation, just as he found it characteristic of him not to have mentioned it. Manning watched R. E.'s face as he told the story, intrigued by his tone. In one way, R. E. was bragging to this table of peers about his unstoppable son, but at the same time he was giving these fathers and grandfathers a glimpse of what it was like to be a father forced into a deeper and more frequent awareness than most, perhaps, of his inability to alter the massive forces at work in his son's life. For a moment, as Manning sat there in his business suit, white shirt, and tie, at a breakfast table covered with a fresh white cloth, he let himself wonder what it would be like to be alone in the woods at twilight, to have to shoot a bear in order to save his life, and then to gut it with a blade clasped in a hook.

"We went down to the creek," R. E. wound up his story, "and I helped him clean up. He was a real mess. Stunk pretty bad," R. E. said with a short, dry laugh.

BEFORE ANY of the farmers took the stand, Weber asked the judge that they be sequestered and ordered not to speak to one another, so that the testimony of each one would not affect the others. Mueller agreed and gave the orders. As for Jones, Weber requested that he not be allowed to appear in court as he was presently dressed, wearing a short-sleeved shirt. R. E. gave him his corduroy jacket to wear, taking it right off his back.

AS WEEK THREE got under way, Betty, R. E., and Steven watched the proceedings with increasing nervousness and anticipation. Finally the witnesses on the stand would be friendly to their cause. There would be plain talk based on direct experience. Now was Manning's chance to try to accomplish in some measure what had been his aim from the start, to show that Steven's was not an isolated incident. To make the point, however, as Manning had explained to the farmers in private, he had to remain within narrow limits. The testimony he elicited from each farmer had to bear on his specific case and not give the impression that the flaw was systemic, because, of course, no single farmer could know that. "We have to walk a narrow road with these fellows," he told the Sharps, "and hope the jury draws the obvious inference. Weber will be watching me like a hawk."

"It's almost like a game," Steven commented, "with all these rules."

"There is a certain sporting angle to it," Manning agreed with a smile indicating that he was not immune to the charm of a high-stakes game.

David McKenna handled the testimony when Donald Joop, the first farmer, took the stand early Monday morning. Sixty-two years old, retired in 1986 due to arthritis, he continued to live on his 350-acre farm in Borup, Minnesota, a small town twelve miles from the North Dakota border. He'd been a farmer all his life, raising crops and beef cattle. He had never traveled farther east than Duluth, nor, prior to flying to Milwaukee, had he ever been on a commercial airplane. He'd bought his Case 1070 (a slightly larger model than the 970 with the same PTO) in the spring of 1973. One morning in June of that year when he had been greasing his baler in preparation for the day's work, the PTO had self-started. He had not even turned on the PTO yet that day. The plunger had begun to rise and fall as he was greasing some fittings, narrowly missing him. Since that first time, Joop said, he supposed the PTO had turned on spontaneously hundreds of times, something that had never happened with any of the other tractors he'd owned. At the start, before he realized that the condition was chronic and irreparable, he'd tried to have it repaired, never with success, and had had many close calls.

Otherwise, he said it was "basically" a good, hardworking tractor, "but it's got the defect with the PTO, and that is dangerous." Although he expected to sell it now that he'd retired, he did worry that "whoever gets it will be careful that he don't get injured." He would have sold it long ago and bought a different brand had it not been for his fear that the new owner might be injured.

During his cross-examination, Weber asked Joop whether the PTO brake—a brake that prevents the shaft from turning—functioned on his tractor. Joop said it had never worked from the day he'd bought it new and driven it fourteen miles home. Why hadn't he got it fixed in the twenty-three years he'd owned it? Weber asked. He'd talked to his "block man"—the local Case representative—several times, Joop said, and had been told that they couldn't fix it. Weber found that hard to believe, and asked repeatedly why Joop had not had it repaired. Joop explained that the Case representative had given him the impression that there wasn't anything to be done. "He says it's supposed to work the way it's put together."

Weber persisted: "He told you it wouldn't do you any good to take it to the dealer?"

"That is right," Joop replied.

The next farmer to take the witness stand was Jeffery Peterson, forty-three years old, from Dassel, Minnesota, a town one hour west of Minneapolis. He had bought his 300-acre farm in 1979 and his father had given him a used Case 1070 "in very, very good shape" in 1982. Max North and David McKenna had visited him in December 1995, a representative for each side. North had taken the PTO console apart and found the broken lever spring. Until that moment, Peterson had been unaware of the spring. Sometime after getting his tractor he had discovered the tendency of the PTO to self-start. Twice he had taken his tractor to a Case dealer and paid to have the unit repaired. Yet the problem had persisted. Now he simply accepted the fact that he had to take great care around the PTO. Otherwise, Peterson testified, he was "very happy with" the tractor.

In questioning both farmers, Weber asked whether the weight of the load on the attached implement affected the tendency of the PTO to engage. Both replied that the load seemed to have nothing to do with it. Thus far, in other words, Weber had little to show for his insistence on calling for these farmers' testimony. The third witness who came to the stand was a thirty-four-year-old farmer named John Pemberton, from Willow River, Minnesota, who owned 163 acres and leased an additional thirty or forty on which he raised crops and maintained a herd of 140 Holstein cows. He had bought his Case 970, used, in 1984. The spring on his PTO lever was still intact but, according to Pemberton, failed to stop the machine from engaging on its own. Unlike the two previous witnesses, who had been phlegmatic in their accounts of their dangerous tractors, Pemberton was very angry about the near miss he claimed to have had.

It had occurred at the end of a working day in late summer of 1992. Pemberton had been checking the blades, the tractor engine on idle, to see whether they needed to be sharpened. First he had run his eye over the twenty-two-inch blades, checking for nicks and scratches caused by rocks or field debris. Then he had reached out his hand to run his thumb along the beveled edges. At that instant, with a loud whine, the knives had begun to spin.

"What was your reaction to that?" McKenna asked.

"I was mad. I was really mad."

"What did you do?"

"I reached in the cab, pulled the off switch, the kill switch on the tractor, walked in the house, which was maybe a hundred feet, and that's when my memory kicked in the fact that somebody had something happen like that apparently somewhere. And also my memory is flooded with the fact we had the PTO fixed in '85 [the problem then had been that the PTO wouldn't turn off], so something had been wrong with it before. My mind's just flooding. You're angry. I'm mad, whatever."

"Were you scared?"

"Oh, yeah. Heart's pounding."

"Did you ever go back and check where the lever was on the PTO control?"

"It was off. The spring was intact. Everything was intact."

In his house, Pemberton had told his mother about his near miss and then, his anger increasing at the thought of how close he had just come to losing some fingers, he picked up the phone and called the president of J. I. Case.

"It would do no good to call the dealership," said Pemberton. "The thing had been to the dealer in '85. They supposedly fixed it. That was within ten years of when it was made. This tractor is in good shape. It had been doing very little, if anything, even in winter work. It looked good. Never had any other problems with it. Wasn't something that had been abused. Dealer had it fixed, supposedly. Obviously, something wasn't right."

"Were you able to reach the president of the company?"

"They handed me to somebody."

"You were passed around?"

Eventually he had talked to someone at Case who "had some power," who had simply told Pemberton to see his dealer to have his machine repaired. A letter to Case had gone unanswered. So he had gone to the dealer, who had told him "it did happen, it happened to people." The dealer had said, Pemberton testified, "Don't use it for a PTO tractor." After the repair, the PTO had never self-started again, but Pemberton said he didn't use it in the way he used to.

After the defense cross-examined the witness, while the jury took a brief break, Weber once again demanded a mistrial on the grounds that Pemberton's testimony that the dealer "implied this was happening to other people on other tractors," had crossed an inviolate line. Now the jury was free to think that the problem with the PTO was not confined to the three or four tractors cited in the case, Weber argued, but that the problem with the 70-series tractors was a pervasive one. To convey such a notion or suspicion to the jury had, of course, been expressly forbidden during the pretrial hearings.

Privately, Manning wondered whether this was why Weber had insisted on the farmers appearing in the first place, in the hope that a slipup such as this might occur and provide grounds for a mistrial. Out loud, both he and McKenna pointed to the trivial nature of Pemberton's statement. It had been short and unremarkable. There had been no follow-up questions. Most likely the jury had not even noticed it, they reasoned. Weber, on the other hand, noting that Pemberton had said it at least twice, declared that an incurable prejudice had been introduced to the trial. The jury was now boiling with speculation, he said.

Judge Mueller agreed that the matter was indeed very serious. "The bell has been rung, and there's no way to unring it," she said. While admitting that curative instruction would just draw more attention to the testimony, she also refused to grant a mistrial.

Weber persisted. "You don't hear me crying wolf a lot in this court, Judge," explaining they had no other way to fix the damage done. "What I'm moving for in all sincerity, Judge," Weber replied, "is to start the trial over." To which McKenna remarked, "I presumed every time you requested a mistrial, Mr. Weber, it was with sincerity."

"Let's cut the crap," Mueller barked. "I don't want to hear that. We're dealing with a serious problem right now."

After more back-and-forth Mueller announced that she would review the transcript to assess the damage and that she would hear arguments the next day.

THAT AFTERNOON, Manning examined Mickey Jones. Forty years old, Jones owned a sixty-five-acre farm at the base of Clinch Mountain on the Appalachian Plateau and rented another two hundred for his crops, beef cattle, and horses. For more than seven years he and his wife had driven a truck in order to raise the down payment on their farm. They had been married twenty-three years and had one daughter. Jones explained the sequence of events leading to his accident. On Thursday, September 4, 1985, raking his hay, he had heard a loud snap, and understood that a tine had broken off his rake, but did not stop to hunt for it. On Friday, while he had been baling the raked hay, about midday, he had discovered that the hay was not feeding correctly between the rollers of the baler. When he had looked, he had found that the baler had picked up the broken tine along with the hay, and that the tine had lodged in the feeder belt, which it was now tearing. He had shut down his equipment and removed the torn belt and took it to town to have it repaired. On Saturday, he had fetched the patched belt, then set out to reinstall it. He had turned on the tractor in order to lower the tailgate of the baler and obtain access to the belt assembly. Then, with the tractor idling, he had crawled under the baler and was feeding the belt over the rollers when the PTO had suddenly engaged, snagging his arm and drawing it between the belt and the roller, nearly severing it.

During Weber's cross-examination, he cast doubt on Jones's account. He asked him whether, when he had removed the baler belt, he had not turned on the PTO and let it run at slow speed to help remove the heavy belt. Jones admitted he had, in fact, done that, contrary to safety rules.

What was to say, then, asked Weber, that he hadn't run the PTO to put the belt back on? The belt was heavy, as Jones had just testified, and cumbersome. Wouldn't the easiest way to put it back on be to feed it to the slowly operating baler?

Jones said that would be impossible. He had been lying on his back under the baler with his fingers threading the belt onto sprocket wheels, he pointed out, something that would have been utterly impossible to do with the baler operating. Weber rephrased his question several times, leaving no doubt that despite Jones's assurances to the contrary, Weber did not believe him.

After all the farmers had been heard, Manning had a cup of coffee with Jones, who, in contrast to his composed appearance on the witness stand, was now very angry. Following his accident he had brought a suit against the Case Corporation, but had received only a small award. Manning had thoroughly reviewed the records of that case when preparing for this one, and he told Jones that he felt he had been inadequately represented by a small local lawyer with few resources.

"What do you think about reopening the case, Bill?" Jones asked eagerly. "Do you think you could do that? It would give me such satisfaction to have you go up against Case for me."

Manning looked at the thin, sad-eyed Tennessean with the mutilated arm. "I don't think so, Mickey. I hate to say this, but you've had your day in court."

Jones paused to absorb the news. The look of disappointment on his face was of a piece with all that had gone before.

CHAPTER TWENTY-SEVEN

EGINNING EARLY on Tuesday of week three, and continuing throughout much of the morning during breaks for the jury, Judge Mueller continued to grapple with the mistrial motion Weber had made following Pemberton's testimony. Weber emphasized the damage done to Case by Pemberton's statement that the dealer had told him other customers had problems with false PTO starts. Pemberton's statements had been minor, Manning countered, and the jury probably hadn't even noticed them. The real prejudice, he emphasized, would be to declare a mistrial over one or two sentences in the midst of weeks of testimony and start all over again, particularly given the thousands of dollars of trial costs that Steven already had incurred.

In the end, although Mueller felt Pemberton's statements were inappropriately prejudicial to Case, she denied Weber's motion for a mistrial and instead instructed the jury to "disregard that testimony" and struck it from the record. Weber continued to protest the result, but the trial had moved on to that day's major event, the testimony of Dwight Saunders.

Settling into the witness chair, Saunders gave the impression of a man ill at ease. He filled the chair as snugly as his chest and massive upper arms filled his taut plaid shirt, and his manner showed his usual straightforwardness mixed with uncharacteristic caution. He had undergone difficult and demeaning depositions at the hands of Scherkenbach and Weber and was wary of what he was about to undergo today. Also, shadowing his resolve to give a neutral and straightforward account of Steven's accident was some uncertainty about what the consequences would be to him personally, for the more clearly he exempted Steven from blame the more blame might be directed against him and his father. He and Stan had recently paid a significant fine to OSHA for infractions of the farm safety and maintenance code, as Weber certainly knew. Could these offenses somehow be held against him here?

After a brief examination by McKenna, who invited Saunders to relate the events of the day of Steven's accident, Weber stepped forward and placed a map of Baker County, Oregon, in front of Saunders. Weber asked Saunders to point out the whereabouts of Baker, Halfway, Richland, and even smaller towns in the area. What was the population of Richland? One hundred and seventy-five. And Halfway? Four hundred and fifty. Then Weber asked how long the families of the Saunders and the Sharps had lived in the valley, and whether they were related in any way. It appeared that Weber's intent was to portray Eagle Valley as an isolated pocket in which everyone knew everyone else, and where the bonds of loyalty were tight, at least toward outsiders, raising the possibility for jurors that Saunders might slant his testimony to defend Steven. Through these questions, the jury learned that the Sharp and Saunders families had known each other for generations; Steven's grandmother had even married Saunders's parents. They also learned that Saunders could be liable for Steven's expenses.

Weber turned to questions about the equipment on the Saunders ranch, eventually focusing on the Case tractor and Heston baler. Saunders testified, as he had during McKenna's direct examination, that he had not shown the safety manuals for either unit to Steven, and eventually acknowledged that the accident would not have occurred if Steven had shut down the tractor before attempting to clear the baler. As Weber bore down, Saunders also admitted that he was aware of the Oregon regulation requiring employers to instruct their employees to "stop engine, disconnect the power source and wait for all machine movement to stop before servicing, adjusting, cleaning or unclogging the equipment."

During McKenna's first redirect, Saunders was able to point out

that he had not been aware of the regulation at the time of the accident, and that it wasn't relevant since Steven had not been servicing,
adjusting, cleaning, or unclogging the baler when he was injured. The
regulation's relevance was also unclear, McKenna suggested and Saunders agreed, because the baler itself had no engine or power source.

Weber returned to ask Saunders whether, after Steven's accident,
they had changed at all the way they used the Case tractor on the
ranch. Saunders said they had not. And despite the horrible accident,
Weber continued, "you still don't think people should shut off tractor
engines?"

"Not if the PTO is working properly," Saunders replied.

During McKenna's final redirect, Weber approached Judge
Mueller's bench, causing McKenna to wonder into what sensitive area
he had strayed. But Weber's maneuver had nothing to do with
McKenna's question, as Saunders discovered the moment he stepped
down from the stand. As he returned to his seat, Weber intercepted
him and thrust a paper into his hand.

"What's this?" Saunders asked.

"We're initiating action against you, Mr. Saunders," Weber replied.

"What do you mean, *action*? What kind of action?"

"I'm sure Mr. Manning or Mr. McKenna can explain this to you,"
Weber replied with a tight smile. He turned and left Saunders staring
down at the document. After reading a sentence or two, Saunders,
clearly worried, looked for Manning, who at that moment, along with
McKenna and Weber, was disappearing into the judge's chambers.

"Debbie," Saunders said when he'd reached her side in the emptying courtroom, "take a look at this. We got us a problem."

In chambers Weber explained to the court and Manning and
McKenna that Case was initiating a contribution action against Saunders for a percentage of the money that would go into any award that
Case might be ordered to pay to Steven. The fact that Saunders was
present in Wisconsin gave the company jurisdiction over him, Weber
explained. "We held off on serving him until after his testimony so that
that would not be an issue in this case," he added.

Later that evening, Manning met with Saunders and his wife in
their hotel room.

"What's this mean, Bill?" asked Saunders in great agitation. He and Debbie, clearly concerned, were sitting on the twin beds in their hotel room.

"It means that if the decision goes against Case and they're ordered to pay an award to Steven, they could come after you for part of it."

"After us? How can they do that?"

"The position they're taking is that they should not be the only ones held accountable. If they have to pay, they're going to nick part of it out of your hide, on the grounds that you were partly responsible for what happened."

"Like, what are we talking here, Bill?"

"Depends on the size of the award, Dwight."

"Could it be . . . *millions?*"

"Yeah, the award could be. Your part, I don't know. There would be a formula."

Saunders was suddenly very angry. "Bill, did you know about this? Did you know that that SOB was going to pull this? Did you bring us here and deliberately not warn us?"

"Dwight, I didn't. The first I heard about it was today, along with you."

"If this goes through, honey, we'll lose the ranch right there," Debbie said.

The room felt too small for Dwight's rage and distress.

"Look, here's my take on this, Dwight," Manning said. "I'm not sure, of course, but I think they're bluffing. For one thing, I don't think they could get this to stick in Oregon. They were able to serve you because you were in Wisconsin, but I don't think it's actionable back in Oregon. Then there's the question of the bad publicity that going after you would bring. I don't think a company like J. I. Case that makes a lot of its money on agricultural products would want to be seen harassing a rancher like you. Nor do they want to call more attention to Steven's accident."

"Yeah, well then, why are they doing this?"

"To intimidate you. Like they tried to intimidate Bud by calling Toro when they heard he was going to give expert testimony. They're a big company, a multinational. Every dealing I've had with their legal department, it's been the same. Hardball. Those guys walk into the room and it's like a collective two-ton gorilla. You saw that in

Scherkenbach, and you can see it in Weber, although their styles are a little different."

"Him, I think he *enjoyed* handing me that paper."

"Dwight, I think he wanted you to feel in your bones that you made a bad choice in testifying on Steven's side."

"I gotta say for the moment he succeeded."

It was well after midnight before Manning left the Saunderses' hotel room. The next morning they flew back to Eagle Valley.

Anxious years were to pass before they concluded that Case had decided not to make good on its threat.

THAT SAME NIGHT, Betty and Steven took advantage of the late-winter thaw to take a walk after dinner. Rather than turning left toward downtown and the courthouse, their usual route, they continued straight ahead, crossed the river, and in three blocks stood in front of the original J. I. Case Company building, the bottom story of which now housed an antique machinery exhibit and the upper stories the executive suites. Above the main door perched the Case mascot, an American eagle, gripping the earth with its talons. They turned left onto a short street that led to a large parking lot and the main building of the corporation, a long, modern, six-story building in glass and steel that flowed in a semicircle around a drive and grassy oval, in the center of which stood a much larger globe gripped by a correspondingly larger and more intimidating American eagle. Originally a mascot for a Civil War regiment, when its name was "Honest Abe," and later the official mascot of the United States, the eagle preened in its present setting as a quasi-national symbol of vast industrial might, no matter that its present owner was a Japanese conglomerate. Betty and Steven crossed the parking lot and gazed at the massive building, its interior offices and corridors brightly lit.

"Somewheres around here, Mom, is the equipment shed where the jury will view the tractor and baler," Steven observed.

"I hope I do all right on the stand tomorrow," Betty said.

"You'll do fine, Mom," Steven assured her. "Just do like Bill said. Be yourself."

"It's interesting to see this place," mused Betty, "actually to stand in front of it."

"Particularly when you think that somewhere inside of it or across the street, there are people working real hard to shoot us down."

"That's scary, don't you think?" Betty asked, gazing up at the sweeping building and its fierce mascot.

"It would have been," said Steven. "We got lucky with our team, Bill and Dave. Look at poor Mickey Jones."

"Right," Betty agreed. "Think of all the injured you hear about all the time with no representation, no one pleading their case."

"I'm one of the few lucky ones."

"Yes, you are, Stevie. Thank God for that," Betty said fervently, more as an admonition than an exclamation.

MORE THAN two weeks had passed since the start of the trial when McKenna called R. E. Sharp to the stand. Fifty-eight years old, he assumed his characteristic posture when seated—round-shouldered, forward leaning, head slightly down, listening hard, favoring his left ear, his right having been damaged by diesel racket and shotgun blasts. He reported that he lived on the family farm his grandfather, J. W., had bought in 1914. His father's health had been declining of late, he said, but Leora, his mother, now in her mid-eighties, was in good health. "She's still taut as a horse." His father had made his living mainly from his fruit orchards—apple, apricot, pear, and peach—but these were no longer commercially viable due to climate change. He himself earned his living from his machinery business, Randy's Repair. He'd learned his trade at first intuitively, as a kid taking apart any machine he could get his hands on, and then in the army, where he'd been a helicopter mechanic, and then at a four-year technical college in Texas, where he'd studied mechanical engineering. Like Steven and his own father, he was dyslexic. "Well, when you're starting to read," he explained to the court, "it seemed like I would mispronounce a word and that changes everything in the whole sentence, and pretty quick, you know, nothing means anything, and so it's quite a problem."

As for his finances, R. E. explained that as with many people in the valley, barter played a big role. To illustrate his point, he mentioned his neighbors, the Forsees. "They hate mechanicing, so they don't use the shop, and I fix their machinery and then they let me work in their shop." He paid them no rent, and in return charged them no fee for repairing their equipment.

"Now, there are some other situations that you are involved with where you trade services for some other services without any money changing hands?" McKenna asked.

"Well, yeah. I know everybody in the country, and one fella I buy a little hay from to feed my own cows and mules, so I worked a little for them, and I get hay from them. If I buy a calf or two, a pig, well, we just kind of trade around."

Asked about his relationship with the Saunders family, R. E. said that while he knew them well, they were not socially close. He repaired their machinery when they asked him to. Two or three years ago, he had replaced the clutch plates on their Case 970 for the second time. How had he make that repair? "There's a unit on the back of the trac-tor," he explained, "and you take the bolts out of it and take it off of the tractor and replace the clutches in it and the gasket and kind of hook it over a little bit, and you just put it back in and away you go." He said the service manuals have "exploded views" of the units, and he used them quite a bit. He doesn't order parts by number, because "I trans-pose numbers so bad that it kind of messes me up. All you got to do is mess up one number and you get something different. So I just tell the dealer what I need, and he sends it."

At the time that he had made that second repair, at Stan Saun-ders's request, he had also welded a steel bar on the baler to make the rollers fit more tightly together. "The hay was pretty slippery, and it wasn't catching in them rows, so I welded that bar on there. It seemed to help a little."

Was R. E. close to Steven while his son was growing up? McKenna asked.

"Yes, we were. We were real close. Of course hunting is what we enjoyed doing, and he really liked to fish, and we done a lot of that, and then we'd run around together quite a little."

"When you say 'run around together' . . . ?"

"Well, run around through the mountains."

"I see," McKenna said.

"I'd put him on an old pack mule and away we'd go."

He and Betty had also taken a great interest in Steven's hobbies, he said. They had attended his 4-H fairs and followed him all over the county when he had been playing Little League baseball. For much of Steven's childhood, R. E. had thought that he might very well have developed into an artist: "He really enjoyed art. He'd draw pictures. I mean, first time I noticed him drawing pictures he was in the backseat of church drawing a few pictures instead of listening, and then he started school and they started him painting things and he got real interested in it." Along with all of his other interests, Steven had been interested in making money, R. E. said. "He was the kind of boy that wanted to have money, a little money to spend, and he always had his own calculator out there, figuring how much them little 4-H pigs was going to bring him. So he was pretty interested in having a little spending money. The rest of the kids always bum a little from him. They'd spend it faster than they made it." Working for the Saunderses was the first steady job Steven had had, he said.

Asked the inevitable question about his and Betty's reaction to their son's injury, R. E. paused, took a breath, and then said softly, "Well, we wasn't so good. I mean, breaks your heart to see a kid lose his arms." He added that Steven, to a certain degree, had alleviated their distress.

"What was Steven's attitude toward all this during the first few months after his injury?" McKenna asked.

"Well, I couldn't see that he was mad at anyone or down. He just . . . That was part of his life, and he just put up, you know, did it. It's real aggravating trying to do things without any hands, but he'd keep working at it till he got her done."

But now, McKenna wanted to know, what was Steven's present attitude, four years after his accident?

"Well, he's really good," R. E. replied. "I mean, he doesn't seem . . . He just works at things and tries to figure out different things he can do, and I mean, you know, I don't know what to say about that. He doesn't seem to be mad at anybody, or he doesn't seem to be happy, he does what he can."

Weber cross-examined R. E. carefully on the various phases of his career, apparently with the idea of showing that, contrary to the impression left by McKenna of R. E. as a mechanic who had not gone deeply into the Saunderses' machine and who had simply carried out a few elementary repairs on it, he was instead a well-trained, up-to-date mechanic.

"So handling farm equipment properly requires some training, right?" Weber asked.

"Yes."

"And requires you to follow that training, right?"

"Yes."

"Because this can be sophisticated equipment, right?"

"Well, not really sophisticated in this day and age, I wouldn't say. It don't have computers and all that kind of thing. Big hammer and screwdriver, you can fix most of it."

"In fact, you went to training classes sponsored by the manufacturer every year, didn't you?" Weber asked.

"Yes."

Having tried to suggest a mechanic fully aware of what he was doing, Weber proceeded to probe the wound of R. E.'s inadvertent role in his son's dismemberment.

Weber began, "Let's talk about the Heston baler next, all right?"

"Okay."

"As Mr. Saunders testified, you put a bead, a weld on that metal roller?"

"Yes, sir."

"And the reason to do that was to make the baler more aggressive in pulling the hay in, right?"

"Yes."

"So it would get a better grip and really pull it in?"

"Yes."

Weber paused to let the full implications of this exchange sink in, then, after a few more questions, concluded his cross.

R. E. stepped down slowly from the witness stand. He was upset, puzzled as to what Weber's point might have been with this last set of questions if not simply to turn the knife in his wound.

BETTY TOOK the stand in a noticeably hushed and attentive court-room. The jury had been observing this apparently serene and composed woman for weeks, but not once had they heard her voice. She sat down, smoothed her skirt over her knees, and looked up at McKenna. "Are you a little nervous about speaking in public?" he asked. "I am pretty nervous," she admitted. Yet she spoke in a calm conversational voice, a slight western twang sharpening her vowels, keeping her gaze fixed on McKenna, as if speaking to him alone.

She had been born in central Oregon and raised along the Oregon coast, in the southwest part of the state, she said in response to his first questions. Her father had been a truck driver, her mother had mostly been a housewife but had held a few odd jobs. After high school Betty had begun working in a nursing home and intended to go on to nursing school, but had moved to Baker City when her elderly grandparents had required care.

"I was the only one that wasn't working at the time in the family, so I went down there to help them out, and met my husband and stayed there." She'd met R. E. in April and married him in August. After her marriage and before her three children were born, she had worked variously at a nursing home, a motel, and a restaurant. Then later, after her kids became teenagers, she had taken a job cooking at the Longbranch Grille in Richland, and done some work at the grade school [she had also kept the books for R. E.'s business, Randy's Repair]. At the time of Steven's accident, she had been bringing home about $300 a month.

Asked about Steven as a boy, she said he had been a normal, busy kid with lots of interests—painting, drawing, raising 4-H animals, baseball, hunting and fishing, earning money—but that his tireless energy had been crimped by occasional attacks of asthma and migraines. The afternoon Steven had been hurt, she had been home alone canning peaches. She had just been about to make a late lunch for herself and R. E. when the call had come from Debbie Saunders.

"From that phone call, did you learn how seriously Steven had been hurt?" McKenna asked.

"Yes. She didn't go into great detail. She said he got his arms stuck in the baler and lost them both."

Manning and McKenna had run through the questions she would be asked on the witness stand, so she was prepared when McKenna posed the inevitable next but scarcely answerable question: "How did you feel about that?"

"Pretty bad," she said simply. An utterly banal and inadequate phrase was all she could trust herself to give and maintain her composure. She briefly described her and R. E.'s arrival at the Saunders farm after Steven had already been taken to the hospital, and their first encounter with him in the emergency room.

"Did you have time up to that point to get any members of your family involved in any way?"

"No. I think they tried to get hold of my daughter that lives in Baker, and she was out of town at the time. Ed that lives out in the valley where we live was contacted and he did come out."

McKenna went on to ask her about the details of the day, the trip to the hospital in Baker, then Steven's flight to Portland.

"Why didn't you or your husband fly with Steven?" McKenna asked.

"There was just room for one of us in the plane, and I felt like we needed to be together, and I don't think either one of us could have driven over there alone. I said we'll just drive over together."

"What was Steven's demeanor and his attitude in the hospital in Baker City before he went to Portland?"

Betty paused to consider her answer. "He was being brave," she said. "He was trying to handle it like a mature young man. He was certainly braver than his father and I were. At one time, I recall him telling me, 'Calm down, Mom. Just calm down. It will be OK.' "

"Did that help?"

"No," she replied, with a catch in her throat.

McKenna went on to establish that for the first weeks of Steven's stay in the hospital, Betty and R. E. had slept in his room, Betty providing much of Steven's personal care and hygiene, which she had continued to do until moving to the nearby Ronald McDonald house. She responded to questions about Steven's heavy pain medication after returning home and his resultant disorientation, specifically on the day he was interviewed by Gerald Beverage, the OSHA inspector. Betty had been upset that Steven was willing to talk to Beverage despite his groggy condition, but she had not intervened.

"Do you consider yourself to be an assertive person?" McKenna asked her.

"No, not really," she replied.

McKenna turned to Steven's rehabilitation, which had been rapid. While he had had no problem accepting help from others, mainly his friends, he had been eager to resume independent control of his life.

He could handle himself alone in the mountains, picking mushrooms, working with a single prosthesis? McKenna asked.

"Yes," Betty answered.

Weber elected not to cross-examine Betty Sharp.

As she stepped down from the stand, her expression calm and her manner steady, Manning realized that he could have spared his worry about her composure. By now, as far as he could tell, beneath her mild appearance Betty had built something like an emotional fire wall. When he had sat preparing her to give testimony, posing difficult and invasive questions of the sort Weber conceivably might have asked, she had not cracked. Her answers had been terse, but there had been no tears. In fact, the only time during this process when he had disturbed her composure, he had done so accidentally. In the course of one of their early conversations, he had asked her about Steven's living arrangements after he moved to Medford, where he had attended business school.

"What was his place like?" Manning had asked, casually.

"It was pretty bad," Betty replied.

"Bad? What do you mean, bad?"

With surprising fierceness, as if her impeccable homemaker's sense had been deeply offended, she enumerated. "Oh Bill, there were broken lightbulbs, a torn lampshade, scratched paint on all the cupboards and drawers, nicks, scratches, and gouges everywhere. Damaged wall sockets. You can't imagine, Bill, the amount of damage that hook had done in a few short weeks."

Of course, Manning reflected, flipping switches and pulling light chains, opening and closing drawers, hooking and unhooking latches, all with something like giant pliers, could do a lot of damage quickly.

"It was terrible," Betty said, her voice breaking as she relived her initial shock and what that shock had abruptly revealed to her about Steven's new life. "But Stevie told me he was getting better with his hook. He was learning to regulate its impact. It would take time, he said, and then he'd get the whole place painted and fixed up again. But the worst thing, Bill, was when he made me breakfast. He insisted on it, wanted to make me scrambled eggs and bacon, toast and coffee, just like at home, you know, I guess to show that he could do it. So I sat there in the kitchen and watched him work and tried to act like everything was normal. But at that point Stevie couldn't really handle a spatula with his hook." Her voice caught. She went on, "Flip it, you know." She took a breath. "So he used his mouth and teeth to hold it. And when he set my plate down on the table, he had burned his face and covered his glasses with hot bacon fat."

As she finished the story, she cried in earnest.

AT DINNER THAT NIGHT, after Betty testified, R. E., in reviewing his and Betty's testimonies, mentioned in his typical low-key manner that he'd been surprised when he was on the stand by the final move of Weber's in emphasizing that R. E. had rendered the Saunders baler more aggressive. Manning looked grim and shook his head, as if sympathizing with R. E. but holding back a comment for reasons he was reluctant to voice. Noting the dark look on Manning's face, Betty interjected in her mild, peacemaking manner, "Well, we can't blame Mr. Weber for just doing his job. Just like Bill's doing everything he can for us, he's doing the same thing on the other side."

CHAPTER TWENTY-EIGHT

NOW MANNING recalled the three Case witnesses who had testified earlier, as well as one new one, Edwin Heys, senior technical specialist for product safety and regulations, and the only Case witness still actively employed by the company. Heys had worked for Case for thirty-one years, and presently, among other duties, he had oversight responsibility for the safety of the 970. Heys had also been supervisor of tractor field testing for Case during the development of the 70-series tractor.

As had been his strategy with the former Case employees who had testified at the start of the trial, Manning sought to establish through Heys that safety had not been an adequate concern during the development and testing of the tractor. Even now, Heys acknowledged, despite his role in safety oversight, he could not name any of the members of the company's executive product safety committee.

Heys also admitted that no one individual had had the "specific assignment" of ensuring that the tractors met applicable safety standards back in 1969. It was not until some point later in time that a particular individual at the company had been formally entrusted with that responsibility. But he also testified that safety was a high priority for all designers and, under later questioning from Weber, emphasized its importance during the specific testing done on the 70-series tractors. "We certainly wanted to know as soon as possible any time any safety issue or anything that anyone thought might be a safety issue would come up so it could be addressed and corrected."

Manning's questions about the adequacy of Case's post-accident investigations also gave Heys the opportunity to make clear that he felt that Steven was solely responsible for his own injuries. From Heys's standpoint, Steven's accident did not raise safety issues about the tractor at all.

"Why not?" queried Manning.

"My understanding from Sharp, if he had placed the lever—if he had done two things: If he had placed the lever in the disengaged position, I don't believe there will be any problem whatsoever; if he had shut the engine off as we instruct, there would have been no problem whatsoever."

Three weeks into the trial, on a Tuesday morning, the jury was to leave the courtroom to view the accident tractor and baler. Manning and McKenna and some aides drove in advance of the bus carrying the jury members to Case's equipment garage. The two lawyers wanted to check on the six-foot cordon the judge had agreed to. Manning wanted the jury to remain at this remove from the baler so as not to be able to lean into it. Walking into the hangar-like building, he saw with alarm that the cordon had been moved so it now stood within six feet of the baler. A Manning team member then started taking photographs of the cordon in its present position, so that the distance was preserved for the record. While strenuously objecting about the whole process to Judge Mueller, Manning caught sight of North climbing into the cab of the tractor.

"Stay out of there, Mr. North," Manning burst out angrily. "We discussed that yesterday," he continued, referring to North's inspection of the baler the previous evening, while the tractor and baler were being set up in preparation for the jury's visit. Manning had vigorously renewed his objections to the viewing just prior to coming out to the site. Now his frustration exploded. For the moment the threat of physical violence hung in the air.

North gave him a startled glance and stepped down from the cab. Manning turned toward the judge and began in seething tones to put his objections on record. "I find it incredible that I mean, here, once again Mr. North is trying to get into the cab of the tractor. And that is just a part of the serious prejudice that's going to be introduced by having the jury look at this equipment."

Before the judge could reply, Manning continued to ride the wave of his anger, strongly objecting to the placement of the cordons around the site, which had been moved closer to the baler by Weber so that the jurors could peer directly into it. "If this is allowed, then absolutely these jurors should be allowed to deal with this lever and see how easily it gets hung up on the back lip, because what we are doing here, what the court's allowing, is a re-creation in effect of Steven Sharp's accident. So we are severely prejudiced now by this view. I'm very concerned about this view going forward."

The judge agreed to move the perimeter back somewhat, so that the jurors could see into the baler but not "lean" into it. The jury members could get into the cab, as the lawyers had agreed earlier, but not handle the controls.

Judge Mueller then turned and signaled to the bailiff to admit the jury, as well as the waiting journalists. Several photographers mounted the high catwalks that crisscrossed the ceiling space and recorded the scene. For the next ten minutes the jury milled about, many of them climbing into the tractor cab. All of them walked close to the baler and leaned over the cordon, moving it forward with the pressure of their bodies, exactly as Manning had feared. He was now constrained to silence, however. He and McKenna on one side and Weber on the other moved casually about on the perimeter of the group with a look of studied neutrality on their faces. But Judge Mueller remained acutely aware of the underlying tension between the two sides, and of the prospect of much retrospective wrangling about the outing. She called a speedy halt to the viewing after twelve minutes.

MANNING BELIEVED that the only weapon in his possession strong enough to counteract the inevitably negative effects of the equipment viewing was Steven himself. Accordingly, as soon as the court had resumed session, Manning called Steven to the stand.* Outwardly,

*For this part of Steven's testimony, liberties have been taken with the order of the testimony to make it easier for the reader to grasp the chronology of events surrounding Steven's accident. Of course, no changes have been made in the actual testimony or in Bill Manning's questions.

Manning's mood had changed radically from the angry one he had shown North and the judge in the equipment hangar. He was calm and composed as he called Steven to the stand. There was almost no color in Steven's face, the tension stiffening him. He wore cowboy boots, simple blue pants, and a short-sleeve blue shirt.

Manning ran through basic background questions about Steven's family and schooling. The give-and-take of question and answer seemed to settle Steven's initial nervousness. He sat leaning forward in the witness chair, his hook resting on his knee, his other stump bare. He kept his eyes fixed on Manning as the lawyer moved around in the open space in front of the bench among his exhibits.

Manning moved on to questions about Steven's familiarity with tractors and balers. Steven said he'd been driving a tractor on his grandfather's farm since he was nine, and baling hay for him since he was a teenager. At the Saunderses', Dwight and Stan Saunders and Barry Neal had all instructed him in the use of the Case 970 and the Heston baler.

In the course of his summer of work, with its three cuttings of hay, Steven had done between 800 and 1,000 bales, each weighing about half a ton. Manning asked him what sort of difficulties he'd encountered, particularly in August, with the third cutting.

The main problem, Steven said, was that the hay was dry and thin, so it tended to bunch up in front of the baler intake. "When you're baling along, you can actually hear the hay smashing as it goes through the rollers. So as you're going along and you quit hearing that sound, you look back to check what's going on. A lot of times the hay would be in front of your rollers and there on the pickup teeth and in front of that, kind of snowplowing.

"You push in your clutch and hit your brake. You look back and make sure everything's fine. You reach up and you run your rpms up just a little bit. Sometimes the hay will suck through and it's a lot better than having to get off and pull it all out. If it don't, you run your rpms back down and turn your PTO off, then park your tractor sidehill, get off, go back there, and clean it out."

Manning then led him through the entire process more slowly, bringing Steven to a key point of emphasis.

"In that process that you've described, did anybody, to your knowledge, ever tell you that when you got off, that you ought to turn the tractor off?"

"No."

"Was that ever mentioned to you in any way that you know in your whole life?"

"No."

Manning asked whether anyone in the valley—his father, or Dwight, or Stan, or even Barry Neal, who had worked with Steven at the Saunders farm—had ever told him to turn off the tractor when removing hay from the intake.

"No," said Steven with quiet emphasis. His voice, which had been low at the start, was now steady and clear.

After a while, Manning focused in on that fateful August day. "And tell us then, if you will," Manning said, "what you experienced on the baler in the field that day."

"Okay. I was baling along and I saw Stan leave for lunch and he waved at me. I probably baled for another fifteen, twenty minutes and I had just finished going down—going up a row and I was turning around and was coming down, and I was about three-quarters of the way down, when I could hear the hay not feeding into the equipment. So I stopped, pushed on the clutch and the brake, looked back, and seen that it was starting to bunch up in front of the rollers. I reached down and I ran my rpms up a little, ran it back down, kicked my PTO . . ."

"When you put your PTO down," Manning broke in, "did you do it the same way that you had done it all summer when you turned the PTO off?"

"Yeah. I pulled the T-bar thing and just slammed her back."

"OK. Go ahead."

"I slammed the lever back and turned it off and I put the thing in reverse, reversed back up the hill, and then I put her in drive and pulled sidehill. Put it in park, reached down, put my emergency brake on, jumped out of the tractor, went back there and I leaned over that bar," he said, pointing to a photo of the baler Manning had standing as an exhibit.

"I'll point it out," Manning said.

"OK. I was standing in front of that bar and I was reaching over it. The bar was about waist high when I leaned down in there, so I had about a foot that I was away from the equipment, and I was reaching down there in front of those rollers, and I reached all the way across. I took my right hand and put it on the rubber roller and I reached across and scraped the hay over to the side where I was standing, so that I could just pick it up and bring it out."

"You put your right hand on a rubber roller?"

"No. I put my left hand on the rubber roller."

"The hay was in front of the rollers?"

"Yes, it was."

"It wasn't in the rollers?"

"No, it was not."

"So you swept that hay?"

"Yes."

"Did you get it?"

"Yes, I got most of it. When you pick the hay up and lift it out, some of it falls back down in front of the rollers, so I had to get that out too. So I walked around and threw the hay back into the windrow so I could come around and do it again. I walked back around and I seen more hay sitting down in here, sitting right about there." He pointed again.

"That was hay that had fallen down when you were pulling out the other hay?" Manning asked.

"Yes. It was just loose hay that was setting down in there, so I reached back down in there again. When I reached down in there there was a little bit of hay that was in between the two rollers and that was just in the process of feeding through when I turned the piece of equipment off. It wasn't stuck in there, and there was very little of it. I always made a practice of cleaning it out real good because it beats having to stop and do it all over again. So I had my left hand in a fist on the top rubber roller . . ."

As Steven started to describe the accident, Manning interrupted. "We're going to go through that process," said Manning, "but before we do, when you were standing there, leaning over that bar, is that something you had done many times that summer?"

"Yes. That's the only way you can get that hay out of there."

"OK. Now let's go back then to your left hand is in a fist," Manning prompted after a few brief questions.

"Yes."

"It's on top of a rubber roller?"

"Yeah."

"And towards the right side you say there's a little hay about this distance?" Manning pointed.

"Right. It's just, you know, kind of feathered out. It was hay in the process of feeding through."

"Did that hay stop the rollers from turning?" Manning asked pointedly.

"No, it did not."

Manning repeated the question in various guises three times, pounding home the fact that there had been no obstructive clog and confirming again that Steven had shut off the PTO.

"Then what happened?" he asked.

"I was just reaching for the hay that was in between the rollers, and just about the time I grabbed it, I didn't have a chance to pull on it or push on it or nothing, because just about the time I grabbed it, the equipment turned on. When it did, it wasn't the hay that pulled me in, it was rollers spinning. It spun my hand down in there, my left one and pulled it in, and almost simultaneously it pulled my right one in and when it did that, it goes up to about my wrist and it slowly pulled me in."

"And did you try to pull them out?"

"Well, see, I really didn't realize what happened at first because it startled me. The thing started up real fast. It was just on. And it went up to about my wrist and my first reaction was to reach over with my left leg and hook it like on that jack and underneath where the baling twine box is." He pointed at the photo.

"I'll show the jury what you're referring to."

Then Manning asked, "How far up on your arms were the rollers at that stage?"

"A little above my wrists."

"Were the rollers still turning?"

"Yes, they were."

Some faces in the jury took on expressions of tension. Betty stared at Steven with great pity as he launched into the difficult part of his testimony, and with great if appalled interest as well. Steven had never told her the details of his ordeal.

"You were obviously in pain," Manning said.

"At first it was kind of a numb feeling like your leg goes to sleep. That numbness went away with time."

"And then it hurt?"

"Oh, yes," Steven replied simply.

"What happened next, if you can describe to us exactly how it happened?"

"Well, the equipment was pulling me in and I think that tractor is ninety horse, ninety horsepower, the PTO, so I couldn't pull myself back out. So as I stood there, it slowly pulled me in. It popped my knee out and my hip out and I had my head stuck up against the straps, trying to hold myself out; and it just slowly sucked me in, and finally it got up to about . . . I don't know . . . about four or five inches below my elbows and I seen my left elbow joint, my right elbow joint, half of it. It pulled half of it off. What it did, you can just see it kind of sucked through the meat and the skin and I saw it go through to the other side of the roller."

"You actually saw your right arm on the other side of the rollers then?" Manning asked.

"Yes, I could. Then it broke this left one here off about three or four inches below my elbow and put the bones on the other side of the roller, but I still couldn't get out because the bones were on one side and the flesh was hooked to the bones and the flesh that was in between the rollers flattened out, you know, your arm's about that wide but because they were so flattened out it wouldn't grind them off. They were still stuck to my stumps at that time. Then I brought my left leg back down. I popped my knee back in. I couldn't get leverage to pop my hip back in because by that time I'd lost the foot of distance between my hip and that bar because it just slowly sucked me in."

"Now, your stomach was up against this bar?" Manning asked, pointing at the photo.

"Yes, it was."

"OK."

"So now it was just the rollers rubbing on the flesh, so there wasn't really much pull. I yelled for help for a while, you know, I yelled for five, ten minutes. No one came. I figured if someone was going to come, they would have heard me by then. I figured I had to get out. I noticed when I was setting in there . . . I was pulling, I was pulling as hard as I could. I noticed when I turned my arm a little bit that the ends of the flesh would flip over itself and grind a little bit of it off. So that, to me, was the way for me to get out."

"How much time had elapsed now before you started cutting off your own arms?"

"Probably five, ten minutes. What I did"—he paused—"I just kept turning them and I kept rotating them and the more I rotated them, the more flesh got ground off on this steel ridge, and the size of the flesh that was in between the rollers just kept getting smaller. I also noticed when I was in there that if I pushed my stumps forward, see, there was much more pull. If I pushed my stump forward in the rollers, the rubber roller would burn and cauterize my stumps so I wouldn't bleed to death. I'd learned in school in health class that you can bleed to death real quick."

"Was there blood?"

"Yes, there was."

"Did the rubber roller burn?"

"Yes, it did. The rubber roller is just made of black charlike stuff. It just built up on my arms and cauterized it."

"To cauterize your arms, you pushed both arms on those rollers?"

"Yes, I did."

"That was something you did through your own effort? In addition to the pull?"

"Yes, I did. But the bad thing about that was, as they cauterized my arms, they were burning my flesh and because of the position I was in, I couldn't get my head away from my arms, so I could smell them, and that was real rough."

Manning glanced at the jury. "Did you, when you were twisting your arms, did you have to rest in between twisting them?"

"Oh, yes. I did it in spurts because I was losing energy. I'd lost a lot of blood and I was thirsty and tired and my stomach hurt and my legs hurt and so I would just take a break. There wasn't much pull, so I would just rest. I set there. Turn and turn and turn. Then I was getting to the point where I was starting to black out so I would just take a break for a while. I probably did that for, I don't know, five or six different times. I kept turning and I'd wait and do it again."

"Turn them, both arms at the same time, or one arm and then the other?"

"Most of the time both of them at the same time. I was, you know, I was doing it quick. I was trying to get out of there. I wasn't just setting there trying slowly. I was jerking and pulling and really trying to get out."

"Were you concerned about keeping your head?"

"Oh, yes. I knew that if I lost my head and panicked that there was a good chance I wouldn't get out."

"Was that why you were resting?"

"Yes. I was resting because of that and also because I didn't want to pass out in that baler because, you know, Stan's up getting lunch. No one else is coming to look for me. Barry's job is done. He went to see his girlfriend. I was there by myself."

"So you knew you had to do it yourself?"

"Yes."

"Tell us how you got out, then. What happened?"

"I just kept turning it and turning it and finally I got to the point where I just couldn't do no more. I gave one more pull and this, the left arm, just kind of came out. As I was twisting it, I finally ground it the rest of the way off. This one here, when I pulled, there was about an inch of flesh that was left that just slipped out between the rollers, and it was kind of weird because right then I got very happy. I thought, man, I got one out. I'm almost there. So I turned around and I went to grab a bar. Kind of weird. I don't know if you guys understand it. There's a thing called phantom pain. You can still feel your fingers. As time goes on, it gets less. I could still feel my hand. I reached up and I grabbed the bar there with my hand."

"What bar did you grab?"

Steven pointed at the photo. "Right there. I grabbed it with my hand. It was weird because I could feel it in my hand. It was cold. I could feel it. I pulled a couple of times. I was delirious. I wasn't think-ing. I was pretty well out of it. I pulled a couple of times. I realized, man, that was kind of stupid, so I reached up with my elbow and I still had my elbow joint, and I hooked my elbow around and while before I couldn't turn my body, couldn't do nothing, after this one got out, I could turn my body and then I could get my right leg underneath me. So my right foot was down here now instead of it pulling me forward, I could turn my body sideways and I could get my right leg against it. I popped my left hip back in. I turned sideways and I started pulling and I was pulling with my leg and my elbow, pulling like this, trying to pull it out. And I gave three big jerks. In between the jerks, I had to rest."

"How long did you rest?"

"Oh, it's kind of hard telling because, you know, you're in and out of it. I lost a lot of blood. My body is wanting to go into shock. I was thirsty. I hurt everywhere, maybe a minute, two minutes, three. I'm really not sure."

"OK."

"On the third jerk, I finally got it out. And as I pulled, I staggered backwards. It was kind of weird because after going through all that, you know, lost a lot of blood, my first reaction was to see what hap-pened, was to turn around, walk over and get in that tractor and see what happened because I had no clue. The PTO just turned on. So I turned around and I walked over to the tractor and I grabbed ahold of the bar with my hand to pull myself in, but of course I didn't have no hand."

"The bar by the steps of the tractor?"

"Yes. I went to pull myself in. It was like there was nothing there so then right then I thought, man, that was stupid. I kind of stepped around and I leaned up against the tire that's right there by the door of the tractor and I caught my breath and got myself settled, got my head about me, and I was pointed toward the house. My first reaction was to start running. I tried running but that didn't work because my balance was off. I couldn't run right and I was afraid if I fell down, I wouldn't get back up."

"You actually tried running, though?"

"Yes, I did."

"Didn't work?"

"No, it didn't."

"Okay. What did you do then?"

"So then there was a fence that ran right up to the house, and by that time, I was losing my sight a lot. I couldn't see far in front of me. I couldn't do a lot."

"Were your glasses on?"

"No. I lost them, them and my hat both, during the thing. As I was walking, I walked over to the fence to get my bearings so I wouldn't get confused as I was walking up there. My left elbow went into convulsions like it wasn't stopping and the extra flesh kept hitting me. That really bothered me, and I finally got it hooked behind my back and got it stopped doing that. I got over to the fence and I leaned up against the barbed-wire fence and rested. I just looked forward and I focused on the fence post because I was losing my sight. I just walked to the fence post. When I got to the fence post, I thought, man, that was pretty good, so I'd focus on another one. I probably took sometimes one fence post at a time, sometimes two at a time until I got up to the gate."

"How long did that take you? Do you have any idea?"

"Probably five, ten minutes. I took a lot of rests. I fell down. I would just lean up against the barbed-wire fence so I could just completely relax, then I'd get going again."

"And then?"

"I got up to the gate. I don't remember going through the gate or going onto the road. Just all of a sudden I came to and I was on my knees. There was a little hill going up to the house. It was only, you know, maybe, two, three feet tall, not much of a grade and I think what happened was, my legs went out from underneath me, I went to my knees, I was on a hill and I kind of came to, so I just rocked backwards back up on to my feet, kind of fell down the hill, got up on my feet, and I tried it again. At that time I was real weak. It was hard getting up that hill. I probably went and tried two or three different times to get up it. Finally, once I got up it, all I could really see was the red house and a kind of green to the grass."

"How did you finally get up the hill? How did you actually do it?"

"I finally had to back up and get a run at it. I finally got up there. And once I did, I put my right shoulder up to the side of the house and walked until I found the edge of the building."

"Couldn't you see?"

"I really couldn't see much, and also that way I could lean up against something so I didn't fall over again because getting back up was pretty rough. When I got to the corner of the house, I turned and went again and just ran my shoulder up against the house till I got to the next corner. Then I turned and the door was open and [after I kicked it] the screen door was open. I walked in the door and Stan was there in his chair and I don't know if he was asleep or half asleep or what he was and I hid my arms behind me because I knew he had a bad heart, and I didn't want to startle him too bad. If he could have a heart attack on me, I couldn't dial the phone. I needed someone to do that."

"Those thoughts actually crossed your mind?"

"Yes, they did. I kind of tried hiding my stump behind me, behind my back. I yelled at him once. I yelled at him again. I told him what happened. He went into shock and fell down. When he got up, he just stood there and looked at me. Then I yelled at him a couple more times to call 911. I said, call 911. The baler chewed my arms off. I need help. Finally, he ran over there and he called 911. You're supposed to stay on the phone. He hung up on them. He couldn't remember his address. All he could remember was Saunderses' ranch."

Manning asked him what he had done while waiting for the ambulance.

"I was bleeding a little bit and I didn't want to lose no more blood because I was going out, in and out of consciousness. I took my stumps and put them on the legs of my pants and I just leaned forward on them and put all the pressure I could on my stumps to help myself from bleeding."

The ambulance arrived.

"They brought the stretcher. I told them I could walk to the ambulance. I didn't want to get on the stretcher. They told me I had to get on the stretcher. I got on the stretcher. They took me out the door. As I got to the back of the ambulance, I told them I ain't leaving without my arms. I want them. I don't think they can put them back on but I want them to go with me. So they grabbed a cooler. A cop was there at the time and I think he got one of the arms and he got the cooler in with me and told me that both the arms were in there so I would go with them."

Manning asked a few more questions about the accident, and handed Steven's questioning to Dave McKenna, who would focus on the damages portion of the testimony. Soon after, the judge called for a recess. Betty and R. E. were both weeping, as were several jury members. Steven stepped down from the stand while Manning slowly put the notebook labeled "Steven Sharp" back into his briefcase.

CHAPTER TWENTY-NINE

A FTER THE LUNCH BREAK, McKenna took Steven through testimony that detailed his active life prior to the accident, from sports and outdoor activities, to school and family and friends. McKenna then moved seamlessly into questions about Steven's post-accident medical history, spelling out the long list of arduous operations and therapies he had undergone. Steven narrated for the jury a video of scenes from a typical day in Steven's life showing some of the difficulties his client inevitably encountered. Despite Steven's remarkable dexterity with his prosthesis, certain basic objects remained difficult for him to handle—items of clothing like socks and buttons, everyday objects like round doorknobs and certain types of silverware. After the video ended, McKenna moved seamlessly into questions about Steven's post-accident medical history, spelling out the long list of arduous operations and therapies he had undergone.

McKenna asked Steven about his continuing problems with phantom pain and neuromas. Three years after the event he was subject to persistent muscle and nerve pain due to the constant stress in his shoulders and back as he bent his muscles to physiologically inappropriate tasks.

To demonstrate this last point, McKenna asked Steven to remove his shirt and show the jury how he operated his prosthesis. Steven had been warned about this request and had steeled himself accordingly. Stoically he pulled open the snaps on his shirt and shrugged out of it without apparent embarrassment, answering McKenna's extensive questions quietly. Several times he had to raise his voice in order to be heard. Later Steven told Manning he'd felt "like a duck on a pond" in taking off his shirt.

Manning was unfamiliar with the expression.

"When you see a duck sitting out there on a pond," Steven explained, "it looks calm as can be, just floating along. Get close, though, and look down through the water at its feet and they're paddling like crazy. Well, when I had to take off my shirt in court and give the jury a demonstration of how everything worked, my heart was moving like that duck's feet. I would of thought you could of heard it."

Once Steven had resumed his seat on the witness stand, McKenna concluded his questions by asking about activities that gave him enjoyment. Did he still hunt and fish?

Yes, Steven replied that he continued to do both, although inevitably with less satisfaction than before. Nevertheless, he would continue to spend a lot of time in the woods and the mountains because that's simply who he was. As for his future work, the picture was far less clear. "Do you know what you are going to do with your life from an occupational point of view?" McKenna asked.

"No, I don't."

"How does it feel not to know?"

"Kind of scary," Steven answered in a low voice.

"Sorry?"

"It's kind of scary," Steven repeated more forcefully, "I said."

"Do you have confidence in your ability to continue to adapt and adjust to these injuries?"

"Oh, yes."

"So do I have," McKenna said as he concluded his questioning.

STEVEN AND his lawyers had now presented as complete a picture of his accident, recovery, and present condition as they could devise. Now it was Weber's turn to cross-examine Steven and wring from him the admissions he had earlier promised to the judge and jury—namely, that Steven had not turned off the PTO and that he had set the baler's rollers in motion by removing the clog that was supposedly jamming them. For Weber, this was the moment, the showdown, the moment to make Steven blink. But facing him on the stand would no longer be the naïve and open Steven of his first deposition. Every evening for the last five days Manning had drilled Steven in question and response, preparing him for his own and McKenna's questions but most of all for Weber's. Placing Steven in a chair, he had run through various sequences of questions, deliberately probing into sensitive areas and using tones of voice and attitudes that might prove upsetting to Steven. He had tried to anger and confuse him, trip him up logically or startle him with something unexpected. "He might try to trip you up with questions about your dad, or the Saunderses, or even Barry, but sooner or later he's going to try to get you to say that the baler was jammed with a clog. Because his whole theory rests on the one point that the PTO stopped working because the baler was clogged, not because you turned it off. And if you didn't turn off the PTO, our entire case is shot. So you've got to watch him like a hawk."

Indeed, Weber did move toward the question of a clog, but so indirectly that at first it was difficult for Steven to follow the drift of his questions. Weber wanted to know very precisely about Steven's posture in front of the baler. How had he been standing when he had first reached in for the hay? How had he been leaning? Had he been off balance? Had he been standing on one leg or two? How far into the intake had he leaned? When Steven's recollection of his movements failed to fit precisely with his deposition account, Weber tried to impeach him. Manning prevented this, however, by demanding that each disputed passage be read in its full context. Meanwhile, Steven was laboriously trying to follow along in the transcript. When this proved too difficult, Manning requested permission to stand at his side and read to him.

Eventually the questioning narrowed down to whether it had been Steven's left or right hand that had first slipped between the rollers. Steven said that his left had gotten caught a second or two before the right, but that the two events had been nearly simultaneous. Weber disputed this and for some minutes a macabre debate ensued as to how quickly and in what order Steven's hands had been captured. Weber's apparent objective with this reconstruction was to suggest that Steven had been standing in front of the baler and pushing on the roller for leverage with his left hand while pulling with his right on the putative clog. As Weber saw it, Steven's left had gone into the rollers in the instant when the right had succeeded in yanking out the clog. The goal of twenty minutes of questioning funneled down to locking Steven into this precise sequence.

But Steven refused to go along with it. On the second swipe, he had balanced himself against the roller with his left hand as he bent down and attempted to grab the remaining hay with his right. But before he could pull that hay out, the roller started moving, pulling his left hand in.

"Would you agree with me," Weber asked, "if you're just reaching in to pick up some loose material that doesn't have any resistance, that you can reach farther if you reach in with one hand and tilt your body toward the side that you're reaching?"

Manning objected that Weber was asking an expert question, but the judge allowed Steven to answer. "The way that thing is set," Steven said, "you can't tilt your body and go in. You gotta go in straight."

"So you don't think it's possible in that baler to tilt your body to reach in farther if you're picking up just loose material, just to sweep in with the one hand with your body tilted toward your hand?"

Steven seemed unclear about Weber's point, but understood it to be a tricky one. "It's probably possible. That's not the way I did it," he said.

Since indirection was not working, Weber tried a more straightforward approach. "Now, if, on the other hand, you are trying to pull out something that is resisting—let's talk about that alternative, OK—that what you're trying to get is not loose but is actually jammed in between the rollers. Are you with me?"

No, Steven said he was not with him. "See," he explained, "the thing with going in with one hand don't make no sense. You have to go in with two to scoop it. You have to go in with both hands to get that little bit you dropped down there."

"Let's talk about a different alternative," Weber proposed for a second time, "that you're reaching in to try to get something that's actually jammed between the rollers, all right?"

"That's not what happened."

Meeting firm resistance, Weber tried a hypothetical.

"OK, would you agree with me, if you were trying to pull something out that's jammed, you might want to put your left hand against something solid so you have some resistance to your pulling motion?"

"You might," Steven replied. "You might want to balance yourself, too."

"And you might want to balance yourself if you're off balance reaching way in, right?"

"You might," said Steven carefully, fully aware that Weber was leading him into danger.

"In fact," Weber proposed, "if you're trying to pull out a stuck drawer, you might put your left hand on the dresser and your right hand on that drawer so you get that push-pull action. Does that make sense?"

"You might."

Having come this close to his desired outcome, Weber decided to make his move toward *clog*. "So if you were trying to pull out hay that was jammed between the rollers," he continued, "it would make sense to put your left hand on the roller to give yourself some push-pull resistance?"

But Steven was waiting for him: "I didn't need any push-pull resistance."

"And when hay is in between those rollers," Weber quickly continued, "those rollers are held together under great force by very large springs, right?"

"Yes, that's true."

"Because those are real large springs that are forcing those rolls together?"

"Yes."

"But sometimes you can pull and even though there's resistance, if you pull hard enough, you can get the clog out, right?"

Clog! There it was, the word Steven had been waiting for, the word Manning had sprung on him unexpectedly during their preparations, over and over, the word he fully expected yet that nevertheless startled him like a rattler when it finally appeared. Steven stalled to give himself time to think. "Well, what are you—? I don't understand what you're saying." Was Weber asking a hypothetical question? Or was he asking about what had occurred?

"Sometimes the clog is so bad," Weber continued in a mode that was both indeterminate and specific, "you actually have to back up those spring-loaded rollers?"

"Yes. That's when it stops the implement."

"But you might not have to get the wrench out and back up the roller if you can pull it hard enough with your hand, right?"

Steven refused the hypothesis: "I don't think I ever did that."

Now, however, Weber was living fully within the scene he had so long painted for himself, and in it he clearly saw Steven yanking out that clog: "And if you pull some out, pull that clog with your right hand, do you know how that changes the resistance?"

Steven gave him a look of stubborn resistance. "I don't understand your question. Resistance on what?"

"On the baler."

"How it changes it?"

"Right."

Steven took one small step into the imagined scene, then jumped back out again. "There would be less resistance," he conceded, "but if you're saying a clog was stopping the baler the day of my accident, that is not what happened. *I know*. I ran that baler for a whole summer. *I know the way it runs*."

Weber had no choice but to switch back into the hypothetical mode. "*If* you reached in and put your left hand on the roller to give yourself some leverage and pulled on that hay with your right hand, you'd agree," he said in a cajoling manner, "that would lessen the resistance of the baler, right?"

"Yes, it would," Steven agreed, "if that was what happened. But then the slip clutches would be activating. I would have heard the slip clutches. You don't miss something like that. Them slip clutches are loud. You can smell them. You can hear them."

But Weber remembered that Steven had mentioned hearing some noise at that point, and he seized it. "Well, actually you did hear something right when you had that right hand wrapped around the hay, didn't you?"

In fact, Steven had never said his "right hand was wrapped around the hay." Paying no attention to Weber's imprecise memory, he stuck to what he remembered. "The only thing I heard was the baler kicking on just a split second before my hands went in."

"You actually heard a click, didn't you?"

"Well, I don't know if I would say a click. It was the equipment turning on. I might have said a click, but it was the equipment turning on."

Weber's imagined scene was fading. All that remained of it was a click. "You agree you might have told us you heard a click?"

Steven saw no harm in granting him his click. "Yes. But a click is completely different than the sound of slip clutches."

Slip clutches! They had been the flaw in Weber's theory from the start. There was no getting around the fact that a jammed baler squeals and shakes and smokes and Steven's had sat silent as a stone. Christopherson was only one of several experts who had pointed out this elementary fact, but apparently Weber had hoped to mesmerize Steven into overlooking it in his testimony. Now that Steven had emphatically mentioned the slip clutches twice, however, Weber had no choice but to change the direction of his cross-examination. And, of course, the slip clutches also blocked him from attempting to get Steven to admit that he had not turned off the PTO. With the jury's eyes fixed on him, Weber was keenly aware that he could not appear to miss a beat, so with the apparent ease of a man dropping a peach pit into the garbage can or flipping a cigarette butt into the gutter, Weber abandoned his beloved clog theory, save for a wistful reference or two in his closing argument.

"Let's move on to a different subject," he proposed briskly.

"All right," said Steven.

But Weber's outward calm may have masked some inner confusion at having been bested in this struggle of wits and wills with Steven, for to outside observers his questions hopscotched from topic to topic during much of the rest of his relatively brief cross-examination. For a few moments he questioned Steven on the OSHA representative's visit, suggesting that Steven's grandmother, previously described as outspoken, would have said something if the meeting had been inappropriate. Then Weber switched to questions about Steven's attendance at his high school farm safety class and what he had learned there, and then, abruptly settling on a new tack, he moved to a series of questions about Steven's purported medical needs. With the video shown by McKenna clearly in mind, Weber asked Steven whether he was aware of a device called a sock donner.

No, Steven hadn't heard of that.

It was a device used by paraplegics to put on their socks. Weber asked whether Steven had ever considered having loops sewn into his socks, which would lessen the risk of his tearing them with his hook when he pulled them on.

No, Steven had not thought about sock loops, either.

Weber moved on to buttons. Had anyone ever talked to Steven about the usefulness of a button hook for buttoning his shirts?

"Yes," said Steven, "they have, in fact."

"Have you had any success with that?"

"No, I haven't, because I mainly just use my left hand. With the button hook, you can't run it with your left hand. Has to be run with your right hand, the way buttons are set up."

"Because on men's shirts they button that way?"

"Yes, correct."

Weber had clearly boned up on gadgetry and was not to be put off so easily. "Anybody ever shown you a freestanding button hook that actually attaches to a table with a suction cup?"

"No, they have not."

Perhaps intending to undermine Steven's testimony concerning the difficulties he experienced on a daily basis, Weber then showed Steven a brochure for a tool for dealing with round doorknobs. Steven glanced at the diagram, then pointed out that he probably would need a hand since the device would entail his unscrewing his hook and screwing in this other device, which would mean carrying around all three devices to handle doorknobs. Also, Steven added, the device looked expensive; he doubted he could afford it.

"Let's look at the description in the catalog," Weber said. " 'Door-knob lever. I designed this lever when trapped in a motel room with a "cue ball" type doorknob. The rubber strap fits around any doorknob, then a simple rotation of the lever tightens the strap and allows you to turn the knob and pull the door open. A handy item for home or travel.' " Weber looked up from the brochure, "Nobody has shown you that before today?"

"No," said Steven, "they haven't."

Weber moved on to Steven's problems with dining, as portrayed in the video. "You mentioned that when you go out to eat, your practice has been to have the person with you or the waiter cut your food for you, right?"

"Yes," answered Steven.

"Has anyone ever showed you a *rocker knife?*"

"No."

These, Weber explained, had been expressly designed for one-handed cutting. Sounding nearly indignant on Steven's behalf, Weber wondered why no one had ever shared with him all the currently available catalogs of practical gadgets for the handicapped. Weber also asked Steven if he had considered the various clinics around the country that specialized in people with problems like his. Steven replied that he had thought about it, "but I've heard they're awfully expensive."

Weber had regained his stride. He spoke quickly, fluently, insinuatingly. Watching him, Manning breathed a sigh of relief, for Weber now appeared to be focused on controlling damages, in both senses of the term—the logical damage to his case and the monetary damages to be assessed on someone, whether Case, the Saunderses, or even R. E. In any event, Weber's implicit message to the jury seemed to have shifted from *Give Steven nothing,* to *If you feel you have to give him something, let it be on the order of button hooks, sock donners, and rocker knives.*

If Weber could not defeat Steven head-on, there still remained the distinct possibility he could spread the responsibility for the accident. The jury would be looking at Steven's and the Saunderses' as well, and if Case was held slightly less responsible than Steven as both counsels knew well, he would lose everything and Case would walk away unscathed.

Weber finished his cross-examination. After a few brief follow-up questions from Manning and McKenna, Steven calmly stepped down from the stand and returned to his seat with his eyes lowered, resisting the urge to glance at Manning or his parents. He felt drained, aware that the testimonies he had given that morning and afternoon had been the most consequential exchanges of his life. Each had required a different kind of mental and emotional control. With Manning he'd had to keep himself locked into the spectator corner of his mind and hold at arm's length the waves of emotion his own words and recollections had threatened to unleash, resisting even the quiet compassion in Manning's voice. With Weber he'd had to sit with an air of relaxed calm while remaining conscious that the skilled lawyer was trying to assail his defenses with his every question, no matter how seemingly innocuous. "Listen to each question," Manning had told him. "Think about it. Take your time. Don't get flustered. Tell the truth."

After dinner Manning and Steven went for a walk. Manning was elated. "Steve, you did it. You backed Weber down. It was beautiful to see."

"Well, we'd been over that stuff often enough, you and me."

"And when you went through your accident, at least three jurors were crying."

"Yeah, that was tough. I generally don't like to do that to people."

"Your mom and dad . . ."

"Particularly them."

CHAPTER THIRTY

D URING WEEK FOUR, the trial nearly done, there was much
expert testimony on medical costs, potential earnings, and the
like. Then, on Thursday, March 14, Weber called his primary
expert witness to the stand: Bobby Clary, the fifty-seven-year-old professor emeritus in agricultural engineering from Oklahoma State University. After establishing Clary's academic credentials, Weber went on
to show how closely connected to practical farming Clary had been
throughout his career, eliciting from him statements about the importance Clary placed on his knowledge of how farmers actually use their
equipment. Eventually Weber brought his witness to focus on the
Case 970 tractor, discussing the mechanics of the PTO, and the fact
that it had been designed to handle literally hundreds of different
implements. "A tractor is just a power source to operate the various
implements that farmers use out on the farm to do the jobs they have to
do," said Clary.

"So, on the basis of your experience and your work in this case,"
asked Weber, "have you reached an opinion about the PTO control
system on the Case 970 tractor as it was shipped by Case back in
November of 1972?"

"Yes," said Clary.

"And what is that opinion?"

"That the Case model 970 tractor as designed, manufactured, and
marketed was not defective nor unreasonably [un]safe [sic]. It was a

reasonably safe product. It met the expectations of users of that piece of equipment." Then he added, "Of normal users of that piece of equipment."

Clary had an equally positive estimate of the warnings posted in the tractor cab and spelled out in the operators' manual, referring particularly to the one that warned: "stop engine before working on PTO-driven machine or PTO shaft or performing any maintenance." He went on to say that Steven should never have approached an attached implement with the tractor running: it was not a normal thing to do. "My personal experience is that farmers don't take those kind of chances when they are working on power-driven equipment," Clary testified. "They don't get off and get into the internal workings of that piece of equipment and leave the power on, as a general rule. It's extremely rare for that to happen."

As for the Saunderses, Clary explained in substantial detail how the tractor and baler had been improperly cared for prior to the accident. He similarly took issue with the training practices on the farm. It was clear to Clary that they had been negligent in maintaining their equipment and in their training of Steven and Barry Neal. In sum, one could conclude from listening to Weber's direct examination of Clary that the responsibility for Steven's accident resided chiefly with Steven, for not having turned off the tractor engine, and secondarily with the Saunderses, with perhaps some responsibility left over for R. E., who had not adequately maintained the equipment.

"Your witness, Mr. Manning," said Judge Mueller.

"Thank you, Your Honor," Manning replied. Then, in an even tone of voice, he pummeled Clary with logically linked questions for the next two hours. He began by walking up to Clary and asking him—it was almost a statement—if he believed "the accident occurred because there was a plug that stopped the baler."

"Based on the testimony, there is a high likelihood of that," Clary replied.

"And what you don't believe is that Steven Sharp caused the baler to stop by pushing the PTO lever back. You believe, your understanding of the accident, is the baler stopped because it was plugged with hay?"

"Oh, I think . . ."

But Manning was not interested in Clary's thinking: "Correct?"

"I think . . ."

"Yes or no. That's a simple question, isn't it? Yes or no?"

"Well, it's not a yes or no. I think the greatest likelihood, based on all of the physical evidence, is that there was probably a plug, but there's also some testimony and some possibility that Mr. Sharp may have brought the lever back to a disengaged position."

Thus, in the first moments of his cross-examination, Manning had forced Clary to step away a bit from what had been Weber's entire theory of the accident and to concede that Steven might well have completely disengaged the PTO. Manning did not let up for the rest of the cross. Clary admitted under Manning's intense questioning, for example, that he had testified for Case previously, and never against the company. Manning also was able to call into question the extent of Clary's knowledge about the Jones accident, as well as his familiarity with the testimony of the other farmers in the trial.

Manning tried to exploit the diagram he had found in Clary's notes during the expert's deposition, emphasizing the short distance between the point of disengagement of the PTO and the point at which delayed self-starts could occur. Clary testified that normal users of equipment like the 970 would understand that delayed self-starts were a possibility when the control lever was placed any place except in the disengaged position.

Manning also returned to Clary's opinion regarding the cause of Steven's accident, suggesting that the expert felt that R. E. Sharp's inadequate maintenance had been partly responsible.

"I believe that Mr. Sharp did not appropriately and properly repair the tractor with regard to replacing the spring, although I don't believe the spring was causative of the accident." Clary explained that R. E. should have gone to the parts catalog to determine what was needed to restore the PTO to its original condition.

CHAPTER THIRTY-ONE

C LARY WAS the final live witness in the trial, though additional testimony was read into the record by the attorneys and shown to the jury on videotape. Judge Mueller then gave the jurors two days of recess so that the lawyers could hammer out an agreement on the verdict form. After much discussion and several drafts, the final result was this:

Question No. 1: Was the Case 970 Agri-King tractor, when it left the possession of the manufacturer, Case Corporation, in 1972, in such a defective condition so as to be unreasonably dangerous to a user? Answer yes or no.
Question No. 2: If your answer to Question No. 1 is "yes," then answer this question: Was such defective condition a cause of Steven Sharp's injuries? Answer yes or no.
Question No. 3: Was the Case Corporation negligent in its design of or warnings accompanying the Agri-King 970 tractor? Answer yes or no.
Question No. 4: If your answer to Question No. 3 is "yes," then answer this question: Was such negligence on the part of Case Corporation a cause of Steven Sharp's injuries? Answer yes or no.
Question No. 5: Did Case Corporation have a duty to issue post-sale warnings on the 970 Agri-King tractor at some point after 1972 but before August 22, 1992? Answer yes or no.

Question No. 6: If your answer to Question No. 5 is "yes," then answer this question: Did Case Corporation breach that duty? Answer yes or no.

Question No. 7: If your answer to Question No. 6 is "yes," then answer this question: Was such a breach a cause of Steven Sharp's injuries? Answer yes or no.

Question No. 8: Have you answered any of Questions 2, 4, or 7 "yes"? Answer yes or no.

Question No. 9: Was Dwight Saunders negligent with regard to providing safe employment for Steven Sharp? Answer yes or no.

Question No. 10: If your answer to Question No. 9 was "yes," then answer this question: Was such negligence a cause of Steven Sharp's injuries? Answer yes or no.

Question No. 11: Was Randolph Sharp negligent with regard to his repair of the 970 Agri-King tractor? Answer yes or no.

Question No. 12: If your answer to Question No. 11 is "Yes," then answer this question: Was such negligence a cause of Steven Sharp's injuries?

Question No. 13: Was Steven Sharp negligent with respect to his own safety? Answer yes or no.

Question No. 14: If your answer to Question No. 13 was "yes," then answer this question: Was such negligence a cause of Steven Sharp's injuries? Answer yes or no.

Question No. 15: If you have answered at least two of Questions 8, 10, 12, or [sic] 14 "yes," then answer this question: Assuming the total fault that caused Steven Sharp's injuries to be 100%, what percentage thereof, if any, do you attribute to:

a. Case Corporation (answer only if you have answered Question 8 yes)

b. Dwight Saunders (answer only if you have answered Question 10 yes)

c. Randolph Sharp (answer only if you have answered Question 12 yes)

d. Steven Sharp (answer only if you have answered Question 14 yes).

Question No. 16: What sum of money will fairly and reasonably

compensate Steven Sharp for his injuries and damages as a result
of the accident in question with respect to:

a. Past medical, hospital, and other related expenses. Answered
   by the court.
b. Future prosthetics expenses
c. Past loss of earnings
d. Past and future pain, suffering, and disability and disfigurement.

Question No. 17: What sum of money will reasonably compensate Steven Sharp's parents, Randolph and Betty Sharp, for the
damages sustained by them before October 10, 1992, which were
the result of the accident, with respect to:

a. Loss of Steven's society and companionship
b. Pecuniary losses.

Question No. 18: If your answer to any of Questions 2, 4, or 7
was "yes," then answer this question: Was the conduct of Case
Corporation outrageous? Answer yes or no.

Question No. 19: If your answer to Question No. 18 was "yes,"
then answer this question: What sum, if any, do you assess
against Case Corporation as punitive damages?

From Friday to Sunday, Manning was generally out of sight of the
Sharps; he was closeted with McKenna, or discussing the verdict form
in the judge's chambers, or sitting in his room, working on his closing
statement. The times when the Sharps happened to catch a glimpse of
him he was moving fast, his face closed and blank with concentration.
Sunday evening, however, he took a break and the four of them had
dinner together. The verdict form was in its final shape and now the
task facing Manning was to assemble all of the testimony of the past
four weeks, much of it technical, into a coherent and manageable
whole.

"That's a big job you've got ahead of you, Bill," said Betty.

"I probably won't get a lot of sleep between now and Tuesday morning," he said, smiling.

"What's your final statement going to be like, Bill?" Steven asked.

"Well, I'll go through each aspect of the PTO, the lever, ramp, spring, and spool; I'll cite all the expert testimony; and then I'll talk about punitive damages."

"Yeah, but you got a main point to pull it all together?"

"What do you think, Steve? You have a suggestion?"

"Well, to us," Steven replied, glancing at his parents, "after listening to this whole trial, we were talking, and it seems to us to come down to one pretty simple question: Who do you trust?"

"Exactly," Manning replied.

And that's exactly how he handled it on the morning of March 19. He presented a detailed review of the testimony concerning the technical aspects of the PTO and then an equally careful and specific indictment of Case's response to repeated reports about the part's dangerous fault. He was passionate in his denunciation. What was it about the Case Corporation, Manning asked, that it had not tried to contact dealers and owners after the Mickey Jones accident, had not taken out advertisements in the farming magazines? The company had done it before, Manning reminded the jury, why not now? Why had it not improved the warnings on the tractor, sent new decals to dealers? "All things that manufacturers should do," Manning told the jury. But not Case. "We don't have to do anything. We can put our head in the sand and ignore what's happening. Blame everyone else." These were people who were "incredibly, incredibly indifferent" to the hazard they had created. They were not evil people. They were simply bureaucrats and company people who did not want to go to the trouble and expense of adequately investigating and evaluating the dangerous machine they had put on the market. They refused to treat it as a safety hazard.

In short, the company had shown outrageous disregard for its customers' safety and should be punished accordingly. It was the jury's obligation, said Manning, to send a message to the company in the form of a punitive damages award large enough to catch its attention.

What should the amount be? In 1994 the agricultural division of J. I. Case had $2 billion in sales. Projected sales for 1995 were $2.5 billion. Ten percent of $2 billion is $200 million, 5 percent is $100 million. He was not going to suggest an award of any of these magnitudes, he was giving these figures for context. Rather, he was going to suggest one half of one percent of the $2 billion sales figure. "We ask you to award

$10 million. Why? Not to harm this company. Not so that anyone loses his or her job. But so that somebody wakes up. So that somebody gets the message."

Having stated his desired outcome, Manning shifted his focus to defending Steven and R. E. and the Saunderses from the charge of negligence. Steven was innocent of such a charge because he had not been doing maintenance on the baler but simply removing some loose hay from the intake, following the accepted and standard practice. There had been no plug, as the defense kept trying to suggest. R. E. had done nothing that in any way contributed to Steven's accident. As for Dwight Saunders, J. I. Case claimed he was negligent because he hadn't maintained the tractor adequately, because he hadn't repaired the PTO lever spring, but neither Dwight nor Stan Saunders had ever known of the existence of such a spring. It was broken and invisible before they had purchased the tractor. In sum, Manning charged, Case was the only negligent party in the case.

After a brief break, Manning turned back to damages, this time in terms of Steven's injuries. What were Steven's work prospects? he asked. What were his future medical expenses—expenses that would continue for the rest of his life? He needed an award that would allow him to live a decent life. Finally, Manning talked to the jury about the pain and suffering Steven had already endured, and the pain and suffering he would continue to endure for the rest of his life. He invited the jurors to try to imagine what it would be like not to be able to do such simple things as remove a speck from their eye, or scratch a hand that itched. "We have to imagine that if Steven is able to marry, what it is like not to hold the hand of your grandchild."

On Steven's bathroom wall, Manning told them in conclusion, there is something from Paul's first epistle to the Corinthians about the qualities of love. " 'Love bears all things, believes all things, hopes all things, and endures all things.' And that's what Steven Sharp has done for four years since this accident, is endure all things, and what he will do for the remainder of his life, however long he lives, is endure all things.

"We ask you help him endure all things and assist him and what we ask is that you give Steven Sharp a full cup of justice. Not a half cup of justice, not a three-quarter cup, but a full cup of justice from this courtroom, the full cup of justice that we very strongly believe he is entitled to."

Manning had spoken for two hours with a single break. Using his exhibits as memory guides, he had spoken virtually without notes. He had built the technical side of his argument as carefully as he could, but ultimately, as he and the Sharps had agreed, it came down to a question of trust.

By a strange symmetry it was also this notion of trust that Weber emphasized in his closing statement. Using trust as a touchstone, Weber invited the jury to pass in review the various experts the plaintiffs had produced, and about each he asked rhetorical questions intended to undermine their testimony. Could Christopherson, for example, be trusted to know something about tractors since his main area of expertise was lawn mowers? Did it seem responsible for witnesses to testify in areas beyond their competence? To none of these or other questions did Weber propose an answer. Instead, he conjured up a vague cloud of suspicion, appealing to whatever latent hostility the jury might harbor against powerful lawyers, because Weber's tone, as he went on, became increasingly that of the plain man speaking plain and simple truth to his peers. He was not one of those fancy lawyers who made expensive videos and flew in experts and witnesses from all over the country. Are you going to trust lawyers like that? Weber asked, later reinforcing the point by reminding the jury to "use your memories of what witnesses said here, not what anybody tells you."

What about the testimony these experts had offered? "Do you want to trust experts who testify literally off scripts?" he asked. "You saw two of the experts up there literally reading line by line from documents they prepared and reviewed with counsel." Why such caution if the truth was so simple? There was one who had even declared that he was speaking the truth. Why would anyone feel compelled to state what should be obvious? "There's an old saying," Weber said. "'The more he proclaimed his honesty, the faster I wanted to count the silverware.'"

The notion of trust also pervaded Weber's review of the testimony offered by the plaintiffs' nonexpert witnesses. Of Mickey Jones he asked, "Do you want to trust a witness who says on a warm September day I was warming up my tractor for thirty or more minutes?" Steven too came in for criticism because of inconsistencies between his deposition and trial testimony.

So far had Weber moved toward embracing the persona of the plain-speaking truth teller that he even stepped back, it seemed, from one of his initial theories of the case. What was all this talk about clogging or unclogging the baler? he asked. "Is that what this case is really about, a play on words? If an operator experiences a problem while baling, gets off his tractor, and goes back and looks inside the baler and says, Oh, well, that just has hay in front of the rollers, so I can climb in there, lean in there and pull it out, no problem, but, oh, if it's called a quote *clog*, however *that's* defined, then I have to go back in the tractor and shut off the engine. I'm leaning in the same place doing essentially the same thing. And if a lawyer calls that a clog, then you have to shut the engine off, but if you just call it clearing hay, then you don't? Now, what kind of sense does that make?" Such distinctions, Weber announced, were "lawyers' stuff," "courtroom stuff."

Weber's defense of his client's tractor also centered on trust. Too many discrepancies in the testimony, he said, to believe that the lever could vibrate forward, particularly since all the pressure on the lever forces it back. The machine just doesn't work that way. "Let's use some common sense here." It doesn't add up that the Saunderses would use the same tractor after the accident to finish up the baling with no problems.

Trust defined Weber's support of Clary, the "gentleman born and raised on a farm." As opposed to the plaintiff's experts, he "operates tractors, baled hay all over the country, taught college students, watches how farmers operate equipment all over the country. If I were concerned about getting advice on how farm equipment works, I'd use Dr. Bobby Clary, not people who don't know what they are talking about."

Weber organized the rest of his closing around the questions on the verdict form and the judge's instructions, explaining to the jurors exactly how they should respond. Focusing on whether the tractor was defective or the warnings sufficient, he said the Saunderses had used the tractor for thirteen years with no problems, no accidents. If you turn off the tractor engine as Case directed, "you can literally have lunch in the baler."

Post-sale warnings weren't necessary, Weber said, given the investigations Case had done into the earlier accidents. But they also wouldn't have done the trick because neither Steven nor the Saunderses, who had bought the tractor used, would have seen them. He questioned their likely effectiveness too, since "they didn't follow the warnings that were already on there."

Weber hit hard at the questions regarding the negligence of Dwight Saunders and Steven. Oregon law required Saunders to tell Steven to shut off the tractor, and Steven testified in his deposition that he would have done so if he had been told. "So if Dwight Saunders would have followed this instruction and warned him to shut off the tractor and Steven would have followed it, then clearly that's causal. Dwight follows the law, tells Steven, Steven listens to him, no accident."

But shouldn't Steven already have known to turn the tractor off? He took the training course in high school. He knew to turn off the engine in other circumstances. The warning was there on the tractor. Between Saunders and Steven, whose responsibility would it be then? Weber asked. "You could divide it between the two of them. Those are the people who could have made a difference." Not Case, he implied.

On damages, Weber allowed that Steven's parents deserved some compensation for lost income because of the time that they missed from work caring for their son, and suggested a nominal amount for their loss of companionship. He also made recommendations concerning an appropriate award for Steven's future medical expenses, and for earnings he had lost prior to the trial as a result of his injury.

For damages for pain and suffering and the disability, which included the cost of prosthetic devices, Weber reviewed the testimony and suggested a range of $600,000 to just over $1 million.

Weber turned briefly to punitive damages, and the "incredible burden" plaintiffs had to carry for such an award. Returning to Manning's closing remarks, Weber argued that Case had been anything but indifferent. He pointed to the two visits that Hartman had made to investigate Mickey Jones's accident, and reviewed his earlier arguments about the warnings and design of the tractor. He reviewed Case's financial situation, concluding that an award of the size suggested by Manning was as "untrustworthy as a lot of the other evidence and arguments in this case."

He closed by thanking the jury for its patience, reminding them to free their minds of "all feelings of bias, sympathy, and prejudice" so that they could decide the case based on the evidence and the law. He had spoken for an hour and a half.

Judge Mueller turned to Manning and asked him whether he wanted to take a break or proceed at once with his rebuttal. "I'm ready now," he said, rising quickly. For the next half hour or so he passed in quick review his experts and their testimony, sharpening the important points, swatting at Weber's innuendos. He was happy, he said, that his opponent had raised the question of trust so forcefully, because he was happy to let the case come down to the simple facts his witnesses had honestly presented. And of these witnesses, none was more important than Steven. Steven had spoken honestly and truthfully to them, and now it was up to the jury to award him his justice.

"In the last three years that Steven Sharp has been in our hands with this case," he concluded, "I have gotten to know him very well. I respect him and I love him. And I have great admiration for his courage and for who he is as a human being and he has been in our hands. We will wait for your verdict, your decision, and hope while we wait that you do justice and read all the law. Now we are offering Steven Sharp from our hands to your hands, where he can either be crushed or he can be set free. He's like a butterfly whose wings, literally, have been clipped. I ask you, please set him free."

CHAPTER THIRTY-TWO

THE FOLLOWING DAY, Wednesday, the Sharps, Manning, and McKenna appeared as usual in the courtroom well before the jury entered to begin their deliberations. The jury arrived at nine and were given the verdict form and their instructions. They were to render their decision by majority rule, noting any dissent on the form. Manning, McKenna, and the Sharps sat in their regular seats and remained until the end of the day, ducking out only for a quick lunch. The jurors eyed them as they entered and left, one or two nodding or saying a neutral hello. Weber, who had told the jury in his closing remarks that he would be "waiting in the courtroom" as they deliberated "no matter how long it takes," was notably absent. Judge Mueller worked in her chambers, occasionally responding to queries from the jury concerning points of law or the interpretation of an exhibit. For the first part of the morning the Sharps and their lawyers engaged in desultory conversation, but by ten they had little to say. They were intensely bored and intensely wound up at the same time. A blink or a yawn could unleash an instant of head-snapping vertigo. During part of the afternoon Manning and McKenna exchanged newsmagazines. Steven and R. E. stared. Betty prayed. In his mind, Manning was beginning to let go of the case, as if fiber by fiber. He had been wound too tightly, too long. He needed to unclench in order to be able to listen to the verdict with a reasonable amount of equanimity.

The same long wait lasted through much of Thursday. Then, at about three, the jury sent word to the judge that they were ready with their verdict. Weber was notified and appeared in the courtroom.

"Members of the jury," Judge Mueller asked, "have you reached a verdict?"

"Yes, we have, Your Honor."

"Would you hand the verdict form to the bailiff, please?"

The form passed hands. The judge gave it a long glance while Weber, Manning, and McKenna studied her face for clues, which were not forthcoming. In view of the length of the verdict, the judge had instructed the courtroom to remain seated. "The following is the verdict reached by the jury," she said, and began reading.

"Question No. 1. Was the Case 970 Agri-King tractor, when it left possession of the manufacturer, Case Corporation, in 1972, in such a defective condition so as to be unreasonably dangerous to a user?

"Answer: No."

She paused and looked straight at Manning. He felt the blood drain out of his face. *Not defective?* How could that be? Had they lost?

Manning and Weber's eyes crossed. Weber flashed him a grin of vindication and triumph. Manning tightened his jaw and shifted his attention to the judge.

Returning her eyes to the verdict form, Judge Mueller stated that since the jury had answered that the tractor was not unreasonably defective, the second question, asking whether the defective condition of the PTO had caused Steven Sharp's injuries, was therefore not answered.

"Question No. 3," she went on. "Was Case Corporation negligent in its design of or warnings accompanying the Agri-King 970 tractor?

"Answer: Yes."

What? Manning was confused.

The judge continued reading in a dry, flat voice: "Question No. 4: If your answer to Question No. 3 is 'yes,' then answer this question: Was such negligence on the part of Case Corporation a cause of Steven Sharp's injuries?

"Answer: Yes."

Manning was scarcely breathing.

"Question No. 5: Did Case Corporation have a duty to issue post-sale warnings on the 970 Agri-King tractor at some point after 1972 but before August 22, 1992?

"Answer: Yes."

Manning took a breath.

"Question No. 6: If your answer to Question No. 5 is 'yes,' then answer this question: Did Case Corporation breach that duty?

"Answer: Yes." Manning shot McKenna a glance.

"Question No. 7. If your answer to Question No. 6 is 'yes,' then answer this question: Was such breach a cause of Steven Sharp's injuries?

"Answer: Yes.

"Question No. 8: Have you answered any of Questions 2, 4, or 7 'Yes'?

"Answer: Yes."

Now came the questions concerning Dwight Saunders.

"Question No. 9: Was Dwight Saunders negligent with regard to providing safe employment for Steven Sharp?

"Answer: Yes."

Uh-oh, Manning thought. How negligent? What was the percentage?

"Question No. 10: If your answer to Question No. 9 was 'yes,' then answer this question: Was such negligence a cause of Steven Sharp's injuries?

"Answer: Yes."

Ten questions into the verdict and nothing really had been decided.

"Question No. 11: Was Randolph Sharp negligent with regard to his repair of the 970 Agri-King tractor?

"Answer: No."

Thank God for that.

"Question No. 12 was therefore not answered."

Now came Steven's turn.

"Question No. 13: Was Steven Sharp negligent with respect to his own safety?

"Answer: Yes."

Disappointment and tension locked gears in Manning's chest.

"Question No. 14: If your answer to Question No. 13 was 'yes,' then answer this question: Was such negligence a cause of Steven Sharp's injuries?

"Answer: Yes."

Manning glanced at Weber, who was staring fixedly ahead. Neither had any cause to rejoice. Now would come the decisive allocation of responsibility.

"Question No. 15: If you have answered at least two of Questions 8, 10, 12, or 14 'yes,' then answer this question: Assuming the total fault that caused Steven Sharp's injuries to be 100 percent, what percentage thereof, if any, do you attribute to: Case Corporation?

"Answer: 50 percent."

Manning clamped his jaws on something between a sob and a howl of triumph. He knew now that Case had lost.

"Dwight Saunders?

"Answer: 15 percent.

"The question involving Randolph Sharp was not answered because he was not found negligent.

"Steven Sharp?

"Answer: 35 percent."

Thirty-five percent, that was a blow. Whatever award the jury had made would be reduced by that percentage.

"Question No. 16: What sum of money will fairly and reasonably compensate Steven Sharp for his injuries and damages as a result of the accident in question with respect to: Past medical, hospital, and other related expenses?"

The jury had been instructed to leave that blank, that the court would answer that question.

"Future prosthetics expenses?

"Answer: $500,000.

"Past loss of earnings?

"Answer: $40,000.

"Past and future pain, suffering, and disability and disfigurement?

"Answer: $6 million."

The defense team and the Sharp family heard the figure and sat as still as effigies while Judge Mueller continued.

"Question No. 17: What sum of money will reasonably compensate Steven Sharp's parents, Randolph and Betty Sharp, for the damages sustained by them before October 10, 1992, which were the result of the accident, with respect to: Loss of Steven's society and companionship?

"Answer: $33,000.

"Pecuniary losses?

"Answer: $1,600.

"Question No. 18: If your answer to any of Questions 2, 4, or 7 was 'yes,' then answer this question: Was the conduct of Case Corporation outrageous?

"Answer: Yes.

"Question No. 19: If your answer to Question No. 18 was 'yes,' then answer this question: What sum, if any, do you assess against Case Corporation as punitive damages?

"Answer: $2 million.

"Dated at Racine, Wisconsin, this 21st day of March, 1996. Signed by the foreperson." There were two dissenting jurors, the judge continued. One with respect to Questions 3, 4, 5, 6, 7, 15, and 18. And a second dissenting juror with respect to Question No. 15. "Does either of the attorneys wish to have the jury polled. Mr. Manning?"

"May I pause one moment, Your Honor?" he asked, looking at the Sharps.

"You may," she replied.

With a glance around, they decided against it. "No, Your Honor, we do not."

"Mr. Weber?"

Surprisingly, in view of the insight it might have given him into the dissension among the jurors, which might have provided ammunition during the appeal, Weber declined as well. "No, Your Honor."

"Anything further from counsel in the presence of the jury before I give them the charge after the verdict is received?"

Manning had nothing more. Weber remained silent.

With a gavel rap, the judge released the jurors, converting the hush in the courtroom to a turmoil of voices and hubbub as all the seated rose to their feet. Manning, McKenna, Betty, R. E., and Steven stood up as if lifted by the same wave, turning and reaching for one another in utter disregard of the flash of reporters' cameras and the noise in the courtroom, their throats constricted and their eyes running with tears. It was a vortex with Steven at the center of it. Obviously he would have stood up whatever the jury's decision, but in the event he felt himself lifted by an immense surge from the new life just granted to him and the vindication it represented.

CHAPTER THIRTY-THREE

BETWEEN STEVEN'S moment of triumph in the Racine County courtroom that spring day of 1996 and his ultimate judicial vindication by the Wisconsin Supreme Court, more than three years were to pass, but the salient moments from that interlude can be quickly sketched. Case appealed the jury's decision, retaining for the process the services of Ralph Weber but hiring in addition one of the country's top punitive damages lawyers to lead the charge, former deputy solicitor general Andrew Frey. Frey objected to the jury's verdict on a variety of grounds, including that its key liability findings were inconsistent. How could they find that Case had built a tractor that was "not unreasonably dangerous" and at the same time find that Case had been negligent in its design or warnings? In her detailed opinion, Judge Mueller ruled, among many other complex aspects of the case, that the two questions were distinct and separable, and the case was passed up to the Wisconsin Court of Appeals in July 1996.

Meanwhile, Steven moved to the city of Medford, Oregon, where, after six months of searching, he found work with a construction company, Randy's Beehive, as an estimator and project manager, using skills he had developed during a training course at Northwest Community College in Portland. The award he had won at trial was held in the form of a bond pending the outcome of the appeal process. If he lost, the money would, of course, revert to Case; if he won, he would receive $2 million in punitive damages plus $4.3 million ($6.5 million minus his assessed 35 percent negligence), which in the interim was accruing interest at the rate of 12 percent a year.

The negligence assessed against him had come about, Manning discovered later, as a compromise on the part of the jury between the majority, who wanted to free him of all charges of negligence, and two jurors, who wanted to find him 100 percent negligent. The more vocal and determined of these latter was the elderly lady in the front row who at the outset had given Manning such reproving glances. Her view was that no one should ever approach an implement attached to a working tractor, and if he did, he deserved what he got. This opinion, immovably held, was not free of ideological coloration, for she buttressed her viewpoint with the fact that her father had not served in World War I in order to hand the country over to be exploited by accident-prone freeloaders.

On a larger scale, a version of this woman's views was being debated in Congress in the spring of 1997. The U.S. Senate Committee on Commerce, Science, and Transportation was holding hearings concerning pending legislation on "tort reform." Big business and big insurance interests were making another of their recurrent efforts to federalize "statute of repose" legislation similar to that already in effect in states like Oregon, which would bar claims against manufacturers of machines or products more than twelve years old. Via the American Trial Lawyers Association (ATLA), of which Manning was a member, he had been in touch with committee member Ernest Hollings, the Democratic senator from South Carolina, and Hollings invited him to make a presentation.

Manning put in a call to Steven, and together on March 14 they appeared in front of the Senate committee, where they explained that if the proposed law went into effect, people like Steven who were injured by a machine more than twelve years old would have no recourse. Manning gave a brief overview of Steven's case, and then Steven made a short, very moving appeal. "Please," he concluded, "do not deprive me, and people like me, of our justice." During the next several days in Washington, Manning and Steven, along with representatives of ATLA, met with approximately twenty senators, congressmen, and their staffs. Steven's photograph and his and Manning's testimonies were printed in a brochure and widely circulated.

This intense lobbying effort, which ATLA continued in the weeks ahead, had two immediately discernible results. The first was that ATLA instituted an annual Steven J. Sharp Public Service Award to a plaintiff and attorney who "helped tell the story of American civil justice and educate state and national policymakers and the public about the importance of consumers' rights." Sharp and Manning were named the first recipients at ATLA's 1996 mid-winter convention. Each year thereafter, the award (which carries no monetary component) has been presented to a deserving attorney and client.

The second result, more immediately noticeable on the national scene, was that the second plaintiff to receive the award, Lois Reinhart, who had been injured by a defective twenty-two-year-old elevator, was invited to the White House to stand beside President Bill Clinton on the day he vetoed the proposed tort reform legislation. Steven and Bill Manning had been invited but could not attend. At the ceremony Clinton said he was vetoing the bill because it "unfairly tilted the scales of justice against American consumers like Steven Sharp."

Steven, pleased and startled at the impact his story was having on important national policy, nevertheless chose not to attend this event or any of the other award presentations made in his name, including the first. "You go, Bill," he said. "I don't need to be there. You can tell my story. I just want to get on with my life. If the award with my name helps those other folks, or helps keep the laws fair, that's good. That's enough for me."

On December 10, 1997, the Wisconsin Court of Appeals upheld the original jury verdict and handed up the case to the Wisconsin Supreme Court but explicitly expressed its disfavor with the prior case law it was obligated to follow on the complicated question of whether Oregon's statute of repose ought to be given precedence in adjudicating the case. If the supreme court decided in favor of Oregon law, the Racine decision would be thrown out. This was the line that Weber had been advocating from the start, on the basis of fairly compelling legal arguments. It was a nerve-wracking moment for Manning. After consulting with Steven, Manning put in a call to Frey in order to discuss the possibility of a settlement. He told Frey he was prepared to discuss compromise figures with Case. Frey returned the call the following day and said the company was interested in seeing the case through the appeal process.

"So be it," Manning replied, hanging up the phone.

In addition to arguing that Oregon's statute of repose should apply, Case's appeal to Wisconsin's highest court again focused on the inconsistent verdicts and the punitive damages. Manning and his colleagues spent the next months researching the complex issues in preparation for their argument, including two "mock" trials for which Manning selected some of the most knowledgeable attorneys in Wisconsin.

At the oral argument on December 1, 1998, Frey spent a substantial portion of his allotted time on the punitive damages issue, which surprised Manning because he was most concerned about the statute of repose. Manning himself, responding to questions from the justices, detailed the various accidents that he felt had given Case notice of a problem with the PTO. With the arguments done, all they could do was wait.

One evening during the spring of 1999, nervous about the impending ruling and a little shaky after an inquiring phone call from Steven, Manning confided to his wife, "You know, honey, if we lose this one, I'll go on, of course, I'll continue to practice law, but it won't be the same. I've put too much of myself into this for that to be possible."

On June 23, 1999, two months short of the seventh anniversary of Steven's accident, the Wisconsin Supreme Court unanimously upheld the lower court's verdict. Steven had won for the third and final time. It was done.

It was over.

CHAPTER THIRTY-FOUR

BOUT A MONTH after the supreme court decision, Manning found a J. I. Case business envelope in his morning office mail. From its standard size and thirty-four-cent stamp it looked like nothing special. He sliced it open. Inside was Steven's award check for slightly more than $9 million. There was no accompanying letter. Instead, stuck to the check was a small handwritten office memo with the words: "You are a fine advocate. Brian Cahill."

Manning leaned back in his office chair, nonplussed by this offhand salute from the head of litigation of the Case Corporation. Thanks for the compliment, Manning thought to himself once he had recovered from his surprise, thinking to himself: Even now you think that it was all just a question of advocacy.

Several days later he welcomed Steven, R. E., and Betty to his office. They sat in a conference room and went over financial details. One of the items on Manning's list of expenses was the purchase of the Saunderses' tractor and baler.

"Does that mean," Steven asked, "that I own that equipment now?"

"Yes, technically, it does," Manning replied. "You paid for them."

"Well, when can I have them?"

Manning gave Steven a searching look. "You don't mean you want them?"

"Well, I plan on doing some farming."

"I think you're pulling my leg," Manning replied with a glance at R. E. and Betty, who in turn glanced questioningly back at Steven.

"Bill," Steven said, "it's just a tractor."

Manning gave the matter a little thought, then picked up his pen and crossed the tractor and baler off the list. "There," he said, "now I own those two things. Who knows, maybe there'll be another trial where they'll come in handy. You want a tractor, buy something else, OK?"

The farm Steven bought was a small one, twenty-five acres on the edge of the minuscule town of Cove, Oregon, population fifty-five, located at the foot of the Eagle Cap Mountains, forty-five miles as the crow flies from Richland on the other side. For a year he farmed, buying a small herd of Angus cattle and planting a large vegetable garden. Raspberry bushes already grew in abundance. He set up a couple of beehives. He lived alone with frequent visits from various high school friends, some of whom he hired on a temporary basis to help him with his farming. He saw a lot of Barry Neal until Barry moved to Washington State, where he'd found work in construction. At the end of a year of farming, Steven bought a few pieces of residential property as investments, and then split his time between caring for his farm and working on his buildings.

Soon he discovered that he preferred remodeling and construction work to farming. It was a more active occupation that showed quicker results and the possibility of higher gains, so he sold his animals and subdivided his land into half-acre building lots, on which he and a contractor, who was now his partner, began building houses. Steven drove the earthmoving equipment and did his share of the framing and carpentry work. He was a busy practical entrepreneur with a hundred irons in the fire. On the weekends he dated various women but was reluctant to marry and settle down. "Time enough for that later," he said. "I got too many projects right now." He stayed in close touch with R. E. and Betty, returning home to Eagle Valley for the major holidays, although the family gatherings at the farm had changed their character with the loss of his grandfather Randolph in the winter of 2000 and his grandmother Leora in the summer of 2002.

Manning and Steven often spoke on the phone in the year following the supreme court decision, working out details left over from the trial. Thereafter, Manning would put in calls to Steven at irregular intervals, every two or three months, to see how he was doing. Manning was concerned about his former client, now his friend, uncertain at first whether Steven would prove equal to the task of managing his finances. Once Manning was fairly reassured on that score, he continued to call, partly out of concern for Steven's general well-being, but mostly because he simply enjoyed talking to him. He found that the quality of heart with which Steven lived his life inevitably lifted his own spirits, just as the way in which that quality manifested itself continued to surprise him.

Talking to Steven in July 2002, for example, Manning was startled to hear that Steven had been training the previous winter to take a long trek by snowshoe. "For Christmas this year," he told Manning, "I plan to head up into those Eagle Caps behind my house and hike home to Richland. Should take me four or five days. It's a lot safer than skiing. I've had a couple of bad falls skiing, so I'm thinking this might be the thing to do."

"Where would you sleep?" Manning asked. "In a tent?"

"No. In a sleeping bag. You dig yourself a little cave in the snow and you can stay warm in there with just a candle."

Manning glanced out the windows of his high corner office at the widespread cityscape beneath him and tried to imagine what it would be like to bed down in a hole dug into the snow high in the mountains. "One thing I have to say about you, Steve," he said, "you remain Steven Sharp all the way through."

"Got no reason to change, I guess."

"Well, you've been through things that would have changed a lot of people. Remember our trip to Washington, talking to all those senators?"

"I look back on all that now, Bill, and I have to scratch my head. You know, I'm amazed at my life, really. All that's happened. Because who I am really is just Steve Sharp, R. E.'s boy, from Richland, Oregon. Nothing that's happened to me has changed that."

"How are your parents?"

"They're good. Sad, of course, after losing Grandma. They took care of her until the end."

"Is R. E. keeping busy?"

"Same as always. Busy fixing equipment."

"You guys still hang out as much together?"

"Sure do. We just got our tags for a two-week hunting trip this fall."

"Where you heading? Out of state for a change?"

"No, we'll stick close to home. We'll take our mules up into the mountains above the valley. There's a little spot up there we always go. I'm sure I told you about it."

"What was the name of that place again? Secret Lake?"

"No, Bill, it's Hidden Lake."

"Right, Hidden Lake."

"Yeah, we love that place."

"I know you do, Steve. Give R. E. and Betty my best."

Steven paused. "Thank you. I will."

EPILOGUE

THREE YEARS after the Wisconsin Supreme Court decision against it, the Case Corporation has neither recalled the 70-series tractor nor sent an advisory notice to its dealers or customers concerning the model's defective PTO. The average life of a tractor is said by the government to be 23.4 years, but many farmers are known to use theirs for thirty to forty years. A sample check of equipment dealers in the fall of 2002 revealed that used Case 70-series tractors are readily available for sale.

Acknowledgments

While writing this book I incurred large debts of gratitude that are now my pleasure to recall. My thanks go first of all to R. E., Betty, Leora, and Steven Sharp for the warmth with which they welcomed me to Eagle Valley and the generosity with which they responded to my requests for information. I talked with scores of people during the writing and researching of this book and I am grateful to all of them. But I owe a special gratitude to a chosen few. My thanks go to Dwight, Stan, and Debbie Saunders for answering my questions about the summer Steven spent working on their farm. Millie Shold very kindly shared her memories of the day of Steven's accident. Kristin Gulick provided background information on Steven's stay in the Portland Shriners Hospital. To my agent, Theresa Park, and my editor, Jonathan Segal, I am more indebted than I can express for their willingness to take a chance on an untried author, and for giving me guidance and encouragement every step of the way.

A Note to the Reader

I met Steven Sharp in the summer of 1999, shortly after the Wisconsin Supreme Court had upheld his 1996 victory against the Case Corporation. Our first interview took place early one Sunday morning in the coffee shop of a downtown Minneapolis hotel. Ten minutes after we had begun our conversation, I knew I wanted to write his story, not primarily because of the dreadful ordeal he had undergone or the remarkable recovery he had accomplished, but rather because of the qualities of courage, humor, and resilience he presently manifested. I suspected these must have been his to a remarkable degree before they became tested, the accident and legal trial serving as a kind of compound crucible that had put them indisputably in evidence. I asked whether I might visit him and his family in Oregon to conduct interviews and he agreed. Steven's character, like anyone's, is, of course, ultimately a mystery, but I wanted at least to take a look at some of the sources on which it fed.

I knew from personal acquaintance and from burrowing into the trial record that in Bill Manning, Steven had found a kind of legal counterpart to himself, a character who showed a comparable degree of grit, energy, and idealism in pursuit of the goal of obtaining justice. That these two characters made contact with each other and ultimately prevailed in court seemed a contemporary American story well worth telling, despite or perhaps because of its anachronistic or strangely serendipitous feel. But to tell it plausibly, unironically, I felt I had to stick as close as possible to the facts of the narrative and the words of the people involved. The conversations reported in the book are either verbatim or faithful to the gist of what was said. As for the trial, the reported exchanges are closer to verbatim than gist, being only lightly edited to remove repetitions and redundancies.

It was my goal when reporting the trial to give a fair picture of both the plaintiff's and the defendant's positions. Early in the writing of the book, I contacted both the president and the chief legal officer of the Case Corporation, informed them of my project, and requested interviews. I made the same request of Ralph Weber, Case's defense attorney during the trial and the appeal. I wrote letters, sent e-mails, and placed phone calls informing Case that I would be happy to present its view of the matter if it would communicate. I received no response. From this I drew the conclusion that Case had nothing to add to what it had presented at trial.

—W. M.
November 2002

William Mishler grew up on a small farm on the outskirts of Cleveland. In 2002 he retired from the University of Minnesota, where he taught Scandinavian languages, literature, film, and culture. He has written extensively on these subjects for journals and anthologies. In 1989 he was the corecipient of the Richard Wilbur Award for the year's best volume of translated poetry. His own poems have appeared in *The Mudfish*, *Denver Quarterly*, and *Chicago Review*. He died in December 2002.

A NOTE ON THE TYPE

The text of this book has been set in Goudy Old Style, one of the more than one hundred typefaces designed by Frederic William Goudy (1865–1947). Although Goudy began his career as a bookkeeper, he was so inspired by the appearance of several newly published books from the Kelmscott Press that he devoted the remainder of his life to typography in an attempt to bring a better understanding of the movement led by William Morris to the printers of the United States.

Produced in 1914, Goudy Old Style reflects the absorption of a generation of designers with things "ancient." Its smooth, even color combined with its generous curves and ample cut marks it as one of Goudy's finest achievements.

Composed by North Market Street Graphics,
Lancaster, Pennsylvania
Printed and bound by Berryville Graphics,
Berryville, Virginia
Designed by Robert C. Olsson